# The Secret Magic of Music

D1507772

"*The Secret Magic of Music* is rich with in̲ ̲ ̲ ̲ ̲ ̲ ̲ ̲ ̲ ̲ ̲ ̲ ̲ ̲ nature of chamber music itself. Through detailed research and interviews with great musical figures of our time, Ida Lichter has produced a book which is highly readable, thought-provoking, and engaging. This is a must-read for anyone who wants to dig deeper into the inner workings of chamber music."

—**JOHN GILHOOLY, OBE,** Director of Wigmore Hall, London UK, and Chairman of the Royal Philharmonic Society

"Secrets shared between two people are always special. Ida Lichter gently coaxes her subjects to reveal the most intimate thoughts on their lives and their art. Fashioned as third-person portraits which are in equal parts biographical and philosophical, *The Secret Magic of Music* lovingly introduces us to an eclectic range of personalities from today's music world."

—**ANTHONY FOGG,** Artistic Administrator of the Boston Symphony Orchestra and Director of Tanglewood Festival

"Lichter has done an admirable job in bringing together some of the world's greatest musicians to personally reflect on their relationship to classical music. The inescapable conclusion is that music serves their spiritual and emotional well-being, and by extension it contributes to ours."

—**DR. RACHAEL KOHN,** Producer and Presenter, "The Spirit of Things," Australian Broadcasting Commission (ABC) Radio National

"The Secret in this book's title unfolds via tantalising glimpses into the insights of stellar professional artists: more than forty of them in all, from Ashkenazy to Wispelwey. I found the title's Magic in the craft that Ida Lichter, like a water diviner, employs to search below the surface for the life-giving flow that is music's essence. As a psychiatrist and chamber music producer, she here becomes our contemporary Music Diviner. Lichter's is the sensibility that unifies the book's individual illuminating moments. She invites us to share her privileged vantage point, profiting emotionally, intellectually, and spiritually."

—**KEN HEALEY,** Pre-Concert Speaker, Australian Chamber Orchestra, since 1988, Lecturer and commentator on Performing Arts

"With her intelligent, perceptive interviews of musicians themselves Ida Lichter explores the place of music in our social and intellectual lives in a way that has rarely, if ever, been attempted. This book will enlighten all those who seek to understand what classical music can add to life; entrenched music lovers will find it irresistible."

—**JAN BOWEN, AM,** Chair, Sydney Youth Orchestras and passionate music lover

"Lichter has produced an intimate, generous, and often very moving collection of portraits of the musician's love affair with their art. Collectively, it amounts to a timely reminder that both great music and great music-making hold out a promise of a higher purpose for our existence, offering insights into what it is be fully human that transcends the merely utilitarian. This is a book which will inspire the agonistic as much as the committed classical music aficionado to open their ears, as much as their hearts, and listen anew."

—**PROFESSOR PETER TREGEAR,** author of
*Ernst Krenek and the Politics of Musical Style*;
founding Chair of the AMF Australia Foundation

# The Secret Magic

*of*

# M·U·S·I·C

# The Secret Magic

## *of*

# M·U·S·I·C

*Conversations with Musical Masters*

## — Ida Lichter —

SelectBooks, Inc.
*New York*

This edition published by SelectBooks, Inc.
For information address SelectBooks, Inc., New York, New York.

First Edition

ISBN 978-1-59079-305-3

*Library of Congress Cataloging-in-Publication Data*
Names: Lichter, Ida, [date]
Title: The secret magic of music : conversations with musical masters / Ida
  Lichter.
Description: First edition. | New York : SelectBooks, [2016]
Identifiers: LCCN 2015004646 | ISBN 9781590793053 (pbk. book : alk. paper)
Subjects: LCSH: Music--Psychological aspects.
Classification: LCC ML3830 .L416 2016 | DDC 781.1/1--dc23 LC record
available at http://lccn.loc.gov/2015004646

*Book design by Janice Benight*

Manufactured in the United States of America
10 9 8 7 6 5 4 3 2 1

*For all musicians, listeners, and arts organizations
devoted to chamber music.*

# CONTENTS

# FOREWORD

As a concert pianist, my purpose is the preservation of classical music and communication of the composer's message. The nature of that transmission is nonverbal. I have therefore held the view that music should be heard rather than discussed. This book, however, shows there is an important place for discourse. It is not an attempt to claim a substitute or equivalent form of expression but to stimulate greater appreciation of music. The enrichment can benefit the knowledgeable, as well as the uninformed listener.

After all, members of chamber music groups, teachers and conductors talk about the music being played, while demonstrating what they mean. The popularity of master classes, radio and television programs about music attest to the high level of public interest and the desire for more information.

Many people are not aware how much pleasure can be derived from classical music and they have a misguided view of the genre as elitist. The artists interviewed in this book speak enthusiastically about its freedom, humanity and beauty. These are universal characteristics that make it accessible to all who want to learn, play and listen.

For those who have been exposed to classical music, the emotional experience can be different for each individual, yet deeply satisfying, and no matter how sad and poignant, the music is ultimately cathartic, positive and, at times, heroic.

Nina Maria Lee, cellist of the Brentano Quartet, explains how the music she plays can be therapeutic: "We might feel the despair in a theme and then follow its transformation through many developments, until finally, when the theme returns, you are a little older, armed with more knowledge." Perhaps music may indeed have healing effects, and in this regard, I have received many letters over the years from grateful listeners.

I am privileged to join my colleagues who have generously contributed their ideas to this book. We are fortunate to be able to spend so much time immersed in the art of music, constantly searching for better ways to serve as conduit from composer to listener.

Successful transmission can be observed in the interaction between performer and audience. This rarely examined aspect is explored by many of the musicians, and there is general agreement that although recordings have an important place, live performance is more satisfying and exciting for players and listeners.

After giving hundreds of concerts worldwide, I have never failed to be thrilled by the emotions shared by listeners and performers when both parties are focused on the truth and splendor of a fine work. These moments are some of the greatest joys.

The musicians in this book also discuss the group experience of a concert audience, when like-minded people, who share a wide range of emotions, can feel a bond, even with strangers.

The author's passion for music and long association with the administration of a chamber music festival have led her to ask the right questions about the role of classical music in society, its transformative potential, and importance in the education of children. Through interviews with thoughtful performers, she explores the interface between composer, performer, audience and teacher. Nevertheless, part of this process may always remain mysterious.

This book is required reading for listeners of most kinds of music, as the means of transmission is comparable. It is of particular interest to anyone learning to play an instrument, and also serves to expose people to the possibilities of emotional engagement through music.

Interviews with authorities on Bach and Beethoven add insights into the powerful communication of two of the greatest composers. In another fascinating discussion, an American pianist and arts administrator outlines how her concert series, largely self-funded, became a successful civic project.

I have devoted my life to classical music and I welcome the author's admirable efforts to build a case for it and make it more widely accessible.

—EVGENY KISSIN
*April, 2015*

# ACKNOWLEDGMENTS

I would like to express my grateful appreciation for the assistance of Musica Viva Australia, patient copyreaders, and members of my family.

# The Secret Magic

*of*

# M·U·S·I·C

# INTRODUCTION

*Music is higher revelation than all wisdom and philosophy . . .*
*Music is the mediator between the spiritual and the sensual life.*[1]

—Ludwig van Beethoven

CLASSICAL MUSIC can excite its passionate enthusiasts. As a devotee of chamber music and founder of a chamber music festival, I have searched for an understanding of audience enthusiasm for this genre and for classical music in general. What is its value and function in Western society, and why does it inspire such a dedicated audience? Music has been described as an inevitable product of human intelligence.[2] The classics, also known as serious or "art" music, are often held up as central to Western civilization, but what does this mean? Is it simply "pure pleasure technology"[3] and "auditory cheesecake"[4] enjoyed by a small elite, or does it embody emotions and ideas? Can people with little knowledge of classical music feel comfortable with it?

In order to investigate questions and quandaries about classical music, I interviewed a number of performing musicians. Most of them are international artists who were touring Australia around the time we spoke. They are not necessarily representative of performing musicians in general, or even of their particular genre, and their responses are personal, anecdotal, and wide-ranging.

Many are members of chamber music quartets and trios. This genre, which evolved as an intimate dialogue between several instruments for performance in private homes, was favored by some of the greatest composers as a vehicle for profound masterpieces.

1

The interviewees were willing to discuss their thoughts and experiences regarding Western classical music. They give sincere and wide-ranging answers, while offering a glimpse into their lives of self-discipline, dedication, passion, and outstanding talent. Some share secrets about the emotional transmission from music score to listener. I have grouped the interviewees into chapters, and as our discussions often navigated to Bach and Beethoven, I have added two chapters for more, but by no means sufficient, information on these titans of music.

Presented in this book are my series of reflections on the interviews. In this sense I have not attempted to quote the interviewees directly, or anticipate the way they might have expressed their ideas. My reflections cover the emotional response to music, the role of performance, and some of the central philosophical and aesthetic aspects of artistic practice.

Such issues deserve consideration, especially in addressing a few of the critical approaches to music developed in the modern era. Since the mid-twentieth century, the concepts of music philosopher Theodor Adorno have become influential.[5] He delegitimized popular enjoyment of classical music, while claiming only the radical, atonal variety was able to convey truth, hope, and social protest. For Adorno, music could become the trigger for change, and take the place of organized revolt. His concept of modern composition had the effect of alienating composers of new music from society, and promoted an elitism that assigned superior intellectual and socio-political value to their works.

More recently, former Oxford English Professor John Carey railed against elitist views and made a case for relativism[6] in his book *What Good are the Arts?*[7] He denounced precious worship of the arts, which he branded a secular religion for the elite and wealthy. He also exposed any moral defense of music by drawing attention to the Nazis' love of the art. At the same time, he conceded it could produce health benefits. As an example, he cited the novelist DBC Pierre, who decided not to commit suicide after hearing a symphony on the radio.[8] Carey's opinions took hold throughout the arts community, where they tended to reinforce the notion that artistic judgment was relative and dependent upon individual taste.

In our age of relativism, the music tradition developed by Bach, Mozart, and Beethoven could be given the same weight as any other musical genre. However, in the Far East, particularly China, Western classical music has been elevated to a cherished part of basic education and cultural life.

Although fundamentally neutral, music can express political aspirations, particularly nationalism. Some music can even threaten political ideologies. During the Cultural Revolution in China, pro-Communist songs and marches were allowed but Western classical music was severely restricted. In some parts of the world today, radical Islamists are challenging secular music.[9]

In our age of spiritual searching, music can inspire contemplation of existential meaning. It wrestles with ideas and tension, and even if one is unaware of the composer's intentions, the music moves us with its inherent nobility and compassion, narrative of human relationships, and reverence for the natural world. The musical landscape offers a harbor in an everyday world buzzing with demands and high-speed activity, but even when disturbing and bleak, great works retain a sanguine core.

Approaching music through verbal language might seem presumptuous or futile; however, discussion can stimulate curiosity and may increase perception and understanding. In doing so, we achieve a deeper engagement, which might explain why pre-concert talks that highlight insights and relevant social history are popular for raising the enjoyment of a performance.

Findings of musicologists and neuroscientists can lead to a deeper understanding of our attachment to art music, yet performers themselves represent an untapped source of information and many welcome the opportunity to contribute their own observations. Their enthusiasm for an art that is ancient and modern, exacting and exciting continues to steer their vision and purpose in life.

I felt encouraged by the many performing musicians and teachers who were eager to discuss the value of music. Many are humbled by the practice of their art and driven by a sincere desire to communicate the wishes and spirit of the composer without self-aggrandizement. Some believe music has transformative power and see themselves facilitating this process.

It can be difficult for non-musicians to understand the bond between performing artist and instrument, a remarkable, often primary relationship. For most artists, music making is an integral part of their personae and their instruments are virtually extensions of their bodies. If the homunculus, the muscular and sensory representation of the body in the cortex of the brain, were redrawn for a musician, perhaps it would also incorporate their musical instrument.

The artists I interviewed have progressed far beyond technical skill. For them, music is primarily a language of emotions and the composer's score an expression of humanity that outstrips the instrument. Great music bundles together emotions in harmonic, melodic, and thematic form. Like choral and operatic groups, instrumental chamber music combinations are able to communicate multiple voices and feelings.

The great composers possessed an uncanny ability to express a wide range of emotions. Some of the artists share their views on the mechanism and give examples of how feelings can be induced, even by the slightest alteration in the score. The emotional power of many works remains undiminished through the centuries and their creators are often regarded with extreme reverence. The legendary conductor Carlos Kleiber reportedly said that some music is so profound it should stay on the page, never to be played.[10]

We are often astonished that Bach, bound by formal structures like the fugue, found infinite freedom within their confines. By contrast, today's composers face no restrictions on liberty of expression. It also seems surprising that Beethoven's daily life was frequently miserable, yet his music is full of generosity and majesty. Equally surprising is how so many acclaimed composers and performers do not necessarily lead praiseworthy lives, despite being constantly in touch with the noble aims of high art. No matter how performers choose to live, however, it is clear most of them are driven to nourish and sustain the music they love and keep it alive through performance.

Interpreting and performing a composition are inspired acts in themselves, demanding full intellectual and emotional effort. Re-creative performers are attentive to the context and emotional engagement of every note in the score. In the process, they distill centuries of pedagogy accumulated by teachers with musical pedigree, and the myriad experiences of their own lives add subtle flavors to the music.

Classical music has led to social changes. It brought purpose and achievement to a group of slum children in Paraguay when they built and played orchestral instruments made out of landfill trash.[11] In Venezuela, the El Sistema[12] national music program has trained about 400,000 children from among the country's most impoverished, creating a network of youth orchestras that diverted adolescents from truancy and crime. Success of the El Sistema music education method has been emulated in other countries, notably in the United States, in award-winning programs such as the Community Opus Project of the San Diego Youth Symphony and Conservatory.[13]

There are many views about the role of music in learning, particularly the positive influence of music lessons on a child's brain and their development of non-musical disciplines,[14] including controversial claims that listening to Mozart improves spatial-temporal ability.[15]

Studies have shown that while listening to music, pleasurable feelings are linked to physical responses, including shivers and altered heart rate and breathing.[16] These experiences are associated with the activation of blood flow to regions of the brain that release the chemical dopamine, a neurotransmitter involved in euphoria, motivation, and addiction. Experiments using brain scanning showed dopamine surged from various parts of the brain when shivers were felt, and during a preceding phase when the music was only anticipated. The pleasure from listening is also self-reinforcing due to activation of reward and pleasure circuits associated with the release of dopamine.[17] Research data suggests that even melancholy music "can lead to beneficial emotional effects such as regulation of negative emotion and mood as well as consolation."[18]

Probing the meaning of art music can be a lifetime journey, but some initial exposure is required. For individual listeners with some familiarity, extensive knowledge is not required for an experience that taps into deep seams of emotion outside spoken language. Re-living old emotions and opening up to new ones can be refreshing and even life changing. Skilled interpretive artists demonstrate how violent emotions can be expressed and controlled. Musicians require years of practice to acquire such mastery, and one can only feel awed by their talent and dedication.

Nevertheless, it is in the field of relationships that music has a special social role. Performers develop bonds with composers while acting as messengers. There is a close tie between musicians and their teachers, who lay the musical world before them, and compress their learning into flexible packages to suit individual students. The relationship between student, instrument, and teacher forms a cozy set not aimed at a specific audience, but focused instead on channeling an interpretation based on fidelity to the composer.

Concerts are more than relaxation and diversion, and many people enjoy the intellectual aspect. From the perspective of the audience, however, the most satisfying concert is one in which performers evoke strong emotions in a safe environment, balance spontaneity with control, and bring their own palette of colors. If the emotions of listeners are roused, then music has done its work by whisking them away from the daily stresses of life into a form of reverie and, perhaps, therapy. And like therapy, the greater the emotional range expressed, the more satisfying and cathartic for the listener, which might explain why the works of composers such as Mozart and Beethoven are so popular.

Another aspect is interpersonal and can be found in the satisfying group experience of the audience members, who come together with a common interest for an emotional journey and communal applause. Historically, music formed an important function for congregations in ancient temple services in Jerusalem, and later in the Christian church, where it was integral to religious worship. In those times, it was a regular feature of people's lives. Today, the connections between performers and audience, and members of the audience with each other, continue this long tradition. Perhaps the mechanism involves stimulation of the hormone oxytocin, the glue that binds lovers and builds feelings of trust, happiness, and benevolence.

Most supporters of classical music simply have an emotional attachment. But without a strong underlying message regarding its social function and value, loyalty to the art will not be forcefully transmitted to future generations. Furthermore, a great deal of public and private funding, often in short supply and becoming scarcer, is required to enable live performances, tours of visiting musicians, and the education of new generations of musicians and audiences. Allocation of these funds needs to be justified. The attraction to classical music can be seen in the widespread popularity of new music stations that play standard classics, although in shortened form, and the common practice of using classical music in film scores. Today, the cinema, Internet, social media, and recordings are vehicles of taste and accessibility not previously seen.

Throughout the ages, classical music has been invested with celestial and esoteric powers. The capacity to comfort, enchant, and excite continues to intoxicate and mystify. Connecting to this art form brings us a little closer to the emotional experiences we crave and the empathy we need to survive.

I have sought to address a number of questions in this book:

* Is music a form of therapy, a religious or spiritual experience, a political weapon, a moral force?

* Does it have healing properties?

* Do composers have a particular philosophical agenda?

* Does great skill in performance require moral character?

* What is involved in interpretation?

* What is the nature of the relationship between players in a chamber music group?

* Why do many people find contemporary classical music unpalatable?

* Does music education and performance warrant the expense to society?

* Is Western style music declining in the West and moving to the East?

* What is the future for classical music?

# CONDUCTORS

# Vladimir Ashkenazy, *conductor and pianist*

Vladimir Ashkenazy is one of the most illustrious living musicians; his joint career as pianist and conductor has taken him all over the world. He tours regularly with the Philharmonia Orchestra and became its Conductor Laureate in 2000. Together with the Philharmonia, he produced the concert series Prokofiev and Shostakovich Under Stalin and the series Rachmaninov Revisited. Ashkenazy is Music Director of the European Union Youth Orchestra and Conductor Laureate of the Iceland Symphony Orchestra and the NHK Symphony Orchestra, Tokyo. In the past, he has held the positions of Principal Conductor and Artistic Adviser to the Sydney Symphony Orchestra, Chief Conductor of the Czech Philharmonic Orchestra, Music Director of NHK Symphony Orchestra, Chief Conductor and Music Director of the Deutsches Symphonie-Orchester Berlin, and Guest Principal Conductor of the Cleveland Orchestra.

Ashkenazy won first prize in the Queen Elisabeth Competition in Brussels in 1956 and shared first prize in the 1962 International Tchaikovsky Competition, Moscow, with John Ogdon.

His discography comprises over one hundred recordings for piano alone and continues to expand. It includes the Shostakovich Preludes and Fugues, which won a Grammy award; *The Well-Tempered Clavier* by Bach; Rachmaninov: Piano Transcriptions; *Diabelli Variations* by Beethoven; and Piano Concerto No.3 by Rautavaara, commissioned by Ashkenazy. In 2013 Decca released a fifty-CD box set titled *Ashkenazy: 50 Years on Decca*, and in 2014, a collection of Ashkenazy's recordings of Rachmaninov's piano music and orchestral music (which he conducts).

His aim to widen the audience for classical music has led to film and television initiatives such as *Music After Mao* filmed in Shanghai, the *Ashkenazy in Moscow* series, *Superteachers*, about working with inner-city London school children, and a documentary based on his Prokofiev and Shostakovich Under Stalin project.[19] He has also worked with producer Christopher Nupen to produce films about composers and performers.[20]

*Music deals with the eternal questions of life and death. When we talk about the great pieces of Bach and Beethoven and many other great composers, we are concerned with the reasons for being here and what we are trying to achieve. We are more than mental, physical, and material beings, as we have perception and the ability to use our brain in a creative, analytical manner. This is our spiritual entity and the highest examples of music reflect that aspect of ourselves.*

—VLADIMIR ASHKENAZY

MUSIC IS TRANSCENDENT and paramount in Maestro Ashkenazy's life, and he fervently hopes others can journey toward spiritual heights through music. Many people gain fulfillment from spiritual aspirations, which outweigh material considerations. Indeed, some of the people who have contributed the most to mankind were satisfied with little more than basic comforts.

Music has always fascinated the human species, possibly starting with singing or animal cries. Until relatively recently, the evolution of music was very slow, but now, with more rapid development, people are keen to express their individuality in musical sounds of increasing technological sophistication.

In the Middle Ages, people probably had to belong to a guild to follow an occupation in music. Instruments were rudimentary, and few could afford to pursue such a profession. Over time, music progressed through the periods of Bach, Mozart, and the nineteenth- and twentieth-century composers. Simultaneously, it moved from rigid restrictions to a gradual breakdown of barriers. But with the removal of constraints, it became more difficult to understand what composers were trying to achieve.

The great composers were gifted with an exceptional understanding of humanity, and the impulse to express it through their prodigious musicianship. Although it is difficult to formulate their spiritual or philosophical mission, it is clear they felt composing music was their purpose in life. In comparison to such ideals, pop music communicates a form lacking in depth, and often dependent on the props of a show, such as dancing, light, and amplification.

Living with the repressions of the former Soviet Union made Ashkenazy more aware of the comfort and consolation music could provide in difficult times. In Soviet Russia, the system kept people ignorant of the outside world, reminiscent of the concepts of control described by George Orwell in *1984*. Most people were unaware of the world on the outside, and they conformed to government regulations in order to cope with everyday life.

But there were those who were dedicated to challenging the system. Some were sent to prison and others were incarcerated in psychiatric hospitals. In the midst of such oppression, the music conservatory was an island of sanity. No doubt the director was a party member, or at least close to the party, and students had to be very careful to toe the official line. There was a Komsomol organization (the youth wing of the Communist Party of the Soviet Union) and a KGB room in the conservatory. One avoided saying anything that could be misconstrued by an informer who happened to be listening. Professors at the conservatory would not speak freely at work for fear of anti-government or anti-Soviet accusations, even by students. Nevertheless, they would often try to defend a student who had raised the suspicions of the authorities. People were still prepared to confide in each other in spite of the dangers, but there was a consuming dread of betrayal, even within the family.

Being a professor at the conservatory and a party member did
not automatically confer any privileges, as became evident for violinist David Oistrakh and his son, Igor, also a violinist. They lived in a
tiny apartment, and although large by Soviet standards, it consisted of
only two-and-a-half rooms in a communal building. When both prac-
ticed, they disturbed each other, so the elder Oistrakh, a committed
party member, went to the central committee of the party to request
new housing. He was flatly refused.

In spite of the miserable environment, Ashkenazy was immersed
in comprehending the great mysteries of Bach, Mozart, and Beethoven and the works of Sibelius, Rachmaninov, Mahler, and other composers. He was always open to diversity in musical expression and
was driven by the desire to comprehend the world of various composers and transmit their message as faithfully as possible.

Beethoven and Mozart had the ability to translate their inner
world and understanding of human existence into a message through
sound. Environmental influences exercised a strong influence, such
as Beethoven's deafness and his lonely life bereft of a marriage to one
of the aristocratic ladies who were above his status. In spite of the
well-known descriptions of Beethoven as gruff and bad-tempered,
Ashkenazy is convinced he must have been a person of the greatest
warmth; the last movement of his piano sonata Opus 109 expresses
a tenderness beyond description, as well as a sense of simultaneously
knowing, accepting, and being part of the cosmos: a supreme wisdom. The second movement of Opus 111 also conveys a final acceptance and feeling of peace.

Performance is the fundamental goal of an artist. Everything is
secondary to this communication, so Ashkenazy pursues it with full
energy. Being absorbed in the music and transmitting its message is
the ultimate fulfillment. It also comes with risks because no performance is faultless, and, in retrospect, performers often think they
could have been more faithful to the idiom, or had a more conducive

state of mind at the time. Performing artists work very hard before playing in public and hope the final effort will deliver what they are seeking to reveal. And the ability to do justice to a work is insufficient. Ashkenazy tries to identify completely with the composer, a never-ending process.

It is the duty of a teacher to impart these principles, but above all to guide students toward spiritual development. This practice requires a similar state of mind in the teacher. Ashkenazy's professors always instilled the spiritual dimension as crucial.

The spiritual side is relevant to the sound production. People are often intrigued by the observation that individual pianists can produce a different sound on the same instrument. Ashkenazy believes it depends on a combination of the physical and spiritual. Pianists might start with a concept of the sound they want to produce and then utilize their particular physical attributes, keeping in mind their limitations.

In all the work that musical expression entails, a broad general education and some knowledge of literature and philosophy might be an advantage, but the most important factor is probably innate talent.

Is there a moral dimension to music? The high ideals of Bach and Beethoven did nothing to stop horrific wars and the evil perpetrated during World War II. Among composers too, not all had high principles. Many were reprehensible but still produced sublime music. Similarly, unpleasant people have been known to perform like angels.

Whatever the character of the classical composer or re-creative musician, the music itself can only have a positive influence, although the degree of impact depends on the individual and the music. For some people, music can be life changing.

*Vladimir Ashkenazy was interviewed by the author in Sydney, Australia, in February 2009.*

# Alexander Briger

Alexander Briger works with many orchestras and opera companies around the world. He has collaborated with soloists such as Alfred Brendel, Murray Perahia, and Maria João Pires during his frequent performances with the Philharmonia Orchestra, London, and worked with the London Sinfonietta, American theater director Peter Sellars, and pianist Hélène Grimaud in the premiere of *Lamentate* by Arvo Pärt.

He is the founder, Artistic Director, and Chief Conductor of the Australian World Orchestra and conducted their highly successful opening season at the Sydney Opera House in 2011. Their recording of Beethoven's 9th Symphony was released on Deutsche Grammophon.

Other orchestras he has worked with include the City of Birmingham Symphony Orchestra, BBC Symphony Orchestra, Bournemouth Symphony Orchestra, Academy of St. Martin in the Fields, Orchestra of the Welsh National Opera, Orchestre de Paris, Strasbourg Philharmonic Orchestra, Paris Chamber Orchestra, Konzerthaus Orchester Berlin, Frankfurt Radio Orchestra, Hamburg Symphony Orchestra, Deutsche Kammerphilharmonie, Rotterdam Philharmonic Orchestra, Gothenburg Symphony, Swedish Radio Orchestra, Danish Symphony Orchestra, Mozarteum Salzburg, Camerata Salzburg, Belgium National Orchestra, Flemish Radio Symphony, Orquestra Nacional do Porto, Japanese Virtuoso Symphony, Monte Carlo Philharmonic, and New Zealand Symphony Orchestra.

Born in Australia, Briger made his debut in 1988 conducting *Jenufa* for Opera Australia, followed by *Madama Butterfly*, *Così fan tutte, The Cunning Little Vixen, The Marriage of Figaro,* and *A Midsummer Night's Dream.*

He has a great interest in opera, and has also conducted *The Tales of Hoffmann* (Royal Danish Opera), *The Bartered Bride* (Royal Swedish Opera), *The Rape of Lucretia* (Covent Garden), *The Magic Flute* (Glyndebourne), *Rigoletto* and *The Makropulos Case* (English National Opera), *The Cunning Little Vixen* (Aix-en-Provence), *From the House of the Dead* (Canadian Opera Company), *The Bartered Bride* (Royal Swedish Opera), *Pique Dame* (Komische Oper Berlin), *La Bohème* and *Carmen* (State Opera of South Australia), Bartók ballets (Opéra du Rhin), and the premiere of Simon Holt's *Who put Bella in the Wych Elm?* (Aldeburgh Festival). In 2012 he conducted the Paris premiere of *Nixon in China* to great acclaim.

Briger won first prize at the 1993 International Competition for Conductors in the Czech Republic. He studied with his late uncle, the conductor Sir Charles Mackerras, and with French conductor and composer Pierre Boulez. Briger is a descendent of Isaac Nathan, the first opera composer in Australia, and of Prince Felix Youssoupoff, who participated in the death of Rasputin.[21]

*Anguish is clearly reflected in Mozart's Sinfonia Concertante.*[22]
*Written in 1779, the two serene and joyful outer movements enclose*
*a slow movement of great pathos, perhaps expressing Mozart's grief for*
*his mother, who had died during the previous year. In this work, he is*
*telling us how he is mourning, and anyone who has had some expo-*
*sure to this music and listens empathically cannot fail to be moved.*

—ALEXANDER BRIGER

ALEXANDER BRIGER believes performing artists have a duty to keep classical music alive. Otherwise, an immense emotional world would be lost. How do composers create this emotion? The greatest, like Mozart, Mahler, and Beethoven, had the capacity to write melodies that could generate feelings. These feelings are physiologically modulated through the brain and the rest of the neurological system. Lesser composers could not do it or were able to do so for audiences of their time but do not have the same effect on modern audiences. When Mozart and Salieri were contemporaries, many people thought Salieri was the greater composer, but today Mozart is recognized as a great genius on par with Shakespeare.

The great musical works have built a legacy of human expression that resonates through the generations. Briger believes people will still listen to these classics for hundreds of years to come, but he doubts whether Beyoncé or Lady Gaga will survive that long. Youngsters prefer contemporary pop culture to classical music because it is less intellectual and more direct, and pop songs last about three minutes, a length that suits the youthful attention span. As teens develop, their attention span increases. Briger associates his own

19

shift to maturity with the time he stopped playing the same Rolling Stones and Beatles songs over and over, although he still enjoys their music. Increasing maturity also makes it possible to identify with worldly experiences and emotions that are more intensely portrayed in classical music than any other musical genre.

Briger is convinced society would be less hostile and violent if the younger generation listened to the symphonies of composers such as Mozart, because they have a calming effect compared to the aggression found in much pop music today. Some gangster rap is clearly belligerent. It deals with rape, pillage, and death, and reflects a mob culture involved with guns and warfare. There is a large market for such music and a number of composers and performers make more money from this genre than a classical musician could hope for in a lifetime.

In order to introduce children to the classics in an easily digestible form, Briger made a cut-down version[23] of the Ring Cycle[24] by Richard Wagner. After the concert he received emails from children to thank him for the *Ride of the Valkyries*[25] they had downloaded. To some, it was so "cool!" Later in life, they might hear that piece again and wish to see the whole opera.

Music can be used to promote a strong political message. Stalin asked Shostakovich to convey sentiments of nationalism and victory in his Symphony No. 9.[26] Instead, Shostakovich scored the work for a smaller orchestra, with more humor, as well as less melody, force, and passion than he had written into his previous symphonies. Briger's uncle, the late Sir Charles Mackerras,[27] conducted the symphony in Edinburgh in the 1950s, and met the composer, who was staying in the same hotel. On one occasion they had breakfast together. Shostakovich seemed very nervous and kept looking over his shoulder. When Mackerras asked him what was wrong, Shostakovich said he was fearful of being overheard, in case he inadvertently said something that would incriminate him with the Soviet authorities.

The comic operas of Gilbert and Sullivan often contain an overt political message, and occasional subtle political subversion has been ascribed to Mozart as well. Politics can also be associated with pop music, such as the songs of Bob Dylan, which aroused young people who protested against the Vietnam War.

Music helps listeners re-experience the full range of emotions and this connection, at least in controlled conditions, might promote personal development. Like poetry, however, much classical music cannot be fully appreciated without a little understanding. At school, Briger studied the English poets but didn't value and love the works without the teacher's guidance. Appreciation of poetry takes time, and therefore it is not well suited for people in a hectic modern environment. On the other hand, music is much more accessible because it is possible to respond immediately to the emotional content, recapturing past emotions and possibly experiencing new ones as well.

Mozart and other great composers were skilled at orchestration and able to produce sounds geared to elicit emotions. Even people who are not familiar with Beethoven's music can respond to his Symphony No. 5.[28] A three-minute pop song might produce a single feeling but Beethoven's symphonies and other powerful pieces of music express a whole range of emotions.

Briger remembers the intense emotional response he experienced when he conducted Mozart's Symphony No. 40,[29] a work he knew well. In the last movement while approaching a particular chord, he suddenly wanted the orchestra to burst out with ecstasy. Indeed, this happened just as he had hoped; perhaps it occurred due to the orchestra's response to one of his physical movements. He experienced a reaction like an electric shock together with overwhelming joy. These were responses he had not previously associated with that part of the symphony. The new emotional insight was illuminating and the experience formed a deeply etched memory.

Group bonding is also important for the audience and for amateurs who either sing in choirs or play in local orchestras. It could explain the popularity of Beethoven's Symphony No. 9, the "Choral." Perhaps "The Ode to Joy"[30] was the first pop song! The concert hall itself can set the atmosphere for a group experience. When it is full, a certain excitement is already present before the performance starts. If only half-full, the audience and performers might feel somewhat despondent from the outset.

In live performance, a fresh approach can be exciting and invigorating. It would be boring to hear the aria "Un bel dì" from *Madama Butterfly*[31] or the slow movement of Rachmaninov's Piano Concerto No. 2[32] always played in the same way. The thrilling and unexpected is also bound to happen in some live performances. Many years ago, as a student in Munich, Briger attended a Berlin Philharmonic Orchestra performance of the Symphony No. 9 by Mahler[33] conducted by Claudio Abbado. The end of the work dies very slowly and then disappears. In this performance, the last note continued for about six minutes, so the audience was uncertain when the music had ended. During that time, the concert hall was completely silent. Even after the last note had ended, the silence continued for a short while. Nobody moved and Abbado stood immobile on the podium. Somehow, he had created such intense emotions in the orchestra that the musicians played their very best and were able to transmit the feelings in the work directly to the audience.

Although Briger had listened to Mahler's Symphony No. 9 countless times and studied the work in detail, he experienced new emotions that night. His wife, also a musician, was with him and she too felt the same intensity. When Briger spoke to members of the orchestra some time later, they agreed that something extraordinary or mystical had taken place. To this day they talk about that particular concert, in which they gave their utmost and produced their best performance of Mahler's Ninth.

It is still difficult for Briger to verbalize what occurred during that concert. He felt a passion he had never known. All the aches of past love had not prepared him for the pain he felt when listening to the final pages of the symphony and the overwhelming despair when resignation descended.

After the concert, he could hardly sleep because his mind was engrossed with profound questions. Could music be transformative and dispel aggression? Could one learn more about religious worship from music than a priest's sermon? The next day he went to his conducting class at the conservatorium in Munich. Many students had decided against attending the concert because the tickets were expensive; they asked him about the performance, but he was lost for words. He simply said they had missed a significant musical event.

The transformative potential of music was explored by Yehudi Menuhin, who established the group Live Music Now[34] to utilize the therapeutic potential of music[35] for people in need. The organization arranges for musicians to perform for people without ready access to live concerts. Briger's wife and her clarinet trio became members of the group. After several concerts in prisons, her trio received appreciative letters from murderers and rapists, and it seemed that the pieces by Mozart and Beethoven had generated calm and prompted self-reflection in some of the inmates. Many had never heard the music before, and it must have presented a strong contrast to some of the aggressive music that was an inescapable part of their prison environment.

Music can be transformative for Briger. Instead of religion, his church is Bach, and in place of a sermon, he listens to the Mass in B Minor.[36] He reveres great musicians, but recognizes a paradox: composers who wrote the most sublime music without themselves being transformed, and conductors like Furtwangler, who could be cruel.

Today, a conductor's aggressive behavior could limit his or her career. Members of the orchestra are often asked to express their opinions on feedback forms, and they might answer "no" to the question whether they would like a particular conductor re-invited. A "no" means a conductor could be out of work and unable to pay off a mortgage, so it is essential to remain amenable!

Briger is aware that the first hearing of a contemporary piece can be distasteful, even for trained musicians, but after study and familiarity, he often develops a liking for it. Explanations can be helpful as well. On one occasion he conducted a piece by the Italian composer, Luigi Nono,[37] for piano, soprano, and orchestra—"Como una ola de fuerza y luz." The composer instructed that it be played as loudly as possible and in clusters of notes. The orchestra complained bitterly until the sound engineer, who had worked with Nono on this piece, informed them that the music was about children in Auschwitz, screaming in pain. From that moment on, the orchestra played with the utmost respect.

People are naturally attuned to pleasing chords and harmonic vibrations, but the ear must be trained for a different distribution of sounds; otherwise, modern music could be misconstrued as ugly. Yet Briger often wonders where atonal contemporary classical music is heading. In contrast, the genre of film music has great influence and is mostly composed harmonically in order to please the average ear and induce emotions.

While some classical works try to depict a story, they usually create a personal emotional journey for the listener. For Briger, Mozart's Piano Concerto No. 23[38] evokes the immense loss he felt at the time his father died, when he became so depressed he was unable to get out of bed for the immediate days after his death. In his grief, he was studying the score of the piano concerto in his mind in preparation for a performance, when the door of his bedroom opened and his father, looking much younger, walked in and sat down next to him! He hugged Alexander tightly and reassured him, saying: "Don't worry. Everything is fine, but I have to leave you now." Although aware he was experiencing a hallucination, he started weeping and begged his father not to leave. After that encounter, he was finally able to get himself out of bed and walk into the next room where his three sisters were sitting. They thought he looked as if he had seen a ghost! Some weeks later, while conducting the Mozart concerto, he felt a sense of peace and comfort in the knowledge that music had helped him adjust to the loss of his father.

In the music of the great composers the transmission of love is evident, as are many other emotions related to love and death. Of all the major classical composers, Beethoven provides the most excitement and adrenaline rush for Briger. Wagner and Mahler, two of the important romantics, are able to focus intensely on feelings of love and passion. But it is Mozart who encapsulates the whole emotional world of passion, joy, depression, and pure excitement rolled up in every work.

*Alexander Briger was interviewed by the author in Sydney, Australia, March 2011.*

# Guy Noble

*BRIEF BIOGRAPHY*

Guy Noble has conducted the major Australian orchestras, Hong Kong Symphony Orchestra, and Malaysian Philharmonic. He is also a pianist, broadcaster, composer, writer, producer, and raconteur and was Musical Director and Musical Supervisor of many musicals, including *Phantom of the Opera, Sunset Boulevard, South Pacific, Man of La Mancha, Gypsy,* and the *Music of Andrew Lloyd Webber.*

Noble has conducted performances of *Great Opera Hits* (Sydney Opera House) *Opera in the Alps* with Anthony Warlow, *Opera in the Markets* with Teddy Tahu Rhodes, *Wallace and Gromit's Musical Marvels* (Sydney Opera House), *Symphony Under the Stars* (TSO), and *Classical and Spectacular* (Sydney Symphony). He also produced a new arrangement and on-field resource for the Adelaide Crows team song and wrote and performed the *Guy Noble Radio Show* for iTunes.

He is a regular presenter on ABC Classic FM, was the host of their *Breakfast* show from 1999–2001, and has worked with a variety of local and international artists, including Harry Connick Jr., Ben Folds, The Beach Boys, The Whitlams, The Pointer Sisters, Human Nature, Dianne Reeves, Glenn Frey, Randy Newman, and Clive James.

Noble has written a book about music (*The Music Explorer)* and writes a regular column for *Limelight Magazine.* He has recorded twelve CDs for ABC Classics.[39]

*In rehearsing with an orchestra, some room must be left for spontaneity. Despite detailed rehearsals, there will be unknowns during performance, like the feeling in the hall and the miracle of communication.*

— GUY NOBLE

CLASSICAL MUSIC CAN BE comforting, exciting, and entertaining. People use it in many different ways and for various reasons, as Guy Noble knows from his experience in radio broadcasting. It might help them get out of the house in the morning and keep their children calm. It can soothe, wind you up, or fill a void in the midst of depression or sadness. Music can bring people together. It might even become an accompaniment to an important time in their lives. That is where pop has a slight edge over classical. If a song came out in 1963 and you happened to fall in love with someone in 1963, this piece of music might be persistently intertwined with that memory.

Occasionally, music aligns with political idealism to produce powerful effects. Verdi's song "Va' Pensiero" from his opera *Nabucco*[40] became an Italian anthem for patriotic unification, nationalism, and freedom from foreign rule, while the Symphony No. 7 in C Major, op. 60 by Dmitri Shostakovich[41] became a testament to the Siege of Leningrad by German forces and the massive loss of life during World War II. In the old days of hand-to-hand battle, music was also used to buoy up the troops. Piccolos, bagpipes, and drums were used to keep battle formation and send soldiers on foot and horseback into the ranks of the enemy.

Music education is now open to everyone and many agree that learning an instrument improves brain function, but Noble believes the most valuable lesson is the development of good social skills. His children are learning modern flute, piano, cello, and saxophone—instruments that are suitable for group music making. In contrast, a pianist misses out on much shared activity. His interests cover a vast range that includes pop, classical, and jazz; he often wonders why certain musicians and listeners confine themselves to classical music. In some ways, popular music has created its own "classics," playing '70s, '80s and '90s pop, not dissimilar, perhaps, to the process undergone by classical music.

We have come to respect Bach, Mozart, and Beethoven as the classics fit for a concert hall. Teaching institutions and orchestras perpetuate these concepts because this music is their staple, but who is to say that a Lennon and McCartney song is less musical and lyrical than a Puccini aria? Yet these examples will never be treated equally with classical music, which is considered on the "high-art" end of the spectrum. Some people actually get their first taste of classical music through the "low" arts. Noble's wife learned a great deal through Warner Brothers cartoons, with soundtracks recorded by musicians, many of whom had escaped Nazi Germany and brought their European culture to bear on Hollywood.

Sadly, this use of classical music in popular culture has almost disappeared. When the "Peanuts" comic strip first appeared in the 1950s, it included a character named Schroeder[42] who played Beethoven and although he was an oddball, it seemed natural there should be a kid who played the piano. Today it is rare to see anyone playing the piano, flute, or cello if it is not an arts program. *The Simpsons* animated sitcom series uses occasional references from the classics, but there are no classical pianists on *Neighbors*!

Deep physical and emotional reactions can be induced by music. People react physiologically to the harmonic scales of octaves, fifths and thirds, the minor sevenths, dominant sevenths, and particularly to a major chord. Because of this deep association with the physics of music, many people don't respond well to contemporary music, even though tolerance for dissonance has increased over the years.

Some modern composers seem oblivious to the audience response to their music. It is almost a badge of honor to be misunderstood, rather than carry on a tradition laid down by Beethoven, Wagner, and Schoenberg. However, they have forgotten that many of those composers were also attempting to speak to an audience and were financially dependent on their patrons. They had to please, even while expressing their own artistic ambitions.

Noble finds intense energy in an audience that comes to enjoy a live performance. However, it is difficult to predict their response and there are no guaranteed ovations, no matter how good the music or performers. The audience has come to the concert for an emotional experience and the worst outcome is a performance that does not touch them.

Pyrotechnics, great music, or simply loud music, can excite, but perhaps there is an overarching comfort about not feeling alone in a shared event. However, not all audiences are equal. Some concerts go very well from the performer's point of view, but the audience doesn't ignite. Fortunately, he is in a good position to speak to them, trying to arouse their interest with talk, surprise, and laughter.

In Noble's experience, a little comedy before, during, or even after a performance can energize an audience through a combination of humor and music, which acts as an emotional release valve. On one occasion, he received a standing ovation and found himself wondering how it was possible that he had just conducted an entire concert without much audience enthusiasm, yet a short piece of comedy roused them!

Performing is a merry dance between the performers and audience. Sometimes he thinks it would be preferable to return to the old

Italian method of paying a few students to boo or shout in order to increase audience awareness and create excitement.

However, an audience can be very responsive to a performer, as illustrated in a concert given by Pinchas Zukerman in London. His playing seemed dreary; Noble thought it was boring and the performance was not working. Then, all of a sudden, Zukerman seemed to wake up and began communicating instead of just playing the notes. He had everyone's attention immediately, and the whole audience seemed to lean in to catch every note.

Noble has no idea how that miraculous change works but he believes it happens in a live music or theater performance due to the "electricity" of a hall. There was an electrifying moment for him in the musical *Billy Elliot,* when the young boy reads a letter from his dead mother to Mrs. Wilkinson, his ballet teacher. In this poignant scene, the ghost of his dead mother walked onto the stage. The audience was transfixed. When this high level of attention produces a "lean-in," the performers onstage can feel it as if they were actually part of that audience. In that moment, a new communication takes place.

On rare occasions, an audience arrives at a concert ready to be involved, but usually people come in feeling a little tired. However excited performers might be, they must work that much harder to help the audience overcome their initial fatigue.

Apart from the music itself, there is a powerful communal aspect for the audience, as well as the need for an "event." People enjoy observing others in the hall and having a drink in the foyer. It is a nice way to spend an evening as long as the performance is good.

There is something very exciting about seeing and hearing how an orchestra works without the editing of a recording. There is also a certain danger, as no recourse is possible in the event of a mistake. In contrast, CDs might have a thousand or more edits on the road to perfection.

For both audience and performers the musical presence is truly ephemeral. Noble always finds it rather sad to go back onto a stage after the audience and orchestra have left, because the energy has dissipated. This energy is derived from the audience as well as the performers.

Sometimes he wonders if the attention span of modern audiences can cope with a long night of art music. He has often thought about a Mozart "Lite" version of *The Marriage of Figaro*[43] that would entail removing some of the more boring parts and having an actor on stage to talk through the action. The opera could be invigorated and repackaged as an irresistible and novel evening of fun. Mozart was writing for a period of time when everything moved at a slow pace. Would it be sacrilegious to speed things up? He thinks not. People tend to be reverential about the great composers and it is worth remembering they were all hard-working musicians who had to make a living. No doubt they were inspired, but you cannot wait for inspiration when you have a deadline for a symphony.

People often ask Noble about his favorite composer. This is like asking, "What is your favorite food?" It is too difficult to choose, although some pieces such as Beethoven's Symphony No. 5 do have a magical appeal. It is the only piece of music that an entire class of 14-year-olds would recognize. Over the years, he has hummed the opening to around fifteen hundred 14-year-olds and asked if they recognize the music. All of them put their hands up. It seems astounding that the four note opening motif is still so powerful that it often features in popular culture.

Beethoven has an extraordinary ability to escalate the tension in his music. These moments often occur at the end of his symphonies when there is a pedal point or sustained tone in the bass, and you know the music is going to burst out into the sunshine again. It can feel like a plane on a bumpy ride while passing through cloud after takeoff, before suddenly bursting through the top of a cloud. The sun is shining, all is smooth, and the seat belt sign goes off. The passengers experience a moment of exceptional joy and relief. As a musician and conductor, he would love to have one of those moments in every concert, but it doesn't always happen.

Stephen Sondheim spoke of these moments. Referring to musicals, he remarked on the need for lots of laughs and a few moments to cry, along with one special moment when members of the audience are aware of a certain joy or the feeling that they understand why they are there. This can happen as a sort of hypermoment within a piece.

Regarding performers, there is no doubt that general knowledge and musical pedagogy have little value compared with communication through the instrument. It is not possible to stop and deliver a lecture with every note. The primary importance of communication through the instrument helps to explain why some actors, and not necessarily the most intelligent, can perform very well; they have a direct emotional connection with their audience. Sometimes children can perform with conviction because they have no constraints and can communicate with simplicity and directness. The advantage of age consists of greater assurance and a better understanding of what composers are trying to say.

Relationships are a significant aspect of performance. It is vital to be supportive and get on well with others on the stage. In Noble's experience the best performers are also the most decent and cooperative people who prefer to keep the drama on stage rather than back stage. Sometimes he wonders why people would put themselves through the torment of being a musician. For most aspiring performers, there is nothing else they want to do, but they have to be prepared for harsh solitary practice, setbacks, and limited possibilities for making a living or a successful career. On another level, musicians belong to an honorable priesthood because music can lift one to a higher spiritual plane.

As an accompanist he used to feel nervous because he was side-long to the audience and their energy. It is easier to turn around and face them, which could explain why singers are often the best performers. They stand in the center of the stage and face the audience with their own instrument, their voice. Some singers today are as good as the singers of fifty years ago, but they are missing out on the great careers that were possible when record companies were producing "stars."

Noble is also quite fearful for the new generation of instrumental performers because they may not get enough work outside of an orchestra. It has become more difficult for musicians to make a living from performing due to less recording and greatly increased costs for marketing and hiring venues. In the future people may prefer to watch concerts on DVDs at home.

Many musicians and listeners feel humbled by the nobility inherent in music and the gifted performing musicians today. Noble is still in awe of the concerts by Vladimir Ashkenazy at the Adelaide festival in 1986, when this great artist performed all the Beethoven piano concertos from memory and conducted Beethoven's nine symphonies in one week! Noble is concerned that such an amazing feat won't be appreciated properly in the future because so much is being "dumbed down." This is a shame because Western traditions in music have taken hundreds of years to build. Every orchestra has developed its own style and sound depending on how they play their horns, oboes, and other instruments.

These days, the number of live performances has dwindled because people can get their music at any time of the day. An iPod containing vast amounts of music can provide entertainment to suit any mood. If someone needs cheering up, they can choose a happy piece of music or if they feel excited, a similar, louder piece. People who seek comfort might find it in a minor key, others in a major key.

Noble enjoys watching people listening to their iPods and can imagine the eclectic range of music they have available, from pop to the classics. Perhaps these modern tastes could give rise to a new type of program for a nibbling society that wants a smorgasbord. Too often, they are given à la carte when all they want is a bit of everything from the buffet!

*Guy Noble was interviewed by the author in Sydney, Australia, in March 2009.*

# INSTRUMENTALISTS

# Alexander Gavrylyuk

Alexander Gavrylyuk regularly tours Asia, Russia, Europe, and Australia as a recitalist and in concerto performances. He has performed with the Philharmonic Orchestras of New York, Los Angeles, Moscow, Israel, Warsaw, Rotterdam, Stuttgart, Netherlands, and Brussels, as well as the Royal Scottish National Orchestra, the Bournemouth Symphony, and the Vancouver Symphony.

He has collaborated with conductors Vladimir Ashkenazy, Yuri Simonov, Vladimir Spivakov, Osmo Vänskä, and Vladimir Jurowski, among others, and recorded all the concertos of Prokofiev live with Vladimir Ashkenazy and the Sydney Symphony Orchestra at the Sydney Opera House. Every year, he returns to Australia for recitals and performances with the major orchestras. In Russia, he has given recitals at the Great Hall of Moscow Conservatory and the Kremlin, and performed with the Russian National Philharmonic under Spivakov and with the Svetlanov Russian State Symphony Orchestra.

Gavrylyuk is well known for his interpretation of Rachmaninov, and in May 2013 he performed all the composer's concerti and the Rhapsody with the Orchestre de la Suisse Romande and Neeme Järvi, and again in March 2014 with the Vancouver Symphony and Bramwell Tovey.

Recordings of solo piano pieces include Schumann's *Kinderszenen*, Mussorgsky's *Pictures at an Exhibition* and works by Prokofiev, Rachmaninov, and Scriabin.

Gavrylyuk was born in Ukraine in 1984 and performed his first concerto with orchestra at the age of nine. When he was fifteen, he won first prize and gold medal at the Horowitz International Piano Competition, and the following year, won first prize at the Hamamatsu International Piano Competition in Japan. In 2005 he was awarded the gold medal and Best Performance of a Classical Concerto at the Arthur Rubinstein International Piano Master Competition.[44]

*Today, with so much emphasis on the material side of life, music has an important role as a reminder of one's inner world. It can open a door to this internal space where universal truths, values, and powerful feelings of love reside. When people come together to listen to a concert, they unite in finding that inner resource.*

—ALEXANDER GAVRYLYUK

I T IS DIFFICULT to define the mechanism of this process in words. When the performer is genuinely immersed, the music can be filled with great beauty and energy; even the spaces between the notes are not experienced as empty. If performers are sincere, nothing prevents them from being true to the music.

Alexander Gavrylyuk grew up in Ukraine and still values aspects of the local culture, such as the love of nature and music. When he was living in Ukraine, society was dominated by Soviet era ideas, including autocratic teaching methods. However, he spent nine years in Australia, and during that time his eyes were opened to freedom of spirit and values based on human rights, individuality, and independence.

Such values, as well as education and upbringing, can be linked to musical development. Gavrylyuk believes they will show through in performance. Life experiences also play an important though subtle part in the development of an artist. Another indirect influence on interpretation is the performer's familiarity with the environment and life of the composer. This background information can assist musicians during the preparation of a piece rather than the performance itself, when other factors come into play.

Regarding performance and communication of the music, Russian actor and theater director Konstantin Stanislavski and his autobiography, *My Life in Art*,[45] became an important influence on Gavrylyuk. When Stanislavski wanted to act a certain part in a play, he would take a few months to try to adopt the traits of the character while continually questioning himself about the way this person would act and feel in a variety of situations. Ultimately, Stanislavski was hardly acting on stage, because he had developed into the character he wanted to portray. Gavrylyuk believes a similar technique can be applied during the process of learning, interpreting, and performing a piece of music.

When pianists stop observing or witnessing their playing, they are getting close to the "sense of truth" described by Stanislavski. It is not an easy course, but very worthwhile. A sensitive audience can experience a greatly heightened emotional transmission if a musician plays in that state of mind. Perhaps this might explain why some performances can be accurate but not transformational, while others can move people to tears even if they don't understand why they are so touched. It is extraordinary that some performers can achieve it without specific training, knowledge, or awareness, and in the absence of good technique or correct dynamics.

During a performance, musicians open up to the stream of music in ways that depend on their instincts, the acoustics, and the special communication between the audience and the music. This openness does not happen during every performance, though Gavrylyuk seeks to achieve it. When he does become aware of a profound connection between the audience, the music, and himself, he feels completely rewarded. These links can occur in spite of limitations in the instrument or acoustics.

As a pianist who often performs solo, he is aware of the intimacy with the audience. This close relationship, reminiscent of the confessional, has a vital place today in a world he believes is suffering from a lack of sincerity. To some extent, this intimacy is also present in chamber music, together with a sense of unity in the teamwork and flow of the music.

The way music can bring people of different cultures together is truly remarkable, and Gavrylyuk would like to believe it could have a positive role in politics. Some composers who lived under Soviet oppression went along with the government but others, like Dmitri Shostakovich and Sergei Prokofiev, were greatly affected by the crimes and brutality perpetrated by the Soviet regime. In their music, they managed to express political dissent as well as the beauty and pain of life, especially in times of war and revolution.

Shostakovich tried and succeeded in using music to expose the deceit and injustice of the regime. In works laden with bold satire, he mocked the political circus that prevailed. Simultaneously, he was able to communicate the emotional and mental state of the Russian people. Some of the music is very bleak, like his String Quartet No. 13,[46] which he completed in 1970. When listeners hear this work, they are usually left with strong feelings about the severe political oppression in the Soviet system. Gavrylyuk thinks it would be a travesty if they walked out of a performance of this quartet and described it as a "lovely concert."

Many other composers reacted to their particular environment and inner lives in personal ways and were able to express their response in musical sounds. Beethoven's music reflects the heroism and stoicism that helped him deal with tragedy in his own life. Throughout the different periods associated with his musical development, his compositions reveal increasingly profound hope and faith in the human spirit. On the other hand, Mozart brought great harmony, childlike sincerity, and otherworldly purity. In Bach we find the foundation of classical music, universal meaning, and a musical manifestation of the Bible. It is celestial and like Mozart's compositions, Bach's music is not entirely of this earth. The music of Chopin

is a whole world of beauty, great suffering, and sacrifice, full of soaring spiritual heights, acute happiness, and sensitivity. Chopin is a
never-ending musical journey, and Gavrylyuk appreciates and loves
Chopin's music more and more over time.

Contemporary music can be very problematic. Gavrylyuk recalls
learning a piece that was so difficult to count that a calculator proved
necessary to follow 12/16 and 7/11 timing. When he heard the composer speak about the way to play this piece, he was surprised to learn
that he instructed musicians to imagine they were smoking a cigarette.
The aim was to play the way smoke unfurls when it is exhaled, ensuring there would be no structure and every performance would be different. He finds it difficult to judge the merit of such a work and other
contemporary pieces, and suspects that the chaos and dissonance in the
music reflects our highly mechanized, egocentric, and cynical society.

Gavrylyuk is convinced that the best classical music is a powerful, positive force in society. Since it has strong emotional and spiritual dimensions well beyond the intellectual, music can impact on
relationships and personal development. The art is also his refuge and
preferred mode of expression whenever he has a problem or needs an
emotional outlet.

In the field of social development of children, music can be a valuable tool for the expression and control of emotions. Research has also
reportedly shown that the study of music can assist intellectual development in children[47] or even reduce crime and antisocial behavior.[48]

In general, music reflects emotional life more than anything else
Gavrylyuk has known, and for a musician it can also lead to special
moments of revelation during performance. When these moments
occur, Gavrylyuk feels an intense, wondrous unity with the audience and almost forgets he is on the stage. This intimate interaction
cannot be reproduced in a recording.

*Alexander Gavrylyuk was interviewed by the author in Sydney, Australia, in April 2010.*

# Angela Hewitt

*BRIEF BIOGRAPHY*

Angela Hewitt is one of the greatest living interpreters of Bach. She performs worldwide as a recitalist and soloist with the major orchestras of the Americas, Asia, and Europe, including the Toronto Symphony Orchestra, Orchestre symphonique de Montréal, Japan Philharmonic Orchestra, Accademia Filarmonica di Bologna, Orquestra Sinfônica Brasileira, the Philharmonia, The Cleveland, Oslo, London, Brussels, Hamburg and Rotterdam Philharmonic, Camerata Salzburg, Washington National Symphony, City of Birmingham, BBC Scottish and Sydney Symphony Orchestras, Finnish Radio Symphony Orchestra, Kammerorchester Basel, Swedish Chamber Orchestra, Australian Chamber Orchestra, and Orpheus Chamber Orchestra.

Hewitt has performed at Wigmore Hall in London, in the BBC Proms, and at the Verbier Festival. She has recorded most of Bach's keyboard works, including *The Art of Fugue*, as well as the music of Beethoven, Chabrier, Chopin, Couperin, Debussy, Fauré, Messiaen, Mozart, Rameau, Ravel, and Schumann. Since 2005 she has organized the Trasimeno Music Festival in Italy, where she performs together with guest artists.

Hewitt began piano lessons at the age of three, gave her first public performance when she was four and won a scholarship the following year. In 1985 she won the Toronto International Bach Piano Competition. She was made an Officer of the Order of Canada in 2000, received an OBE in the Queen's Birthday Honors in 2006, and was named Artist of the Year at the 2006 Gramophone Awards.[49]

*Music can provide comfort as people age. They concentrate more on the most meaningful aspects of life, while triviality falls away. What was significant when they were younger can become important again, so that people who studied music in their youth often return to it in later life.*

—ANGELA HEWITT

WHETHER ONE IS a Buddhist, Catholic, or practitioner of any other religion, it is possible to feel in touch with a higher presence through music. Angela Hewitt believes this spiritual connection is attainable, especially through the music of Bach. It is so miraculous and his faith is so strong that its spirituality is expressed with immense power. Even if listeners are not inclined to the spiritual, they become aware of this quality in his music. Hewitt refers to the way Bach manages textures with great ease. The intertwined voices[50] and the dialogue between them are evidence of his endless musical invention. There is also great beauty in his melodies. One often becomes absorbed in the way Bach combines them in counterpoint, yet the melodies themselves are incredibly expressive, and he conveys much joy through the song and dance that remains the source of most music.

It is unlikely that many of the great composers had a particular philosophical agenda. They were practical people who wrote music to earn a reasonable living, and composing was hard work. Bach had deadlines for cantatas he had to write every week for the Sunday church service. Mozart organized subscription concerts and wrote piano concertos as a freelance artist. At the same time, he was looking for a permanent position with a patron. In those days the main patrons were the royal courts and the Church, and much of the music was written for specific occasions. Bach's keyboard music was composed not only as pedagogical material for his children and students, but for music lovers to refresh their spirits.

Great composers such as Bach express powerful emotions in their music, although some avoided displaying them in everyday life. Hewitt draws attention to Ravel, who hid his feelings but was free and passionate in his music. Beethoven also communicated intense emotions in his music. In the last movement of Sonata No. 31 in A-Flat Major, Op. 110,[51] the "Arioso Dolente" (or 'sorrowful song') is full of notes and rests that sound like sobs. When the melody is repeated, there are more sobs and hiccups, as if the music is describing a person attempting to breathe, while life is ebbing away. Of all the Beethoven sonatas, this movement is one of the most graphic and intimate.

Memory for music can be remarkably enduring. In the last years of his life, Hewitt's father was in a home together with many Alzheimer patients. One Easter Sunday, she played an Easter hymn for the patients on her father's ward. To the great surprise of the staff and visitors, a patient who had not spoken a word to anyone for two years suddenly started singing all the words of the hymn, bringing everyone to tears. Perhaps many people who suffer from dementia can still relate to music—its retention being held in a different part of the brain than other forms of memory.

For some people, specific themes are strongly linked to commercials or organizations, and the association of a tune with memories of a personal occasion can resuscitate feelings from the time of the event. For an audience, the strength of memory for a piece of music is probably related to the power of the emotional transmission by the performer, and Hewitt believes an artist must feel the music very deeply, many times more intensely than a listener, in order to transmit the emotion successfully. Giving a little bit of themselves won't do; performers must give a great deal. This does not imply they should throw themselves around while playing, but rather focus on identifying with the composer, especially if the composer was renowned as a keyboard player. A performer who is playing Beethoven, Mozart, or Liszt must try to inhabit the maestro in some way. It takes time, and an artist must play a great deal of a composer's music in order to become more familiar with his or her personality and musicianship. Knowledge of the social and political history of the time also plays a subtle part in the eventual performance of a piece.

For Hewitt, performance can be compared to acting. Like a good actor, a successful musician has a fine sense of timing and the ability to shift between different styles and moods very quickly. Some of the best-known actors—John Gielgud and Richard Burton, for instance— had impeccable timing and inflection. To some extent, these skills can be learned but they are also instinctive. Young children may possess a natural musical instinct that is easy to recognize, but the talent needs to be carefully nurtured and developed through hard work. Even the most gifted actors have to work to develop their skills.

When Hewitt is preparing a piece, she notes the style or taste of the period, as style and tradition were important considerations in the past. At the same time, she is constantly thinking of the dynamics, the kind of sound she wants to produce, and the emotions expressed in the music. Her aim is to create the most interesting and colorful sound, using musical imagination to hear the desired result in her head before producing it on the keyboard. Ultimately, the audience might be able to hear the piece the way she hears it.

Hewitt is very sensitive to audience response. Sometimes Japanese audiences are totally silent throughout the performance until they come alive at the end. The silence can seem deathly, but it is full of expression and tension, as people hold their breath. Some listeners might be surprised to learn that many performers are extremely sensitive to the feedback from an audience. This is not unexpected when one considers the artists on the stage are in a state of acute concentration—trying to communicate with the immediate environment as well as the music.

Artistic skills are not dependent on character and some great artists may not have wonderful personalities to match, but Hewitt has rarely come across a musician who doesn't show his or her true character on stage. Usually, this is evident in the playing and attitude, because the individual is closely linked to the performance. Sometimes it is possible to discern personal characteristics from someone's playing; a shy and insecure person might not project during a performance, whereas an outgoing and secure person might show more authority.

Is interest in Western style music dwindling? Hewitt is aware that people are often preoccupied with their computers and the Internet, and a piano in the home is becoming increasingly rare. Music education in schools is also declining. As interest in religion has waned and Western society has become more secular, fewer people attend church, and so they are missing out on the music played during services. In the past, the hymns sung in the congregation and choir were an important part of life.

The situation in Asia is very different. There is a vast young audience for music and many parents in Asian countries encourage their children to play an instrument because it is a valued part of a good education. In Korea and Singapore, about two thousand children have attended Angela Hewitt's concerts. Perhaps these children will form a large portion of the audience for classical music in the future.

Many excellent performers of classical music are also emerging from Asia, but it might be difficult for someone from another culture to play Bach, as it requires some understanding of church music. Such knowledge is, of course, unnecessary for members of the audience, who simply respond as listeners.

Music has emerged as a source of value for young people in some deprived societies. The El Sistema music education[52] movement showed how underprivileged children in Venezuela were able to form one of the best youth orchestras. This hugely successful program is being copied throughout the world.

To some extent, the preservation of classical music and advocacy for the art depends on performers. First, they have to be excellent players, and then they must excite the audience with their interpretations and personalities on stage.

Hewitt is convinced that these days it is incumbent on performers to do more than just play the music. In the past, an artist gave a concert and disappeared off the stage. Now they speak to the audience, become more involved in writing and talking about music, and use social media to reach existing and potential listeners.

*Angela Hewitt was interviewed by the author by telephone in December 2013.*

# Stephen Hough

*BRIEF BIOGRAPHY*

British-born pianist Stephen Hough performs worldwide in recital and as a soloist in major world venues with the greatest orchestras. He is also a frequent guest at music festivals, including Salzburg, Mostly Mozart, Edinburgh, Tanglewood, and the BBC Proms, where he has performed over twenty concertos. Apart from his career as a concert pianist, he is also a composer, writer, and painter, and was chosen by *The Economist* and *Intelligent Life* as one of Twenty Living Polymaths.[53]

His awards include first prize at the 1983 Naumburg Competition in New York and the Royal Philharmonic Society Instrumentalist Award in 2010. In 2001 he became the first classical performer to win a MacArthur Fellowship for exceptional merit and potential.

His recordings, which number over fifty CDs, have won many international awards such as the Diapason d'Or de l'Année, several Grammy nominations and eight Gramophone Awards, including a Gold Disc and two Records of the Year.

As a composer, he has received commissions from the Berlin Philharmonic Wind Quintet, Wigmore Hall, Musée du Louvre, Musica Viva Australia, Indianapolis Symphony Orchestra, National Gallery of London, Westminster Abbey, and Westminster Cathedral. He has written for *The Times*, *The Guardian* and *The Independent*. His blog for *The Telegraph* UK attracts a global audience.

As an educator, Hough holds the International Chair of Piano Studies at the Royal Northern College of Music. He is also a Visiting

Professor at the Royal Academy of Music and a faculty member of the Juilliard School, New York.

In 2014 he was appointed a Commander of the Order of the British Empire (CBE).[54]

*Some composers had a religious agenda. They perceived a transcendent relationship between religion and music. For humans who want to search deeply, to live meaningfully, just eating and sleeping is not enough. The material world alone does not satisfy or give the explanations people crave, but music can often open a door to this world.*

—STEPHEN HOUGH

S TEPHEN HOUGH BELIEVES there is really no function to music. It is simply there, beautiful, uplifting, and outside of us. People die but the music remains. Beethoven died but his music remained. Like everything else in this world, it doesn't really belong to anyone; we are only caretakers.

However, music can bring a heightened awareness, whether merely mood-changing or life-changing. There is always a danger of living life on a mundane and prosaic level, thoughtlessly doing ordinary things each day with routine and boredom. But music has the potential to lift us out of this environment even if only for a short time, enabling us to experience a sort of ecstasy—literally being outside ourselves while we listen or play.

Hough observes that no one really knows how this works or why some music reaches deep inside and other music stays on the surface. But there is no doubt that life begins with rhythm, with the beating of our hearts. Some sort of pulse is one of the main attractions in any music. There are times when we enjoy the quickening of our heartbeats and we take part in activities that make this happen, but a healthy, happy life should be accompanied by a heart that beats with a certain regularity.

Melody is also attractive and humans seem to be the only mammals that sing in any kind of nonuseful way. It is interesting that people from different backgrounds will respond positively to classical music, even if they have not known it from childhood. Like all art, music is referential and people unfamiliar with certain developments of Western art, particularly in the twentieth century, might not appreciate it, or fully understand its significance.

Hough would like to believe music can have a moral purpose, but he doesn't think it is a clear or independent one. The most harrowing examples of this disconnect are the infamous evenings of Schubert songs for the guards at Nazi death camps. After organizing the shoveling of bodies into ovens all day long, they went home, sang Schubert, loved the music and were deeply moved. These were sensitive souls on some level, not brutes without human feelings. Regrettably, it seems that music does not have a directly civilizing influence; it cannot be used as a moral teacher or compass.

Music does, however, have positive effects; it can improve focus and concentration in a modern world full of distractions. In the past, people would spend quiet evenings at home, reading, doing needlework, talking, or playing games together. Today, television and the Internet offer the possibility of endless diversion, but there is a real danger that people will not only fail to find true satisfaction from such superficial surfing, but also lose the ability to concentrate on anything at all. Learning a musical instrument, especially for a young person, encourages focus and provides a skill that will last a lifetime.

Music can engender a deep self-awareness and an extraordinary realization of simply being alive on this magical planet. It alerts people to their bewildering insignificance in a huge universe, yet also to their precious connection with others through the emotions we all share. Although music does not necessarily offer easy solutions to our deepest questions, a group of people sitting in a concert hall on a particular night can somehow celebrate the marvel of existence together—our shared fragility, our shared ecstasy.

These days, there is a choice of listening to live or recorded music, but they are distinctive art forms. The musical works might be the same, but the products are very different. There are exceptions, and some recordings of live performances are wonderful, but there is a difference in the way people listen when they are aware of the dangerous possibility of a musical calamity on stage, or that the interpretive choices they are hearing were made once and for all on one evening—a different kind of accident. It is impossible to create that sense of risk in a recording made in a studio—we already know the outcome! There is also the option to stop listening in the middle of a recording, which cannot be contemplated during a concert . . . except for walking out.

In the past, when people had their major musical experiences in the concert hall, the 78-rpm gramophone record was like a postcard souvenir of the performance. Some 78s are superb and even matchless, but the mentality of listening to recordings is different today. Probably over 95 percent of people listen to music in recordings now and only 5 percent listen "live," so they expect to hear something similar to a recording when they sit down in a concert hall. This is unfortunate because a concert can never replicate a recording, nor should it try to. The experience should be something of the moment, less perfect perhaps and less well balanced sometimes in the orchestral textures, but alive, involving risk and spontaneity.

Many young performers feel compelled to try to sound like a perfect recording. They worry about wrong notes without remembering that recordings are usually full of edits—no one can play perfectly all the time. Even the greatest darts player in the world never hits a bull's eye every time! Hough loves recording but doesn't always enjoy the laborious process of aiming for faultlessness while still trying to capture the frisson of a performance in a studio's sterile environment.

Artistic risks are always necessary. Some musicians aim artificially to sound distinctive, others are in such awe of the work that they never take any daring interpretive risks. Musicians must begin by knowing the score extremely well and then take it on a long journey. Like diplomats working for their country, they need to be well-versed in the party line yet able to be creative in the way they put across their positions. Difficult diplomatic situations require quick thinking. Similarly, a performer must be adaptable, open to fresh ideas, while playing the same pieces every night.

Hough asserts that a performance must never be routine, no matter how many times an artist plays the same work. When a musical voyage begins, the direction might seem clear but there will be countless roads and choices yet unknown and some of the greatest music can be taken in many different directions. Perhaps the process is like a metaphor for daily life: we know our set path when we leave the house in the morning, but there is nothing stopping us from taking a completely different turn along the way.

When he is playing, Hough doesn't focus on a "story" in a piece of music but more on abstract emotions—for example, tenderness, doubt, or despair. He aims to share these emotions and touch the audience, while giving people space to be with their own thoughts, sometimes stimulating contemplation about bigger human issues. There is an additional element of entertainment and he hopes there is space for a smile or two in the course of the performance!

Music probably goes way back to the earliest human settlements. People want to be with others in a group or village and musicians are like the local jugglers or storytellers. There has always been a place for artistic people in society and those who can lift us into another realm of imagination have always been in demand. It also seems that people want to listen to things together and this is one of the reasons why recordings will not completely supersede live concerts, which are essentially theatrical experiences characterized by a certain group electricity.

In recent years, people have expressed concern about attracting more young people to classical music concerts. All possibilities should be considered but Hough is not sure it is just the formality or stuffiness of the concert halls that drives people away, nor will it depend merely on having more people on stage in torn jeans or performers who chat in a familiar way to the audience. Sometimes it is the very distance of an artist on a stage that can create a magical allure, a theatrical moment. This also applies to magicians and other performers. There is that special moment when the lights dim and the hall falls silent for a few seconds of anticipation, just before someone walks out from the wings, sits down, and begins. The charm of that ritual will never disappear.

He has sometimes wondered mischievously if people would be more likely to attend a concert if it were more "exclusive" and tickets were only available by limited invitation. It is one of those strange quirks of human nature to want to do something restricted, such as entering a nightclub where the doorman selects only a few clients, keeping most people outside and thus creating huge queues of hopefuls snaking around the block.

Music must never be seen as elitist and should be made available to everyone, but it does often require some preparatory work. It takes (and should take) a little effort to enjoy a concert fully. All arts and crafts involve work, time, and care—this is true across all cultures, from Japanese ceramics to African masks. And to play an instrument or respond to a piece of intricate classical music will never be easy. It's a challenge like running a marathon. A young person might take a lot of persuading to get out of bed on a Sunday morning and yet be fired up for taking a trip to work for orphans in Africa. Difficulty is not the problem, rather apathy. Classical music's challenges may well be its greatest asset.

Middle-aged people are usually the ones trying to decide what young people want to do and they tend to get it wrong. In the end, musicians have to trust in the quality of the music they play, without apology but with maximum encouragement and unrestricted access. Even if concert audiences are mainly in their sixties, seventies, and eighties, Hough is not concerned because they keep replenishing themselves. People often come to classical music at a later age, when they have more time on their hands.

He likes some popular music even though its emotional range can be limited. A number of the Beatles songs are extremely poignant, and "Eleanor Rigby" is really an art song. However, much pop music is uninteresting, as it keeps the same, unchanging beat with the same, unchanging chords in every song. In general, it functions more like background music and is not intended to be listened to with a totally focused ear while doing nothing else. Much contemporary jazz is fascinating and can be even more appealing than contemporary classical music because it has such a deep connection with the roots of rhythm.

Modern classical music, like modern life, has changed hugely in the past thirty years. Fashions and trends have become much less restrictive than they were in the 1950s and 1960s, when only one kind of new music (or size of lapel) was acceptable. Its innovations were often disconnected from the main body of classical music and deliberately detached from ordinary listeners. Looking back, Hough thinks audiences were often right in criticizing what sometimes seemed like mere alienating noise—but composers were right to make that iconoclastic challenge. Much was demolished in those complex, post-war years. He doesn't long for a simplistic return to tonal music prior to the early twentieth century, but is happy that tonality now has its place in the writing of more recent composers. After all, atonality exists only in relation to tonality. Without the contrast, the argument, the conflict, the tension and release, music simply floats in space with nothing to tie it down. Contemporary

music cannot be fully understood or appreciated at first hearing. Composers should be given the benefit of the doubt, but they have to earn respect, too.

Since beginning to compose more seriously, Hough feels a different sort of responsibility to composers whose works he plays, and he is increasingly aware of wanting to communicate the music through an interpretation that conveys the original message. Composers write in different ways; some are quite free in their notation and intention while others are more specific and prescriptive. Liszt was mostly free because much of his music came from improvisations hastily jotted down, whereas Beethoven, despite equal improvisation skills, was more concerned with concretizing his musical ideas on the page. His compositions are rigorously logical and built with a keen sense of architecture.

Composers like Beethoven and Liszt represent something deep and fundamental to Western civilization, but much contemporary discourse, especially in universities, has focused on the Western arts being only a fraction of a bigger picture that includes African, Asian, and other ethnic art. This discovery has been immensely enriching (think of Debussy hearing *gamelan* music for the first time!), but there is no longer any need to be defensive about the Western canon. More people now love and learn classical music in Asia than in the lands where it was born. This delights rather than disturbs Hough.

Classical music and great art in general are not designed to be uncomplicated or simply restful. Beethoven is never relaxing, nor, for that matter, are the late self-portraits of Rembrandt. They are challenging and full of melancholy, seeming to question the worth of a single life with its loss of time and beauty. The last sonata by Beethoven is full of that same struggle. The first movement is short, with tense agitation, but the second movement, three times as long, depicts transcendence—a stirring up of the waters before allowing them to be purified.

Music can also offer a language beyond words. As Hough observed in a home for Alzheimer patients in London, those suffering were often responsive to music even when they were unable to communicate verbally. On another occasion, he gave a concert for young offenders, who proved to be a very restless audience. Some walked out but others stayed on to listen quietly and were visibly moved. There has been much research into music therapy and now more is generally known about the way physical ailments can have psychosomatic causes; is it possible that music can have a healing effect on the body as well as on the mind?

Music can also be depressing and create unbearable nostalgia. Elgar, for example, often makes Hough feel sad in a way that is a mixture of pleasure and pain. Like Rachmaninov, Elgar's music is deeply emotional. Both composers felt out of place in the new world following that period of incredibly rapid change in the first two decades of the twentieth century. This period, encompassing World War I and the Russian Revolution, also became identified with explosive changes in social life, women's liberation, jazz, the motorcar, and electricity in the home.

Some composers relished the new styles and mores, but for others, these conjured up poignant feelings perhaps similar to a grandfather wanting to understand his grandchild, but knowing he cannot really share her enthusiasms, or of parents saying goodbye to children leaving for university, aware they are about to change irreversibly through new relationships and ideas. Musicians often try to express some of these feelings, as well as those of ecstasy, joy, and particularly love, which has stimulated much popular music. To be a musician is to be at the heart of what it means to be a human being. Music's vibrations are intangible in the air but profoundly felt in the soul.

*Stephen Hough was interviewed by the author in Sydney, Australia, in October 2011.*

# Evgeny Kissin

Evgeny Kissin tours regularly in Europe and the United States. He has appeared with the greatest orchestras in the world under conductors such as Herbert von Karajan, Riccardo Muti, Carlo Maria Giulini, James Levine, Lorin Maazel, Daniel Barenboim, Seiji Ozawa, Vladimir Ashkenazy, and Christoph von Dohnányi.

He is the recipient of many awards, including the Crystal Prize of the Osaka Symphony Hall for the Best Performance of the Year in 1986, Musician of the Year Prize from the Accademia Musicale Chigiana in Siena, Italy in 1991, Musical America's youngest Instrumentalist of the Year in 1995, the Russian Triumph Award, Shostakovich Award, and many honorary doctorates of music from universities around the world.

Awards for his recordings include Diapason d'Or, Edison Klassiek and Grand Prix of La Nouvelle Académie du Disque. He won Grammys for Best Instrumental Soloist in 2006 for recordings of music by Scriabin, Medtner, and Stravinsky (RCA Red Seal) and in 2009 for Prokofiev Piano Concertos Nos. 2 and 3 with the Philharmonia Orchestra conducted by Vladimir Ashkenazy (EMI Classics).

Born in Moscow in 1971, Kissin began to play the piano when he was two years old. At six years of age he entered the Gnessin School of Music and commenced studies with Anna Pavlovna Kantor, his only teacher. He made his debut with orchestra in Mozart's Piano Concerto K. 466 when he was ten, followed by a solo recital the next year. At the age of twelve, he performed both Chopin piano concertos in one concert with the Moscow State Philharmonic under Dmitri Kitaenko. His outstanding talent and dedication to music is the subject of Christopher Nupen's documentary film, *Evgeny Kissin: The Gift of Music.*[55]

*My life is devoted to music simply because I couldn't do otherwise, but from time to time, I question why people need the music I love so much. To some extent, this question is answered by those who write to me, saying that my music has helped them overcome problems in their lives.*

— Evgeny Kissin

Evgeny Kissin is aware that classical music does not play an important part in everyone's life. Some people are highly intellectual and spiritual, but not sensitive to classical music—the novelist Vladimir Nabokov, for one. There are also many people for whom classical music does not feature in their lives simply because they were never exposed to it.

The great Russian pianist Sviatoslav Richter[56] claimed that good music and good performance would always reach any listener, but Kissin disagrees with Richter's hypothesis. In this context, he draws attention to the work of Mikhail Kazinik. A violinist and pianist of Russian Jewish descent who now lives in Sweden, Kazinik has devoted his life to promoting music. In his book (Russian), he recalled his efforts to introduce classical music to new listeners and test Richter's hypothesis.

Kazinik started by giving away free tickets to a recital by Richter. The recipients were fourteen young men who were students at a technical high school. These youngsters had no knowledge of classical music, and could not be considered intellectual or spiritual in any way. The concert program included the *Hammerklavier Sonata* and Sonata Opus 111 by Beethoven. Afterward, Kazinik asked the group to write down their impressions of the concert. They all made similar comments: "A man came out, sat down and played the piano. It was very boring. The audience clapped. I think they were just pretending. Nobody can like this. Never."

Faced with this response, Kazinik began teaching the young men about classical music, and after several sessions, he came to Beethoven and played Richter's recording of Sonata Opus 111.[57] Everyone in the group was adamant that the man who performed at the concert they attended had not played this music! They insisted the concert had been particularly boring and the recording they were listening to now was undeniably beautiful.

In light of this investigation and its outcome, Kazinik suggested that great art, classical music in particular, can be comprehended by most people, but requires a process of familiarization through education. He illustrated this view with a story about Victor, a childhood friend and neighbor two years older than himself.

Even though the families were neighbors, it would be difficult to imagine two more different households. Mikhail's parents were always taking him to concerts, theaters, and museums, whereas Victor's father was an alcoholic who beat his wife and children and spent his money on vodka. In order to support the family, Victor's mother did the washing at cut prices for people who lived in the same building.

Although still a teenager, Victor was already in trouble with the police. Mikhail's parents took pity on him and often invited him to their home for meals. One day, when his parents were out, Mikhail and Victor sat poring over Mikhail's collection of postage stamps. It was during the late 1940s, and no one in the Soviet Union, apart from diplomats, could envisage traveling abroad. In this environment, stamps offered a certain vicarious enjoyment. At some point in the evening, Mikhail went into the kitchen to check on the food his mother had left for both of them, and after dinner, Victor left.

The following morning, Mikhail was horrified to discover that his stamps had disappeared, but he was so naïve and full of fantasy that he imagined himself sleepwalking and giving them to strangers during the night. His parents, more sensibly, confronted Victor, who returned five of the stamps but admitted to selling the rest. He was terrified of being reported to the police. As he was already in trouble with the law, Mikhail's parents felt sorry for him and did not press charges. However, they stopped inviting him to their home.

Kazinik, who was fourteen at the time, was studying the piano. He was learning the *Moonlight Sonata*[58] by Beethoven, and loved the piece so much he played it constantly. About six months after the stamp incident, Victor rang Mikhail's doorbell and bashfully asked if he could come in and listen to Mikhail playing the *Moonlight Sonata*. Over the following days, he often returned. He was also keen to know more about the music, and one day, he questioned Mikhail about the possibility of learning to play the same piece! As Mikhail did not want to give him false hopes, he explained it would depend entirely on motivation and could only be achieved if Victor's aspiration to play the *Moonlight Sonata* was powerful enough to suppress all competing desires.

So this sixteen-year-old boy with an alcoholic father, a police record, and no previous contact with classical music started on a frantic quest to play the piano. For two years he worked hard on scales and études until finally he was able to start playing the first movement of the sonata. Then he was curious to know if Beethoven wrote any other sonatas, so Mikhail told him about the composer's total of thirty-two piano sonatas. Over time, they listened to a recording of the complete set at Mikhail's home. Eventually, Victor became a lifelong enthusiast of classical music, and when he got a regular job, spent most of his salary on recordings.

Kazinik had another story that demonstrated the effect of great art on people who had never been exposed to it. He was invited to give a series of lectures on great music at a Swedish university. Just before he was due to start, the organizers warned him about a young girl who would probably attend. They described her as erotically obsessed, restless, and likely to leave the room at any time. Kazinik heeded the warning, but the girl sat still throughout his lecture and listened with rapt attention. The next day, she came to see him, carrying a gift of poems she had written in response to his talk.

When he read through the poems, Kazinik was impressed. As he thought his Swedish was not good enough to pass judgment on the poetry, he got the advice of a Swedish linguist and literary critic. This authority immediately recognized the high order of the poems. The young woman was obviously endowed with much creative energy that had been expressed sexually, but she had never been introduced to the world of great art. Much later she went on to become an important writer.

In another anecdote, Kazinik wrote about a concert and lecture for students at a regional Russian university during the Soviet era. When he and his pianist colleague arrived the day before, they expected to see posters advertising their event. There were none to be seen, so they went to the director of the university, who explained that the university was really keen for students to attend Kazinik's lecture, but they had shown very little interest in classical music. In an attempt to change their attitude, the university staff had thought up a strategy. They invited a local sexologist and announced he would be giving a talk on sex techniques, even though this was a taboo subject for public discussion in communist times. Instead of publicizing the lecture concert, they had put up posters advertising the sexology talk.

Though Kazinik was baffled, he had a few friends among the students of the local theater school and met with them for consultation. The following day, the auditorium filled with students just before the two events were due to start. Backstage, Kazinik, the pianist, and the sexologist met, and then all three went on stage together with the director, who announced the sexology talk was about to begin. He introduced the visiting musicians from Moscow and suggested the students listen to the music lecture, at least for the sake of the tradition of local hospitality and courtesy. At this point, some of the students yelled out, "We don't want music, we want sex." Kazinik's student friends in the audience countered with "No, we want music now. We want to listen to the musicians." The director deliberated for a moment before presenting a solution: the musicians and the sexologist would have alternate sessions, ten minutes at a time.

Kazinik started his talk and the students began to listen attentively. Ten minutes passed, then fifteen and twenty. Nobody interrupted him, but the sexologist was getting irritated because Kazinik's ten minutes were long over. Then a member of the audience piped up proposing that the musicians be allowed to continue their presentation. After all, the sexologist lived locally and the musicians had come all the way from Moscow, so why not listen to them now and have the sexologist give his talk another day. A slanging match started for and against the plan, and finally the director decided the sexologist should give his talk in the same hall and Kazinik and the pianist should move to another, smaller auditorium.

The lecture concert went on and on for about five hours with more and more students coming over from the larger hall. At the end of the event, one of the students asked Kazinik to sign a poster that had advertised the sexology lecture. Kazinik was so moved that he was roused to compose a poem then and there. It ended with the words: "the human body should be loved not through technique, but through music"!

Kissin admires the way Kazinik is able to talk about music and stimulate interest in the subject, as he often finds such attempts very limited, and even vulgar. He just plays it. Ever since he can remember, he has responded to music with every fiber of his being, and while playing, feels in touch with some of the deepest and most positive emotions.

How does a musician convey the emotions in the music? For Kissin, there are few visual associations. He has no visual memory for music and only memorizes by ear, but occasionally, as in Rachmaninov's lyrical works, the music arouses the same feelings as those he associates with the Russian countryside.

Except for program music, like Schumann's *Carnaval*[59] and *Kreisleriana*,[60] or Mussorgsky's *Pictures at an Exhibition*,[61] he is not usually aware of a storyline. After a concert in the United States, however, when he played Liszt's B Minor Sonata,[62] his piano technician exclaimed: "What a story you have told!" Clearly, it was not a story in the literal sense but one that journeyed through profound emotions in a language beyond words.

It is difficult to be categorical about how a piece should be performed. As a young virtuoso, Josef Hofmann[63] once asked Anton Rubinstein,[64] founder of the Russian piano school and the St. Petersburg Conservatory, how a particular piece of music should be played. He replied, "In sunny weather, play this way; when it rains, play differently!"

Knowledge of events at the time of a composition could influence a performer's approach. Kissin has always loved "Sonata-reminiscenza" by Nikolai Medtner,[65] but when he began to study the piece and learned more about the composer's circumstances at the time of writing, he became aware of new elements in the music. The sonata was written after the Russian Revolution when Medtner and his wife were staying at a friend's house in the middle of a forest. It was midwinter. The civil war was raging, food was scarce, and they had to make do with whatever potatoes they could find. The nostalgic feeling imparted by this music probably reflects Medtner's response to the loss of the old Russia he had known all his life, a Russia that was quickly disappearing in a bloody civil war. As a result, the future was looking very uncertain.

All experiences, however insignificant, can influence a musician's interpretation, even though he or she may not be aware of it. Kissin has two examples from his own experience, both in relation to the Piano Concerto No.1 in C Minor by Shostakovich.[66] In the summer of 1989, he played this concerto at the Lucerne festival, and in the same building as the concert hall, there was an exhibition of twentieth-century paintings. Although he cannot recall any of these, they somehow drove him to play the concerto differently.

On another occasion, he played the concerto six months later in Amsterdam. The day before the concert, he heard the news of Andrei Sakharov's death, and his grief influenced the way he played. By that time, Kissin had performed the concerto so often that it felt a little jaded, but the news of Sakharov's death shook him profoundly and injected fresh emotion into the piece.

Music is about emotions, which Kissin finds much more difficult to convey in a recording studio compared with a live performance. This is why he was not happy with his recording of Schumann's *Kreisleriana*. He needed to feel especially creative in order to play it well, and missed the presence of an audience. Not all musicians feel the same; some play equally well in a recording studio or a concert hall.

Being a performing musician is all about sharing things he loves. Some journalists have asked him what he would do if he weren't a musician. At first, he used to dismiss that question because he couldn't imagine doing anything else. Then he realized that in the absence of musical talent, he would have liked to work as a tour guide or freelance journalist, and, on reflection, he realized what these three disparate professions had in common. In each case, they involved sharing what he loved with others. The insight also helped him understand why he had loved reciting children's poetry and Tolstoy's fairy tales so much during his childhood.

From a very early age, he loved playing for people. His first solo recital took place in Moscow when he was eleven years old. As the tickets were free and many people were interested to hear a child of that age giving a concert, the six hundred seats were quickly filled. More seats, closely surrounding the piano, were added on the stage to accommodate extra people.

During the interval, he kept asking when the second half would begin, as he was anxious to get back on stage and continue playing. After the concert was over, his piano teacher asked him if he had felt uncomfortable with so many people sitting close to him on the stage. "No," he replied, "They were helping me!" Indeed, he felt energized by their presence.

Communicating the love and elevating experience of music to an audience is his raison d'être, and music is the dearest thing in the world for him, but he is skeptical about any ethical claims for the art. Although he might wish it had moral value, he sees no evidence for it. Nazi leaders were no less evil for listening to music, and Stalin liked certain poetry and opera. According to Maxim Gorky, Lenin marveled at Beethoven's "Appassionata" Sonata,[67] but music also got on his nerves. He said it prompted tender thoughts of stroking people and whispering sweet nothings, while it was in fact the time to beat people on the head without pity, even though he was basically against any violence.[68]

Music is morally neutral although emotionally powerful. In a talk on television, a prominent Russian priest remarked that religion, like all great art, could be used for good and evil. He spoke of the Spanish Inquisition as a wicked abuse of the Christian religion, which he held sacred. Similarly, music can be misused.

*Evgeny Kissin was interviewed by the author in Sydney, Australia, in September 2011.*

# Paul Lewis

*BRIEF BIOGRAPHY*

Paul Lewis is the recipient of many awards, including the Royal Philharmonic Society's Instrumentalist of the Year, two Edison Awards, three Gramophone Awards, the Diapason D'or de l'Année, the Preis der Deutschen Schallplattenkritik, the Premio Internazionale Accademia Musicale Chigiana, and the South Bank Show Classical Music Award.

He is a soloist with the greatest orchestras in the world, such as the Boston, Chicago, London, and NHK Symphony, Bavarian Radio Symphony, New York, Los Angeles and Czech Philharmonic, and the Royal Concertgebouw under conductors including Christoph von Dohnányi, Sir Mark Elder, Bernard Haitink, Jiří Bělohlávek, Stéphane Denève, and Wolfgang Sawallisch.

As a recitalist, Lewis has performed at Alice Tully Hall and Carnegie Hall in New York, Royal Festival Hall, London, Concertgebouw, Amsterdam, Theatre des Champs-Élysées, Paris, Musikverein and Konzerthaus, Vienna, Berlin Philharmonie and Konzerthaus, Tonhalle Zürich, Palau de Musica Barcelona, Oji Hall, Tokyo, Sydney Opera House and Melbourne Recital Centre, among others.

He regularly performs at major festivals, including Tanglewood, Mostly Mozart in New York, Salzburg, Schubertiade Schwarzenberg, Lucerne, Edinburgh, La Roque d'Anthéron, and the Klavier Festival Ruhr. In 2010 he performed a complete Beethoven piano concerto cycle at the BBC Proms.

His recordings for Harmonia Mundi include all the Beethoven piano sonatas, concerti, and *Diabelli Variations*, as well as works by

Liszt, major piano works by Schubert, and the three Schubert song cycles with tenor Mark Padmore.

Lewis studied at the Guildhall School of Music and Drama in London and later with Alfred Brendel. He is artistic director of the Midsummer Music chamber music festival in Buckinghamshire, UK, together with his wife, Norwegian cellist Bjørg Lewis.

Lewis received an honorary doctorate from the University of Southampton in 2009.[69]

*Today, people demand immediate benefits, usually those of a larger, faster, noisy and more colorful variety. These attitudes can be seen in television programs that encourage attraction to the loudest, most accessible disposable content that shuts out depth and contemplation. Schubert could not be further from these values, which encapsulate so much popular culture and mainstream media. He reminds us of our basic need for more introspective engagement with the world, and many people respond to this message.*

—PAUL LEWIS

PAUL LEWIS WAS interested in classical music when he was a schoolboy. This interest was an important part of his life, with music like a close friend, bonded in a relationship of mutual understanding. He believes this closeness is part of the power of music and does not happen at the level of speech.

To some extent, it is illustrated by the experience of his wife's sister, who plays in a string quartet in Norway. Her son went to a nonselective local school with no music curriculum, so she decided to develop a children's mini-music course that included a group violin class every week. Some of the children had never considered playing an instrument or even taken an interest in classical music, yet there was an unexpected benefit outside of the classes. After a few months, it was observed that many of the academic underachievers in the group had become more interested in their schoolwork, and the teachers concluded the music project was a small investment for a large return. This project illustrates the value of exposing children to music, because it promotes their sense of achievement and enjoyment in learning and performing classical music.

It appears music assists learning by stimulating parts of the brain, a process especially beneficial for children. The study of music helps them learn social skills, such as the ability to listen with empathy. Research has reportedly shown that children who are bilingual are more likely to see both sides of an argument[70] compared with those who only speak one language, and Lewis wonders if music could act like an additional language, resulting in a "bilingual" effect on the brain.

The brain also appears to store music together with emotions and strong associations, which might explain the powerful memory for songs. Lewis remembers hearing pop music on the radio when he was a child but took no interest in it at the time. These days though, he feels nostalgic whenever he hears 1980s chart music, as the songs transport him immediately to his childhood, complete with the associated sensory memories of taste and smell.

Apart from any learning function, music performance presents a dynamic in which the performer and audience react to each other, giving and receiving energy. This might explain why making a recording is such a different experience from a live performance. In the recording studio, one has the opportunity for a very high level of technical achievement, but music flourishes in live performance because the audience and performer are jointly engaged in its production. Nonetheless, Lewis is grateful for the availability of recordings, as they assisted his youthful searches in music before he started going to concerts and commenced playing the piano.

Performing musicians need to find suitable teachers, and after progressing to an advanced level, Lewis had the good fortune of studying with Alfred Brendel,[71] a pianist who has explored music's multifaceted relationships with other arts and life itself. Mentoring of such a high order deepened his approach to the expression of universal human feelings otherwise difficult to articulate in the music he plays. The great works seem to be independent of the constraints of time or place and fundamentally concerned with human issues. Some music can be more explicit, such as the works of Shostakovich, but Lewis admits it is difficult for someone like him to fully comprehend the pressures people experienced under Stalin's regime.

It may seem counterintuitive, but music is also independent of the composer's character. Wagner was repugnant, with obnoxious ideas, but he was still a great composer. The conductor Wilhelm Furtwängler may have believed in an abhorrent ideology, yet some of his performances are miraculous, even though they have been captured on a primitive recording with grainy musical colors. Richard Strauss appears to project himself as a hero in his symphonic poem "Ein Heldenleben" (A Hero's Life).[72] It is probably one of the most egocentric pieces of music, but the work is great in scope and feeling.

For an audience, listening can be challenging in many ways, particularly in the appreciation of contemporary music. These works are harder to understand given their more abstract nature. They might be puzzling at first, but they attempt to say much that is similar to traditional classical music. The difference lies in the language. Even Beethoven's fugue from his *Hammerklavier Sonata*[73] can sound bewildering, and it would be interesting to arrange a program that combines this sonata with modern pieces.

Context is quite important, and when Lewis plays modern music, which is not very often, he tries to include the pieces in a program connecting the unfamiliar to better-known works. He has done this successfully with György Kurtág,[74] a modern Hungarian composer, whose music contains much humor. Haydn, Beethoven, and even Mozart's works include humor, and it is possible to draw quite precise parallels between the ways these composers capture this aspect of music. Erik Satie[75] is another composer who expressed a sense of humor and wrote for the amusement of listeners as well as the entertainment of players.

When planning programs, Lewis looks for connections and contrasts. They should add up to more than their sum, and to that end, it is necessary to build a musical experience with a common thread. People are curious to make sense of things and they enjoy a well-constructed, insightful program.

Musicians are often attracted to particular composers. As a teenager, Lewis was devoted to the music of Alexander Scriabin,[76] a composer who was heavily into mysticism and was probably aided by copious quantities of alcohol. Scriabin wrote beautiful music he hoped would push beyond the accepted boundaries. When he died at the age of forty-three, he left the unfinished *Mysterium*,[77] an ambitious, innovative synesthetic work that included light, sound, touch, and smell, as well as active audience participation.

Of all the composers, Schubert is the one to whom Lewis feels closest. Although not exclusively inward-looking, Schubert's real strength lies in introspection. Some of his most intense work is black, and deals with despair, horror, and death. This is not done with the intention of adding darkness to people's lives, but is about articulating ideas often difficult to express in words. In his songs, the most complex emotions are immediately comprehensible on a profound level. Schubert's music doesn't always reach out; instead, it invites attention in a distinctive and irresistible fashion. If Schubert is on a concert program, people should not expect to be entertained. Listening will require some effort but the rewards can be great.

Some music can have a controlling influence on a person's mental state. As a young man, Lewis was greatly affected by Schubert's song cycle *Die Schöne Müllerin*.[78] The story focuses on a simple young man who starts out on a journey without a care in the world, follows a brook to a mill, and falls in love with the miller's daughter. She spurns him for a hunter, and the young man, broken-hearted, throws himself into the brook, which sings a gentle, rocking lullaby. On one occasion, Lewis was lying on his bed in the middle of the day, enraptured while listening to these songs. The concept of innocence interwoven with death seemed chilling, and for a couple of hours, he lay there unable to move.

This depth of emotional experience belongs to music, rather than painting, sculpture, or literature. It is a very personal response, and depends on how receptive people are to its message. Lewis describes his own relationship to music as one of necessity. He could enjoy it without playing, but he plays because he can. There was never a decision to become a pianist; it just happened. He doesn't have a mission to convince or convert people, but as a performer, he believes he has a responsibility to transmit the music without hypocrisy or special effects. In that regard, he gets very irritated when he recognizes aspects of playing that are superfluous to the music and calculated to draw primary attention to the performer.

A convincing performance demands that a musician conveys the music honestly. Clearly, the level of skill is vitally important in order to enable emotional transmission. It is a thrill to watch and hear a virtuoso play, but a blast of fast octaves and rapid arpeggios is not enough to sustain lasting memory of a piece.

Music can transport listeners on an emotional voyage with intrusive elements. An example occurs at the end of Schubert's great A Major sonata, D959.[79] This work passes through a landscape of deep feelings, especially in the brutal slow movement. Later, during the last movement, Schubert takes his time, as he always does, never in a hurry to develop ideas, meandering to allow reflection in the moment.

Finally, the end of the work approaches, but he seems unable to let go.

The theme recurs throughout this movement; the listener has come to know it as a close friend, and it is heard again with a slightly different harmony: an F natural instead of an F#. It is unsettling, even disturbing, as if to say all is not well, not straightforward. Ever since he heard that semitone change, Lewis has thought of it as a farewell to a dear, dear friend. When we listen to this section, it seems as if someone is trying to say goodbye to a friend, but unable to part, wanting just a little more time with the person. After all the emotional turmoil of the journey, we come to this point of departure without resolution, and in typical Schubert fashion, we are left to resolve this separation later, in our own time.

Beethoven employs similar elements, but unlike Schubert, he gives more answers to questions. His solutions entail a different approach and destination, depending on the period of his life. Initially, he manages to conquer adversity with determination and sheer force of will, and eventually he finds a more introspective, spiritual path, which makes his late work so compelling.

In Beethoven's last work, the Piano Sonata No. 32 in C Minor, Op. 111,[80] the first movement is turbulent, traumatic, and so driven it hardly stops for breath. The second and final movement, the *Arietta*, is a huge contrast to the first movement in terms of character and the emotional world it occupies. The listener is in a very different space now, and becomes aware of the emotional effect of the high trills. They are alarming, and act like vibrations that induce a feeling that could almost be described as spontaneous, effortless levitation. This is Beethoven's form of resolution, but it is not Schubert's way. There is no end to discovery with these compositions, and Lewis feels if he returns to the Schubert sonatas in ten years' time, he will probably find many new revelations. But increased maturity and life experiences might not have any direct impact on the way he will interpret these sonatas in the future.

He can, however, recall major life events he associates with certain pieces—in particular, the time his wife went into labor with their first child. They were at home, and, while trying to hold off going to the hospital, they listened to a recording of Beethoven's Fourth Symphony.[81] The clarinet solo in the slow movement made a deep impression on him, and now, whenever he hears this music, he is brought back to an event that completely and permanently changed their lives.

*Paul Lewis was interviewed by the author in Sydney, Australia, in July 2010.*

# Aleksandar Madžar

*BRIEF BIOGRAPHY*

Aleksandar Madžar was born in Belgrade in 1968. He started playing the piano under the guidance of Gordana Matinovic and later
studied with Arbo Valdma, Eliso Virsaladze, and Daniel Blumenthal
in Novi Sad, Belgrade, Moscow, and Brussels. He won prizes in the
Geneva, Leeds, Ferruccio Busoni, and Umberto Micheli competitions, and made his debut with the Berlin Philharmonic Orchestra
under Iván Fischer in 1990. Since then, he has enjoyed a rich and
varied career in recital, concertos, and chamber music, performing
regularly all over Europe and occasionally touring North and South
America, South Africa, Australia, and the Far East. Madžar teaches
at the Royal Flemish Conservatoire in Brussels.[82]

His discography includes Chopin Piano Concertos No. 1 & 2 (Classic
FM), *Chabrier: Complete Piano Works* (Arion), *Dufour Performs Mar-
tinů, Prokofiev & Hindemith* (Harmonia Mundi), *Louise Hopkins and
Aleksandar Madžar Play Elliott Carter, Sergei Rachmaninoff and Alfred
Schnittke* (Intim Musik), and two CDs of Brahms Violin Sonatas and
Schumann Violin Sonatas with Anthony Marwood (Wigmore Hall
Live).[83]

*Musical communication could be perceived in terms of a psy-chogram, or psychological map, made up of successive states of mind, and different for individual listeners. Rather than sim-ply evoking sadness or melancholy, the total effect might be seen as a cocktail of feelings, and if there is real contact with the audience during a performance, listeners could experience a whole palette of emotional responses. The Schubert Fantasie in C Major D934, for example, might be represented as a giant diagram of varying colors and intensity.*

—ALEKSANDAR MADŽAR

OZART'S MAGNIFICENT MUSIC reflects many emotions and states of mind, even though he limited himself to the more positive aspects of life. In contrast, accord-ing to Aleksandar Madžar, Beethoven revealed the whole spectrum of human experience, and his music exemplified a route for the expression of social rebellion and nobility of pur-pose in confronting an oppressive environment. Schubert's world is a more introspective, otherworldly landscape. In this realm, we might feel as if we are traveling toward a goal, yet the destination is an illusion because there is no end, only a long tunnel toward infin-ity. Apart from the music itself, the accomplishments of the great composers are also admirable as monuments to hard work and com-plexity. Verdi took about two years to write *Otello*, which runs for two hours and ten minutes.

The ideal exposure to music simply requires being open to it, and the listener's permeability to pieces can be fostered through increased familiarity with the works. If a concert is successful, the audience should feel some joy or perhaps elation, even if the music itself wasn't joyful. Some of the most tragic pieces usually contain a glimmer of light, particularly the compositions of Mahler, Beethoven, Chopin, and Brahms.

Some believe that music could influence people to change their attitudes or behavior, and it is conceivable that a listener who has just heard a fine performance of a Beethoven quartet might leave the concert a more thoughtful person. General transformative power seems doubtful, and it is more likely that music could help us re-evaluate some aspects of ourselves for the duration of a concert in the absence of extraneous preoccupations.

There is no doubt, however, that music has much to offer the development of concentration and self-discipline. Self-knowledge may grow too, as it would be very difficult to play a Beethoven sonata well without some understanding of how the piece relates to you as a person.

Musicians develop these attributes while dealing with the technicalities and the re-creative task. In preparing a piece, they receive a certain "charge" that needs to be discharged during performance. Visual imagery like films, which nourish artistic imagination, can assist performers with this release. It is interesting that the structure of films shares some similarities with musical pieces, as both represent a progressive journey or story on many levels, punctuated by a succession of strong emotional and dramatic moments.

It can be informative for musicians to read about the life of a composer, but this knowledge is unlikely to influence a musician's technical prowess. Similarly, an extensive general education may indicate a lively mind, which is an asset, but not a necessity for great artistry. Maturity might also seem to be an advantage, yet there could be a downside in the contamination that comes with experience, and the loss of freshness and spontaneity that is inevitable in a repertoire played many times.

Even those who are gifted as musical prodigies may not progress into mature artists, as development depends on the strength of their connection with the music. In some cases, parental reinforcement could foster brilliance, but the desire to perform and communicate the music is essential.

Maturity is irrelevant for many musicians and other artists who peak in their teens. The Viennese poet Hugo von Hofmannsthal[84] is such an example. Today, he is best known as the librettist of the operas *Rosenkavalier*[85] and *Ariadne auf Naxos*[86] by Richard Strauss. At the age of sixteen, his first poems were published under a pseudonym. They were received with great acclaim, and people were astonished when they learned the author was still in high school. Von Hofmannsthal spent the rest of his life trying to live up to his brilliant teenage flowering, yet he ultimately found fulfillment in his work with Strauss. It offered a new direction that steered him away from living up to the expectations of his early promise.

On one level, musicians are entertainers, but they could also be envisaged as priests or messengers. Perhaps Madžar's first piano teacher had this in mind when she avowed that music was a precious and fragile sacred commodity in need of careful nurture and appreciation.

Although most listeners are not extensively trained in music, they can hear the difference between a major and minor chord. Between the seventeenth and early twentieth centuries, this was a fundamental musical tension. When it was abandoned later in the twentieth century, the musical language that emerged was unfamiliar and bewildering for many people.

Contemporaries of great classical composers such as Beethoven and Liszt considered some of their works incomprehensible, but after a generation or two, the music was fully accepted. Similar integration is yet to come for much of twentieth-century music, and some pieces are as difficult to comprehend today as when they were first written.

At present, there is a tendency to throw all categories of music together. In the French media, a new term, "*les musiques*," the plural of *la musique*, has come into use to encompass all genres, whether classical, jazz, pop, or world music. Nowadays, a newspaper in France might head one of its arts pages with *Les Musiques*, featuring a variety of articles, concert reviews and so on.

Clearly, there is enormous talent and passion evident in diverse forms of music but classical musicians have a responsibility to keep the many centuries of art music alive, not only for its intrinsic value, but also for the collective bonding it gives listeners. Musicians should be proud to defend their tradition and the composers who perfected a craft over many years.

Other cultures have their own venerable music traditions. Some societies though, particularly Japan's, have responded enthusiastically to the Western concept of classical music. This process may be underway in China today.

*Aleksandar Madžar was interviewed by the author in Sydney, Australia, in November 2012.*

# Kees Boersma

Apart from holding the position of Principal Double Bass with the Sydney Symphony Orchestra, Kees Boersma performs as a soloist, often in new works written for him. These include the Double Bass Concerto *Young Tree Green* by Colin Bright and the *Lake Ice: (Missed Tales No.1)* concerto by Mary Finsterer. Other performances with the SSO include Mozart's concert aria *Per Questa Bella Mano* with Teddy Tahu Rhodes and Bottesini's *Passione Amorosa* with Alex Henery.[87]

As a keen chamber music player, Boersma performs with the Australia Ensemble and the Sydney Soloists, and was a member of the contemporary music group ELISION that premiered works by Franco Donatoni, Richard Barrett, Liza Lim, and Brian Ferneyhough.

Together with his wife, double bass player Kirsty McCahon, and colleagues from the Sydney Symphony Orchestra, he is a member of The Four Basses quartet.

He has played with the Orchestra of the Age of Enlightenment in London, the Australian Brandenburg Orchestra, and Pinchgut Opera, and has been a regular Guest Principal Bass of the Hong Kong Philharmonic Orchestra, the West Australian Symphony Orchestra, and the New Zealand Symphony Orchestra. Prior to joining the

Sydney Symphony Orchestra, he was Principal Bass with the State Orchestra of Victoria and the Australian Chamber Orchestra.

Boersma studied at the Victorian College of the Arts and the Sweelinck Conservatorium in Amsterdam, where he performed with the Royal Concertgebouw Orchestra Amsterdam under conductors Bernard Haitink, Nikolaus Harnoncourt, Antal Doráti, Carlo Maria Giulini, and Riccardo Chailly.

He is a Lecturer of double bass at the Sydney Conservatorium of Music and a tutor for Australian youth orchestras.[88]

*Music is one of the greatest accomplishments of humanity and a high point of civilization. It brings out the best in the human spirit by touching that part of us which is only accessible through music. Can music change behavior? Perhaps not directly, but it is definitely enabling.*

—KEES BOERSMA

KEES BOERSMA WAS BROUGHT UP in the Netherlands, one of eight children. His family moved to Australia when he was a boy, and although none of them were involved with music, it became the driving force of his life, a reason for living, and the channel for much of his energy.

Compared with one's children, good food, or exercise, music generates different strength and enjoyment because it deals with more spiritual needs. Boersma believes the great composers such as Mozart, Bach, and Beethoven are able to fulfill some of these needs by connecting with people in very personal, intense, and mystical ways.

Beethoven in particular sends him into a different space or disposition, which he describes as spiritual because he doesn't feel altered in a physical or emotional sense. It is more akin to a different way of thinking about life, and his receptiveness to this state of mind has grown over the years.

Classical music expresses many emotions, including love, jealousy, anger, and sadness, as well as concepts like courage; yet a composer such as Beethoven does much more. He can make the listener feel like a person who is empowered. There is a majestic, heroic strength in his music, which is particularly evident in the slow movements of the symphonies. The second movement of Beethoven's Seventh Symphony[89] is a good example of the portrayal of struggle and fortitude.

Performers and listeners can identify with the sentiments evoked by such great music and in that sense, it can be seen as a form of therapy as well as a mechanism for changing one's mood or worldview.

As a performing musician, Boersma finds himself on an endless quest to improve his understanding and interpretation, and continually strives for maximum communication with the audience. This process constantly evolves and has no definable end point, as there is always much more to comprehend and value.

Like the visual arts, music is only beneficial if people respond to it, but this requires a little education. Boersma understands the need for music education very well, as he was not brought up in a musical environment and gained much from the opportunity to study the art.

For many years, he struggled to comprehend the merit of certain composers. The music of Anton Bruckner, for example, had always sounded bombastic and simplistic to him. This view changed quite suddenly some years ago when he had the good fortune to play in several seasons of Amsterdam's Royal Concertgebouw Orchestra, which holds Bruckner's symphonies in particularly high esteem. The series of concerts included Bruckner's Seventh Symphony[90] under the baton of the distinguished Dutch conductor Bernard Haitink. At one point in the rehearsals, a feeling of comprehension came over Boersma with an intensity that was difficult to describe. This experience completely changed his appreciation of Bruckner's music, which he now finds incomparably grand and spiritual.

Since his undergraduate years in Melbourne, Boersma has enjoyed performing all genres of classical music. Regular exposure to the works of composers such as Haydn, Mozart, Beethoven, Brahms, Wagner, Mahler, and Strauss made him aware of their common tradition and influence on each other. The style of composition was similar and their craft evolved slowly, with gradual accretion of additional ideas. In Haydn's time, people recognized new elements, such as the composer's introduction of Turkish music in his

*Military Symphony.*[91] When they encountered Beethoven, they heard his new ideas in the context of music that was already familiar to them through Haydn and Mozart.

Since that time, the direction of music has changed considerably. The great schisms in compositional schools, which occurred early in the twentieth century, resulted in a huge stylistic diversity that continues to this day, and demands great flexibility on the part of orchestral musicians.

Boersma has played some very complex new music, which can appear to inundate the performer with a maximum number of notes. In some of the compositions of Brian Ferneyhough, simply progressing from the beginning to the end of a piece could feel like an achievement. In contrast, Boersma premiered a concerto for double bass and orchestra[92] written for him by Mary Finsterer.[93] An exploration of textures and beautiful sound worlds, this music differs from the vast complexity and extremes of many contemporary works.

His choice of instrument might seem unusual, but he was attracted to the double bass early on. When students were invited to select an instrument in primary school, Boersma walked past the violins and trumpets, as he was drawn to the double bass. Initially, he was fascinated by the look of the double bass, and afterwards, by its sound as well.

The intense physicality is particularly enjoyable for performers—perhaps endorphins are released by the central nervous system in response to playing such an imposing instrument! Moreover, the double bass underpins the sound of the orchestra with a solid melodic and rhythmic foundation, and a voice, which is essential in driving the tension and drama.

Whenever possible, Boersma enjoys playing chamber music, exploring intimate works in ways that are not possible in larger ensembles. In a small group, the immediacy and ease of close communication engenders a very different experience to orchestral playing.

Adapting cello parts for the bass has given him an opportunity to perform works he never anticipated for the instrument. In a performance of the C Major String Quintet by Schubert, written for two violins, viola and two cellos,[94] Boersma played the second cello part on the double bass. The replacement presented a challenge to sound convincingly "cello-like," while allowing the natural lower, more resonant qualities of the instrument to make a positive contribution.

Boersma is a great advocate of classical music education for children, in the belief that the body of work bequeathed by Bach, Mozart, Beethoven, and the other great masters represents the peak of human creation. He feels especially privileged for having had the opportunity to appreciate music and pass it on through teaching.

Initiating a string music program at a local Sydney school has been one of his most satisfying experiences as teacher and mentor. Together with his wife, Kirsty McCahon (Principal Double Bass in the Australian Brandenburg Orchestra) and several similarly motivated and energetic parents, a string ensemble was established at Leichhardt Public School (LPS) in 2005.

The enterprise, which was set up to be self-funded through parental and community support, started with weekly lessons for fourteen violin and cello players from kindergarten and year one. A range of donated instruments was also offered for hire. Currently, the LPS Group, consisting of students aged between five and twelve, comprises four levels of ensemble: Mozart, Vivaldi, Beethoven, and Paganini. They perform regularly at school functions and have featured at the annual Instrumental String Festival in the Sydney Opera House. Some of these young players have gone on to join more established youth ensembles and music camps, and Boersma is hoping that one or two of them might eventually become his colleagues in the symphony orchestra!

*Kees Boersma was interviewed by the author in Sydney, Australia, in September 2013.*

# Ole Böhn

*BRIEF BIOGRAPHY*

Violinist Ole Böhn has performed regularly with orchestras through-out the world and worked with conductors such as Moshe Atzmon, Herbert Blomstedt, James Conlon, Lukas Foss, Michael Gielen, Franz Welser-Möst, Marek Janowski, and Oliver Knussen. His wide repertoire spans baroque to contemporary music. He champions new music and composers such as Elliott Carter, Niels Viggo Bentzon, Noël Lee, Ib Nørholm, Pascal Dusapin, and Arne Nordheim have all written works for him.

Elliott Carter dedicated his violin concerto to Böhn, who premiered the work with the San Francisco Symphony Orchestra in 1990 and subsequently performed it with the leading orchestras in Europe and the United States. The Gramophone nominated his recording of the concerto on Virgin Classics as one of the best records in 1992.

He is a regular guest at many chamber music festivals, performs numerous solo recitals, and was first violinist of the Vigeland Quartet and a member of the award-winning Trio du Nord and Leonardo Quartet. Ole Böhn is an acclaimed teacher who has given classes in many music schools, including the Eastman School, Hartt School and Oberlin Conservatory in the US, the Norwegian State Academy of Music, Tokyo University of the Arts, the Oficina da Musica de Curitiba, and the Cinves Festival, Juiz de Fora in Brazil. Currently, he is professor of violin at the Sydney Conservatorium of Music.

He was a member of the jury in competitions including the Sparre Olsen Competition in Norway, Edvard Grieg International Composer Competition, the Concert Artists Guild Competition in New

York, Canadian Music Competition, Concurso Nacional de Cordas Paulo Bosisio in Brazil, the Kendall National Violin Competition in Australia, and the London International String Quartet Competition.

He is the artistic coordinator and curator of the summer concerts at the Vigeland Museum in Oslo, and was awarded the King's Medal of Merit in gold by King Harald of Norway.

Böhn has held the position of concertmaster of the Norwegian National Opera, the Copenhagen Symphony Orchestra, and for shorter periods, the Oslo Philharmonic Orchestra, Teatro la Fenice, Venice, Teatro Municipal do Rio de Janeiro, the Residentie Orkest in the Hague, the Beethoven Orchestra in Bonn, and the Hamburg State Opera.

He studied at the Juilliard School of Music, the Royal Danish Conservatory of Music, and the Staatliche Hochschule für Musik in Cologne.

Böhn plays a violin made by Giovanni Battista Guadagnini in 1766, acquired for his use by Nordea Bank of Norway.[95]

*Bringing people to a chamber music concert is the best way of advancing classical music. The performers are in a relatively small room, close to members of the audience, and they feel as if the musicians are playing exclusively for them.*

— OLE BÖHN

USIC HAS ALWAYS BEEN a part of Ole Böhn's life. He was brought up in a musical household and never questioned the value of music. On reflection, he thinks there are two main reasons for appreciating the art. First is the physiological effect, experienced by some listeners as an emotional release, and which is used in various therapies, including drug and alcohol rehabilitation.[96] Second, music has social connotations; many people like to attend concerts to socialize and spend time with like-minded people. Listening to recorded music is fine, but he prefers the full advantage of live music that utilizes many senses and offers social interaction.

Apart from the social side, one shouldn't underestimate the value of the well-being or the pleasure that listeners derive from music. People often turn to it, particularly during hard times, to help them express emotions and escape everyday worries. Almost everyone has been involved in or exposed to it in some way because it is part of everyday life. People sing and listen to recordings. Today, classical music is a high form of art, with powerful emotional and intellectual content that stimulates and challenges.

Some believe music can also heal. There is some anecdotal evidence for the healing power of music, and Böhn became aware of this dimension while playing at a center for drug addicts. The concert consisted of short pieces by Mozart and Beethoven. One of the young male patients expressed a great deal of interest in the music and told Böhn which piece he liked best. Several months later, he heard that the behavior of the patient had changed following the concert. He was currently off drugs and had left the center. Had the music set in motion a wish to change that was already present?

On another occasion, Böhn was performing in a retirement home where most people seemed too ill to respond to anything but the most basic interactions. While he was playing, he noticed that an old man who had been lying completely immobile started to move his hand in time to the music. No spoken language had been involved in this response.

Music has no barrier due to spoken language or national borders. Anyone can respond to the feelings it conveys. People in India might relate better to their traditional music than to Mozart; however, this doesn't preclude an interest in Western music. People of many cultures watch Western movies that cleverly use classical music in the film score. *Amadeus*, the film about Mozart, created much interest in the classics. People remained in the cinema after the film ended because the music had touched them, and they wanted to hear the complete recording of some of the pieces in the soundtrack.

In spite of classical music in popular films and even as background music in public places, many people are under the impression that this music is elitist and highbrow. Yet Böhn has noticed a wide spectrum of people can be moved by recitals, symphony concerts, and operas. His involvement with a nightclub in Oslo became an interesting experiment. "Stravinsky" was the most popular, trendy bar in the city, although very few patrons knew anything about the composer after whom it was named. The owner, a friend of Böhn's, decided to introduce some classical music in addition to the regular pop, and suggested Böhn should play in the nightclub every Tuesday.

At the time, he was working in the opera orchestra, so he came to the club after work and brought a few musicians with him to play some chamber music. Surprisingly, the Tuesdays with classical music were no less popular than the other nights. Some clubbers even asked Böhn if they could go to the opera, so he started to distribute tickets for opera performances as well as chamber music concerts. Eventually, many patrons of "Stravinsky" became regular concertgoers.

He is disappointed when people express distaste for classical music and recommends they listen more attentively and without prejudice, allowing their feelings to connect with the music through mental associations such as images, events, or relationships. The emotional ride may bring them considerable enlightenment. When he is trying to promote classical music, he refers to its emotional appeal. Today's society is hectic and many people face financial difficulties. Often both parents have to work, leaving little time for the children. Daily life needs to be well organized and controlled if stress is to be avoided. Music allows for some emotional release. The process has the potential to change attitudes to problems and see beyond them.

Böhn runs a series of concerts in Norway aimed at attracting a wider audience to the classics. People are invited to attend and experience the emotions aroused by the music. Later, he suggests how their responses could be utilized. He starts with a talk, a story, or a few keywords to identify some aspects of a work. Using musical examples, he might remark: "You should listen to this. It comes in the middle, and see if you can recognize it." Then he plays a few phrases, points out a modulation, and invites the audience to listen carefully and detect it. He might go on to say: "You will feel it in your skin when that happens. Don't be shy to let it loose, because you will gain something of value, like a very good meal, a pleasurable encounter, or perhaps a thoughtful chat that broadens your knowledge and horizons."

He usually tells untrained concertgoers to focus on listening to the music without thinking or analyzing excessively, in order to reject the impulse to interpret, understand, or form an opinion. Then he plays a piece and asks them to think a little more about their experience: "Does this remind you of something? If it does, can you make it a little more concrete?" One participant told him a particular piece reminded him of the mountains. Even though the music had nothing to do with mountains, it had obviously triggered a memory.

When Böhn had to raise money for a music project in Norway, he invited some business people to lunch at his home and arranged for children to play a few short pieces. Before the concert started, he asked the guests to try and feel the music when it was being played. It must have worked, because he achieved his objectives for the project!

The traditional classics are much easier to promote than contemporary music because the general structure and individual chords are reminders of music people have heard since childhood. New music is more difficult to accept; it is unlike the chords in tunes one enjoys singing in the shower. Nevertheless, Böhn finds that young children, even those in kindergarten, are happy to hear him play the most avant-garde music by Elliott Carter[97] and Krzysztof Penderecki.[98] These children may respond positively because they don't have any preconceived ideas. They are still open-minded and less likely to be influenced by their parents and the dominant culture. It seems they are responsive to musical intervals and rhythms in contemporary music that often seem strange and edgy to older people. Böhn doesn't differentiate between historical and contemporary composers with regard to emotions. Modern composers are also focused on emotions, but they are more difficult to recognize, as the music is new, complex, and not easily compared with that of earlier periods.

If people are not trained to appreciate contemporary music, they may need to listen to a composition several times to access the feelings. Unfortunately, many are constrained by the belief that serious study is required before music can be enjoyed. This is a fallacy. One doesn't need in-depth knowledge of paintings or sculptures to enjoy an art exhibition. People respond very personally. Böhn admits he has no expertise in the visual arts, yet the paintings by Picasso affect him emotionally. For these reasons, he believes there is a comparison to be made between listening to great music and looking at paintings. He loves to visit the Prado in Madrid and when he leaves that museum, he feels a better person for it. Music can also have this effect.

The emotional aspects of music can be quite complicated, but some instruction can help people feel the ups and downs, become aware of the work as a whole, and follow the musical threads. They can learn to recognize the many layers of voices, like those in the finale of the second act of Mozart's *Don Giovanni*.[99] In this sextet, each voice sings a melody that represents a separate character and forms part of a larger unit. Verdi achieves a similar effect in the quartet from *Rigoletto*.[100] Most people who listen to these sextets and quartets are not often aware of the voices as separate melodies with different emotions because they hear every chorus as a single, unified entity. Listening carefully to the sextet in *Don Giovanni* can reveal the individual voices of Donna Anna, Donna Elvira, Leporello, Don Ottavio, Masetto, and Zerlina. All these characters have different agendas that are reflected in their words and musical lines.

Similarly, the four instruments of a string quartet often represent different emotions presented simultaneously. Attempting to hear the voice of each instrument in a string quartet can be quite challenging. Böhn encourages people to spend some time with this genre, even if they prefer the large sound and visual activity that comes with operas and symphony orchestras.

In any music, the composer takes precedence over the performers. The artists are required to interpret the work faithfully and put aside any notions of music as a vehicle for the ego, which could distract the audience from the music. Even a distinctive outfit might divert attention and is the reason why most orchestras prefer their members to be dressed in uniform. There are famous performers who seem more interested in appealing to an audience than conveying the message of the composer. Sometimes an audience can be impressed with an artist's physical appearance, technique, or fabulous instrument, even if a performance lacks genuine quality and feeling. However, it is unlikely that people could be moved to tears in the absence of a sincere performance. Occasionally, there might be an inexplicable, magical element as well. Both performers and listeners can often sense it coming and it makes one feel as if time is standing still.

The idea of a truthful or genuine performance was brought home to Böhn through a personal experience. He used to play regularly with an American pianist. Prior to one concert, he told the pianist how nervous he was feeling. The pianist turned to him and snapped: "Ole, stop thinking of your personal success. Think more about the music." This incident left a deep impression on Böhn, and he has often repeated this comment to his students.

From a very early age, he was taught to be sincere regarding musical interpretation and he has tried to impress this value on his students. First, they have to learn how to study a piece of music and closely follow the composer's markings, which are usually written in Italian, French, or German. When he asks his students about the meaning of the markings, many have no idea. Then he reminds them that they would read the instructions before using a new washing machine. Similarly, the composer has written directions in the form of dynamics such as crescendo and decrescendo. These dynamics are some of the basic tools needed to pass the composer's message to the listener.

The process of teaching students with explanations and demonstrations is an important learning experience for Böhn. He also learns from the students themselves, who contribute new ideas and associations with the music. In his teaching, he emphasizes the importance of accepting individual limitations as musicians and the need to work hard to improve. The same values could be applied to life in general!

Musicians are privileged because they can spend time with composers such as Bach, Beethoven, Mozart, and Brahms. These masters influenced each other and were dependent on previous traditions. Bach provided the bedrock for all, but there would have been no Beethoven without Mozart, and no Brahms without Beethoven. Apart from the music, they were ordinary people. As composers, many were driven by great talent, skill, and profound connection with the human spirit.

Böhn's exquisite 1766 Giovanni Battista Guadagnini violin was acquired by the Norwegian Nordea Bank for exclusive use during his lifetime, or at least while he remains a serious violinist. He gave some thought to the way music could assist the bank in its work and came up with the concept of short concerts associated with business meetings. The bank decided to experiment with the idea and the president arranged several concerts. During a break in business discussions, Böhn would arrive with his accompanist, talk briefly about the violin, and then play for ten to fifteen minutes. These mini concerts invariably broke the ice, initiated a change in the atmosphere and conversation, and somehow helped to clarify problems and solutions. Similarly, he performed in New York some years ago during the negotiations for Norway's membership in the UN Security Council. Humans can be touched by music and crave some sense of the experience, which could explain its power to alter the mood of a meeting.

*Ole Böhn was interviewed by the author in Sydney, Australia, in May 2012.*

# Edward Dusinberre

Edward Dusinberre is first violinist of the Takács Quartet, in residence at the University of Colorado, Boulder. The Quartet tours the world and performs eighty concerts a year.

Their recordings of Beethoven's string quartets, released on the Decca label, have received many awards, including a Grammy, two Gramophone Awards, BBC Music Magazine's CD of the Year, a Chamber Music of America award, and three awards from the Japanese Recording Academy. Their live recordings of the complete Beethoven Quartet Cycle at the Southbank Centre of London was chosen best performance in 2010 for the Royal Philharmonic Society's Chamber Music and Song Award.

Apart from performance, Dusinberre's interest in communicating chamber music has led him to announce the music from the stage, adding relevant and entertaining details. He developed a program combining philosophical readings from Philip Roth's novel *Everyman* with the music of Schubert, Arvo Pärt and Philip Glass. The Takács Quartet, together with Philip Seymour Hoffman, performed the work at Carnegie Hall. In another program in 2010, the Quartet collaborated with playwright David Lawrence Morse and the Colorado Shakespeare Festival on a presentation of the possible environmental influences on Beethoven during his composition of the string quartet Opus 132.

Dusinberre has written articles on the Beethoven quartets for *The Guardian*, *Financial Times,* and *Strad* magazine.[101]

*For some listeners, music provides an escape from the bur-dens and banalities of everyday life by taking people to anoth-er space. It is amazing that a mere musical phrase can trigger memories of a particular time, place or person. In this way, music offers a means of staying in touch with the past.*

—Edward Dusinberre

L ANGUAGE IS NOT always the best way to communicate emo-tion. Edward Dusinberre believes that one of the great strengths of music is its ability to help people articulate and tap into emotion, especially on hearing a piece that connects to particular experiences. Most of Dusinberre's teenage memories relating to music are very positive and linked with playing in the National Youth Orchestra of Great Britain.[102] Participation in this full orchestra included the opportunity to work with top conduc-tors during three two-week residential courses every year during school holidays. Certain pieces, like the Symphony No. 1 in B flat Major by William Walton and the Symphony No.4 by Shostakovich, are now firmly associated with that period of his life, which was full of excitement and youthful infatuations with girls.

Apart from connections with specific memories, music can be enlightening and elicit new, liberating, even somewhat dangerous feelings. A perilous potential of the art is reflected in Tolstoy's disap-proval of the first movement of Beethoven's *Kreutzer Sonata*.[103] He felt this music was emotionally destabilizing in ways that worked against the achievement of social harmony.

Some listeners shy away from certain pieces because they fear where the music will take them. This speaks to its immense power. On the other hand, musicians enjoy the intense involvement, often forgetting about themselves and even losing track of time. Dusinberre finds it tremendously liberating to be released from a suffocating sense of self when playing or listening to a great piece of music.

It is difficult to know if a specific state of mind is required to be moved by music, but there are times when Dusinberre walks on stage and feels that this particular audience is ready for an adventure. A Sunday afternoon audience probably has a different dynamic, especially if they have just had a glass of wine with lunch. The way people listen also depends on their knowledge of the structure, themes, and harmonic progressions of a piece. They might be waiting attentively for their favorite passages. Moreover, hearing a piece for the first time can be a revelatory experience. Dusinberre was a schoolboy when he heard the Piano Concerto No. 1 by Tchaikovsky for the first time on the radio. Enthralled, he stopped doing his homework to listen. So far, he declares, no subsequent performance has quite matched that experience!

Some audiences are willing to let the music take them somewhere disconcerting, like the territory of Beethoven's *Große Fuge*.[104] Dusinberre believes this piece is best placed at the end of a six-concert Beethoven cycle. After the audience has heard all the previous quartets and experienced the range of emotions, they are primed to cope with the craziness, conflict and ultimate resolution of the *Große Fuge*. When the Takács Quartet played it at the end of a Beethoven cycle in London, the listeners responded with immense enthusiasm—a tribute to the musical voyage the quartet and audience had taken together, as well as Beethoven's triumph in overcoming hardship.

There are times when the audience might be tired, want to be elsewhere, or are anxious about plans for the next day. They may find their mind wandering or otherwise filled with mental chatter. Although not an ideal starting point, it is the task of performers to convince the listener to stay and focus on the music for the course of the performance. They must engage the audience and take them elsewhere.

Members of the audience can have a distinctive individual experience as well as a shared one. Comparing individual responses is revealing: when hearing the same melody, one person might see the color yellow while another feels homesick. An indication of the depth of shared involvement can be inferred from the way an audience listens to the end of a slow movement. An intense, sustained silence might signify a more profound and reflective experience.

During each performance, Dusinberre is intensely focused and the energy level of the other members of the quartet can affect his playing. All of his senses are tuned in to every moment on the stage; he is alert to miniscule changes of a crescendo or diminuendo or whether one of his colleagues spontaneously wishes to play with more or less momentum. Firmly in the moment, he is not worried about what might occur in the next movement of the piece, nor does he dwell on something that did not go well thirty seconds ago. It is in this space that he feels truly liberated and transported.

Music can be transformational for the player and listener in different, highly personal ways; its capacity to provide solace is particularly important for many people, especially those who live lonely lives or are trying to come to terms with a traumatic change. After the Takács Quartet played Schubert's great and last String Quartet in G Major[105] at the Wigmore Hall 1997 Gala held in honor of the two hundredth anniversary of the great composer's birth, a woman from the audience came up to Dusinberre and said: "Thank you for your music. I don't have a happy life and your concerts give me something to look forward to."

There is a spiritual element in music; some of Dusinberre's favorite passages and phrases seem to explore the miraculous part of life, or ponder questions about the mystery and wonder of existence. These are some of the reasons he enjoys Beethoven's music so much.

The structure of the works also offers much to consider and analyze. In the composer's later quartets, the transitional passages between one theme and another are not simply a bridge from A to B. Instead, they form a digression that is often more fascinating than the themes themselves. Perhaps there is also a message here for a more spiritual approach to life: an appeal to spend some time in contemplation of life's mystery rather than moving directly from one point to another.

Beethoven's *Hymn of Thanksgiving* in the Quartet Opus 132[106] is a more concrete example of a spiritual communication, and many listeners, even those without religious beliefs, are able to recognize and respond to the composer's perception of awe and beauty.

The range of emotions in music is enormous, and there are more feelings translated into music than one can express in language. Generally, listeners are drawn to pieces that have the richest emotional spectrum, rather than the alien, the one-dimensional, or the superficially cheerful. Beethoven deals with a wider range of emotions than any other composer and can even create an impression of forgiveness, which is an unusual emotion to express in music. It may have been a response he developed through massive personal trials and suffering, culminating in the mastery of his circumstances and emotions. When Dusinberre plays a Beethoven quartet, he is aware of a deep well of emotional intensity waiting to be tapped.

The magnificence of the music is also a constant reminder of one's own insignificance and self-centered pursuit of individual happiness. He is aware it is a privilege to be in the service of something far greater than oneself and associated with an art of such scale, beauty, and even healing properties. Recently, he put together a CD of various pieces for a person anxious after being diagnosed with a chronic disease. In spite of minimal past exposure to classical music, he found the music diverting and soothing.

The emotional effect of music depends on one's sensitivity. Harmony can do it, or the texture and tension of a particular chord. A soaring melodic line can speak passionately, and contrasts can create particularly strong reactions. Following the sublime *Hymn of Thanksgiving*, Beethoven wrote a somewhat pesky march that bursts the bubble of holiness. It is an extraordinary moment in the piece: a shock for the audience, but for the performers a welcome release after all the reverence!

There is a whole palette of color in music. Dusinberrre is often moved by the shimmering transparency of a passage: for example, the opening of Ravel's *Daphnis and Chloe*.[107] For string players, there are two extremes in the color range. They can use a lot of bow and make a sound containing much air but without immense focus. Alternatively, digging into the string produces a richer sound with more powerful overtones. These dark, warm sounds are vital, but as a violinist who enjoys playing very high notes, Dusinberre tends to be drawn to the transparent, clear, rather liquid sounds, and is particularly drawn to the masterful recording of Edvard Greig's Piano Concerto[108] played by Norwegian pianist, Leif Ove Andsnes. Throughout that piece, he produces a gorgeous liquid transparency.

Many of the most beautiful instrumental colors arise when a performer ceases to sound like an instrument, and the audience is focused on the music alone—for example, when a pianist is able to make listeners forget they are listening to a piano. If Dusinberre sounds too much like a violinist, it is a problem. Singers have a different aim because they are often trying to imitate instruments.

Chamber music groups have various ways of managing the balance between instruments, with some aiming for a supreme unity of sound. Although the Takács Quartet has received compliments for projecting a singular purpose, Dusinberre points out they are four very different individuals whose challenge is to produce a unified sound and an interpretation that still permits independent personalities to come through on stage. Each member is sensitive to the interactions and atmosphere in the group, and he feels the quartet would be unable to give a good performance if they weren't getting on well. They place great value on each other, not only as musicians but also as people. Dusinberre believes this attitude is the main factor in generating the good working relationships that make it possible for the quartet members to debate and criticize each other freely. This process is a vital, even enjoyable part of rehearsals and the evolution of a unified sound and interpretation.

Nonmusical aspects of performance have become more important in recent years. Following a concert, a woman came to say she missed the patent leather shoes Dusinberre had worn previously! There is also a greater expectation for performers to talk from the stage. In addition to the content, the audience would like to glean some idea of the performers as people. Some performers believe there is a need to break the ice with the audience, as if playing the music were inadequate. There are indeed times when talking about an unfamiliar piece can be helpful in removing some of the audience apprehension. Dusinberre enjoys talking on stage but feels it is no substitute for communicating through the music.

Transmitting the emotional message relies to some extent on the interaction between the players, as manifested by their body language and facial expressions. This dimension is lost in recordings, but the process of recording helps musicians deepen their knowledge of a piece and the closeness of microphones in the studio can induce players to try colors and dynamics that would not project in most concert halls. For some listeners, hearing music in the intimacy of one's own home with superb audio equipment is a powerful experience. For these reasons, recordings have immense artistic value for both players and listeners.

The Takács Quartet has avoided becoming immersed in the contemporary repertoire, unlike the incomparable Kronos Quartet, which has made a career in that genre. Usually, it is the composer's feeling for melodic beauty that drives Dusinberre's interest in a contemporary piece. In the Bartók quartets,[109] the Takács emphasize the humanity, warmth and humor in the music, without underplaying the roughness or ugliness of certain passages. Sometimes Dusinberre wonders how many people in the audience are prepared to brave the elemental ugliness, terror, and alienation portrayed in the music. It is no less appropriate to confront these feelings in music than in certain paintings or movies, as long as there is balance: he would wish to hear some consolation in a terrifying piece.

Good contemporary composers are aware of a need for balance, so they include both lyrical and more rhythmic writing for strings. A good example is Australian composer Carl Vine, whose String Quartet No. 4[110] is a piece characterized by contrast, variety, and a strong musical language of its own.

Creating a context for contemporary compositions can prove useful and illuminating. The Takács Quartet commissioned a young American composer, Daniel Kellogg, to write a work based on the theme from the slow movement of Schubert's *Death and the Maiden*.[111] This piece, which is about fifteen minutes long, is an imaginative exploration and meditation on Schubert's music, and audiences were able to connect well to the work. The Quartet has had mixed experiences with other contemporary music, and Dusinberre has a low tolerance for new music that is very difficult to learn, especially when the audience response is poor. On the other hand, both of these characteristics could apply to Beethoven's *Große Fuge*, so any new piece deserves repeated playing and listening before a verdict is reached!

For Dusinberre, some modern composers seem to have lost touch with the need to create a wide emotional range. A number of new compositions do not communicate well and appear to be restricted by abstraction, mathematical formula, or textural gimmicks. However, there are many exceptions, like the works of Thomas Adès, which are particularly attractive and challenging pieces. Naturally, personal taste plays a huge part in these judgments!

Dusinberre has never been very interested in atonality for itself, which he concedes is probably his own failing, and he is more sympathetic to a modernist composer like Debussy, who believed that any type of sound could be considered music; but then, he did have exceptionally good judgment in its use.

*Edward Dusinberre was interviewed by the author by telephone in November 2012.*

# Donald Grant

*BRIEF BIOGRAPHY*

Violinist Donald Grant studied music at St. Mary's Music School in Edinburgh and at the Royal Northern College of Music, where he won the Eleanor Warren Salon prize, the John Webster strings prize, and a Concerto Award. He also won scholarships from the Dewar Awards, Loan Fund for Musical Instruments, and Foundation for the Sports and Arts.

He was guest leader of the Britten-Pears Chamber Orchestra, performed with the Scottish Bach Consort, Camerata Scotland, Hertfordshire Chamber Orchestra, Mendelssohn on the Mull Orchestra, and Meadows Chamber Orchestra; and worked with artists Catriona McKay, Kate Rusby, and Roy Bailey.

He is co-founder of the Elias String Quartet. The quartet has toured the United States and Australia and performed widely in Europe and the UK, including a five-concert series at the Wigmore Hall, London, with associate artists Leon Fleisher, Jonathan Biss, and Pascal Moraguès. They have also collaborated with other artists such as Michael Collins, Ralph Kirshbaum, Alice Neary, Ann Murray, Anthony Marwood, the Jerusalem Quartet, and Vertavo String Quartet.

In September 2009, the Elias Quartet's recording of the String Quartet No. 6 by Mendelssohn was given highest rating on BBC Radio's *Building a Library,* and their *Live in the Wigmore Hall* CD of Schumann and Haydn has received great acclaim.

The Elias Quartet was recipient of the 2010 Borletti-Buitoni Trust Award and was chosen to participate in BBC Radio 3's New Generation Artists Scheme.[112]

*During periods of stress, we have a greater need for music to provide an escape from everyday life, or to tap into more positive feelings. It does not have to be joyful. Even the most melancholic music can make us feel better by accessing our emotions. People who come to see the quartet after concerts often tell us how much comfort they have received from music while trying to deal with cancer or a death in the family.*

—DONALD GRANT

ERIOUS OR CLASSICAL MUSIC, especially a work of genius, can expand the heart and soul in inexplicable ways. Even without any depth of knowledge, the first contact with great music can be overwhelming.

Children seem to have a natural instinct for musical sounds. Even as infants in a pram, they reach out with their arms as if to touch the music. When they are older, they like to dance to the music. For teenagers, music is an expressive outlet and lessons are a time for freeing up emotions, which could explain why music students have such close relationships with their teachers.

Donald Grant is not a religious person; yet when he plays or listens to music such as Beethoven's String Quartet in A Minor, Op. 132,[113] he is drawn to pondering the big questions of life. When he was nineteen years old, this was the piece that induced him to dedicate his life to playing chamber music, particularly string quartet music. It is full of hope, and leads one on a mighty journey. Everything in this work makes sense. In his youth, Grant was also overwhelmed by the Schubert String Quintet in C.[114] It is a perfect voyage through many emotions that are evoked by extraordinary harmony, melody, and the wonderful bass sound of two cellos.

112

While rehearsing such musical masterpieces, musicians attempt to enter the mind of a composer of genius through the markings on the page, the structure of the piece, and the harmony. In the Elias Quartet, they share opinions and analyze and experiment with different ways of playing, but leave a certain amount of freedom for spontaneity during performance. Otherwise they are simply recreating something rehearsed. During performance, the players feed off the acoustic and audience response, when listeners seem to focus on every note and are emotionally involved. Acoustics are important; a very live acoustic could force players to slow the tempo and articulate more in order to avoid blurring.

It is vital to learn how to practice and rehearse well. When they were younger, members of the quartet talked more during rehearsals, but these days, they communicate more effectively through playing, and even a slight movement can indicate an idea that would have needed verbal communication in the past. At all times, they strive to maintain the same direction and a blended sound. No matter how gifted the performers, quartet playing is hard work, and people are often shocked to learn how long it takes to master a piece.

Grant is devoted to the re-creative work and firmly believes the string quartet repertoire probably represents the greatest music. It is very spiritual, but the performer is greatly aided by a good general education and life experience. Natural musicians, however, are able to create emotions they have never known. Music also has the capacity to connect people to past times and tap a deep reservoir of emotions. This is important for performing musicians, as they must give everything when they play. At the same time, they preserve control by "witnessing" the music.

The effect of the music on an audience is all about emotions—thrills and tears. The more absorbed the listener, the more nuances one is able to hear. People have become accustomed to perfection in recordings, but emotionally, the opportunity for "something magical" is much greater with live music. In order to spark the magic, musicians need to risk slightly different interpretations during each performance—for example, one member might play a different quality *pianissimo* with the rest following suit. Other similar changes could involve tempi, dynamics, phrasing, or different bowing and fingering.

In the past, members of the quartet communicated mostly through looks, but over the many years they have been together, their interaction has intensified to such an extent they can anticipate a change, particularly an emotional one, even before the other person has made it.

Compared with soloists, string quartets usually get on well with other groups. This camaraderie is at work in chamber music competitions, where quartets are generally supportive of each other. In general, musicians within a chamber music group cooperate well. Perhaps it is due to good working relationships, both musically and in terms of business decisions.

The Elias Quartet has a special affinity for Mendelssohn, and they champion his chamber works in the belief he is an underrated composer whose genius deserves to be promoted. Beneath the lightness, there is amazing harmony and complexity in his music. These qualities become more apparent when his pieces are played slowly, but they are often too intricate for an audience to recognize at full tempo.

The younger generation is usually more receptive to contemporary music, but most people need to hear it several times before it becomes familiar. This has led to some concert programs featuring the same piece twice. There are some wonderful modern works, such as *Ainsi la Nuit* by Henri Dutilleux,[115] which many consider a masterpiece.

Music is a common language that has the power to heal through group experience and teamwork, perhaps, even leading people in the audience to listen more attentively to each other. For Grant, dedication to music is intrinsically good, and for the greater good. Playing for children or teenagers who have never heard live music can only have a positive effect, with a message separate from commercial interests and bare ambition.

The Elias Quartet embarked on an exciting venture, the Beethoven Project,[116] after they received the 2010 Borletti-Buitoni Trust Award. This grant is usually donated to young artists for a specific project, and the quartet decided on learning and performing the whole cycle of Beethoven quartets. It fulfilled a long-standing dream. The project was also designed as a bonus to complement their concerts and create a personal link, so people who attended would come to know the quartet and feel connected to them.

For four years, the Quartet had been resident at Sheffield's Music in the Round. During that time, they formed personal relationships with members of the audience through concerts and work in music education, but they hoped for even closer contact with their listeners.

A website seemed an ideal vehicle to break down the barrier between audience and artists, and a place where the quartet could appear in everyday clothes in the room where they rehearse. Not only does the group post their concert performances of the Beethoven quartets, the audience also has access to clips of rehearsals and intimate chats about the music and composer. Watching the progress of ideas during rehearsals helps people understand how group decisions are made regarding interpretation.

At the time of the six-concert Beethoven cycle, the quartet asked a number of writers to contribute program notes for each concert. Some journalists also wrote articles on other aspects of the music, for example Tully Potter's[117] extensive piece on historical quartet groups, their members, recordings, nationalities and schools of playing.

The website features a blog with a wide variety of articles, some by members of the Elias Quartet. The viola player Martin Saving has written many blogs about technical issues, including an article on Beethoven's metronome markings.[118] The quartet is hoping that a database of articles promoting knowledge about the composer will foster even greater enjoyment of his music.

So far, the feedback about the project has been very positive. Eventually, they would like the website to belong to all quartets, and to this end, the quartet invites other players to contribute as many different opinions as possible. They have interviewed David Waterman from the Endellion String Quartet and Peter Cropper from the Lindsay String Quartet.

As the Beethoven quartets present some of the most soul-searching music, Grant and his colleagues return to the drawing board again and again. Even after playing the same quartet many times, they are keen to try out new ideas, and they will never be satisfied because the music has such great depth.

Some of the most emotional moments occur in the slow movements, particularly the *Cavatina* from Op. 130, and the slow movement (*Hymn of Thanksgiving*) of Op. 132.[119] In the late quartets[120] there are territories where one is transported far away, losing all sense of time and reality. It is music of immense meaning, and subjective for performers and listeners.

The personal connection with the quartets is particularly strong for some music lovers, who have heard many concert cycles and keep noticing new details. These fresh observations are a reflection of the density that makes it possible to hear these works differently every time.

When it comes to use of the Internet, classical music seems to be lagging behind the rest of the music world. Perhaps the new website could help to bring in a wider audience, especially the younger generation, for whom this medium is crucially important. Reaching out to youth was another reason for launching the project.

Beethoven's emotional transmission in the quartets is a subject of endless fascination. Although often technical, the insights are accessible and stimulating for the listener. It is remarkable how some harmonic changes are there to produce an intense emotional effect. Quartet Op. 59 No. 2 in E Minor[121] is a case in point. The last movement is in C major, which is unusual because one would expect the first and last movements to be in the home key of E minor, or perhaps E major. The key of C major is very distant from E minor, and would have been shocking when first heard. Listening to it now, one might not be surprised or even aware of the key, but subconsciously one knows something is not quite right and it is disturbing.

The quartet discussed this question during rehearsals, and came to the conclusion the choice of key may have been related to Beethoven's personal situation at the time of writing. He had just announced his deafness to the world, contemplated suicide, but finally chose life. The first and third movements are quite dark; the last movement in C major is exuberant, but there is more than joy. Perhaps the odd choice of C major personifies joy in the face of adversity.

The next String Quartet, No. 9, Op. 59 No. 3, is in the key of C major. When Beethoven was writing the previous one, was he looking ahead to the quartet in C? Perhaps he contemplated all three "Razumovsky" Op. 59[122] quartets as a set, even though they are very big works in themselves.

Talking about Beethoven's music can be difficult because it is complex. Various emotions are expressed at the same time, creating a unified whole, as in opera. Sometimes, a quartet does seem to function like four characters in an opera. One character is singing about her lost love, two are providing a commentary, and the other is doing the sweeping at the back of the stage.

*Donald Grant was interviewed by the author in Sydney, Australia, in September 2009.*

# Clive Greensmith

Clive Greensmith was Principal Cellist of the Royal Philharmonic Orchestra in London prior to joining the Tokyo Quartet in 1999. He has performed as soloist with the London Symphony Orchestra, Royal Philharmonic, English Chamber Orchestra, Mostly Mozart Orchestra, Seoul Philharmonic, and the RAI Orchestra of Rome. In chamber music, he has worked with András Schiff, Midori, Claude Frank, and Steven Isserlis.

He has taught at the Royal Northern College of Music, Yehudi Menuhin School, and San Francisco Conservatory of Music, and he currently teaches at the Manhattan School of Music. His CD *Brahms: Two Cello Sonatas; Schumann: Five Pieces in Folk Style* with Boris Berman was released on Biddulph Recordings, and *Beethoven: Trio op.11; Brahms: Trio op.114; Weber: Grand Duo, op.48* with Jon Manasse and Jon Nakamatsu, on Harmonia Mundi.

The Tokyo Quartet[124] won many awards for their recordings, including the Grand Prix du Disque Montreux, Best Chamber Music Recording of the Year from *Stereo Review* and *Gramophone* magazines, and seven Grammy nominations. It disbanded at the end of the 2013 season following the decisions by violist Kazuhide Isomura and second violinist Kikuei Ikeda to retire.

Following a decision not to replace Isomura and Ikeda, Greensmith formed the Montrose Trio with pianist Jon Kimura Parker and Martin Beaver, first violinist of the disbanded Tokyo String Quartet.

*Musicians have a responsibility, if not a moral duty, to keep the music truly alive through concert performances, and if music does indeed have beneficial effects, live music should be made easily accessible and affordable for all.*

— CLIVE GREENSMITH

USIC HAD VARIOUS ROLES over the centuries. In the sacred realm, it was written for specific occasions. These days, with so much commercialism in the world, Clive Greensmith is aware of a certain yearning for deeper, spiritual values. People are aspirational and look for meaning. In some respects, classical or serious music deals with such issues by expressing the longings and frustrations of mankind, not only in program music but also in abstract works like the Bach Cello Suites.[125] As in the visual arts, people are often moved, soothed, and nurtured by music and, at times, challenged.

For children with learning difficulties[126] or severe mental disabilities, music has been known to improve communication.[127] And as a powerful agent of social change, the El Sistema[128] music education project in Venezuela has been successful in rescuing disadvantaged children from descent into drugs and crime through music training and youth orchestras.

Some music has political connotations, like national anthems and the *Eroica* Symphony[129] that Beethoven dedicated to Napoleon. National and political associations were also part of the Tokyo Quartet's background, and reflected in the interesting mix of a Canadian violinist, British cellist, Japanese violinist, and Japanese viola player.

Kazuhide Isomura, the violist, started to play a musical instrument after 1946, when his mother vowed her sons should have nothing to do with war. Music seemed a healthier alternative and she encouraged her four sons to play instruments. It was after the grave events of World War II that music emerged as a source of high value to the Japanese people.

The shared Japanese background of Isomura and violinist Kikuei Ikeda added special qualities to the quartet. They were the middle voices and, although these two musicians had spent most of their lives in the West, the Japanese communal philosophy worked to produce a unity of spirit, sound, and musical purpose over many years.

An interesting cultural challenge arose as rehearsal of Western music requires a combative approach at times, and Japanese culture restricts open expressions of disagreement. This constraint was lifted in the 1980s following the appointment of a Canadian, Peter Oundjian as first violinist. As a result, members of the quartet started communicating in English, which enabled a more confrontational style and opened up possibilities for airing divergent opinions. Of course, cultural differences were not relevant in transmitting the universal emotions conveyed in the music.

Historically, much Western music developed in the religious singing tradition of the Christian church, even though it went in and out of favor with the authorities. At the same time, the oral tradition in music was a vital part of life for many communities, as folk songs were part of harvests, weddings, and funerals. We have Béla Bartók[130] to thank for collecting many of the folk tunes that originated in Eastern Europe and were embedded in his scores.

Certain pieces may carry tremendous meaning and transformative power. They have the capacity to change the listener's outlook, not unlike the potential in literature to present new and challenging ideas. A piece of music can also link a person to a certain time in life.

Greensmith has a particularly strong memory of the quartet's performance of Beethoven's String Quartet Op. 132[131] in Riga, Latvia. Beethoven wrote the quartet after recovering from a serious intestinal illness, and marked the third movement, "Molto Adagio— Andante," with the inscription *Heiliger Dankgesang eines Genesenen an die Gottheit, in der lydischen Tonart* ('A Convalescent's Holy Song of Thanksgiving to the Divinity, in the Lydian Mode'). While Greensmith was playing this movement, he thought of his father, who had passed away ten years earlier, and felt so overwhelmed with emotion it was difficult to hold back the tears. After his father died, Greensmith's mother found comfort in the cathartic power of music that helped her grieve and move on.

In music, listeners share the exploration of similar ordeals, and some composers have been able to give expression to the human struggle in accordance with their own personalities. Mozart tends to speak to the individual, whereas Beethoven talks to all mankind with strength and vision. In his Symphony No. 9[132] he chooses themes of universal love and the brotherhood of man, ideas that he also conveys in his sixteen string quartets.

The effect on emotions is particularly powerful in pieces like the Bach cantatas, Schubert *Lieder*, or the Mozart *Requiem*, but some of the best music making can be associated with the most abstract music. The emotional content usually comes through even if the listener is not aware of the reasons for the composer's state of mind at the time of composition. In the case of Edward Elgar's Cello Concerto,[133] it was written when he was melancholic and suffering from the passing of his wife as well as the losses associated with the end of the Edwardian era. But it is not essential to understand the reasons for his anguish, as one could still respond to the feelings conveyed in the music. Perhaps music has a way of expressing emotions that are best not articulated and musicians should simply allow the music to transport listeners through time on the wings of emotion.

In a way, music speaks about immortality because the great composers live on through their music. When a performance goes well and the technical side is forgotten, the music seems to come alive. While performing at this level, Greensmith has the sense that his instrument is somehow inconsequential and he is overwhelmed by pure music. At this re-creative peak during a performance, the composer is regenerated. These high points illustrate why live concerts are so important.

Other factors also play a part in the thrill of a live performance. Spontaneity is exciting, and there is a certain adventure, risk, and even danger entailed in walking onto the stage. Most performances are scripted, and musicians who play the same program on tour for many nights have to do something different to avoid becoming stale. Live concerts often produce very interesting results, as the music evolves in unexpected ways. Sometimes it is a challenge with hits and misses, but occasionally the composer's vision builds up and becomes more vivid with each performance.

There might be one or two concerts in a season when all the elements in a particular movement of a quartet come together successfully. Musicians live for these soaring experiences; re-creation of these heights is very difficult, if not impossible, in a recording studio. A musician might sound impressive and perfectly in tune, yet the special moments are absent.

Greensmith can recall such moments in association with the quartet's performances of the String Quartet No. 2 in A Minor by Felix Mendelssohn.[134] The music, written when the composer was a teenager, starts in a meditative way and then goes on a journey through many different landscapes. At the end, the listener comes full circle with a sense of great relief when the music returns to its original scene. When the last A major chord is reached, the music gradually dies away.

There were many times when the quartet performed this work and there was no applause or sign of movement from the audience at the end. People seemed entranced. On one occasion, Isomura got up to take a bow, then promptly sat down again because the audience was motionless. Perhaps the last moments of this work convey an inner calm, much like the beneficial effect of a tonic, or perhaps feelings of redemption. This view was borne out by the many people who came to see the quartet after a performance of this work to tell them how much the music soothed their nerves.

There are also occasions when the music even overwhelms the players, but musicians are most effective when they maintain control of the performance. Only after a work has been well rehearsed and digested are they free to fully experience the music and witness the performance, as if others were playing.

Combinations of instruments, personalities, and their evolving roles in the group characterize chamber music. It is exciting to hear the various creative alterations in a theme being transferred from one player to another. Like four actors in a dramatic production, the members of a quartet are required to be very adroit at changing personality. It is, of course, thrilling to watch an orchestra play with a conductor, and yet the absence of a conductor can lead to more intimate and direct communal music making.

The inherent philosophies of the great composers revolve around the nobility of human love and relationships, as well as wonderment and reverence for the natural world. Haydn expresses these sentiments most beautifully in his oratorio *The Creation*.[135] The first melody takes shape softly, followed by an explosion of sound to the words "Let there be light." At one of the first performances in Vienna, the sick and aging Haydn was carried into the concert hall to rapturous applause, whereupon he reportedly gestured upwards and said, "Not from me—everything comes from up there!"[136] This music is still enthralling and seems to soothe and humor.

Greensmith believes Haydn's immense contribution to the development and repertoire of the string quartet is underappreciated and he enjoys conveying the composer's wit, changes of mood, inventive-ness, and economy of expression. Haydn can take the tiniest theme and discover myriad ways to develop it. Moreover, the slow move-ments in Haydn's late quartets are astonishing and as revelatory as late Beethoven.

Haydn expresses an amazing level of wit and gaiety. In the final movement of the first of his quartets written for the King of Prus-sia,[137] he teases the audience by appearing to finish the piece, only to start it again, before finally ending with great merriment. People laugh, giggle, and clap louder for that piece than almost any other, as if to say that was a good joke!

The natural world was an inspiration for many composers, par-ticularly Beethoven, who came to represent the nineteenth-cen-tury ideal of man in relation to nature. Some of Schubert's chamber music also contains references to the sounds of birds or water, as in *Die Schöne Mullerin* (*The Fair Miller Maid*) song cycle.[138] Schubert's abstract chamber music can also take the listener from blind rage to tranquility within minutes.

In his operas, Mozart had the ability to portray human nature in the most revealing fashion. His chamber music is also sublime. Some of the dialogues and counterpoint between instruments in his late string quintets are reminiscent of duets from operas, where he explored themes of jealousy, bitterness, romance, reverence, and love of mankind. In doing so, he exposed the naked truth about human motivation and behavior.

Some pieces of the French repertoire, like the Ravel String Quartet in F Major and the Debussy String Quartet in G Minor, are particularly ravishing. Debussy was one of the most revolutionary composers of his time in the way he used color, and evoked nature and imagery in abstract music.

Composers can allude to nature and human emotions in various ways. *Papillon*[139] (Butterfly), a piece for cello and piano by Gabriel

Faure, creates a powerful illusion of a scintillating butterfly in the cello part. The great French cellist Paul Tortelier was moved by Schumann's ability to express kindness in music, and this quality is evident in Schumann's String Quartet in A Major No. 3. Every movement of the quartet evolves as a perfect journey, embodied with kindness, tranquility, and peace.

The first duty for musicians is to reveal the contents of the score as honestly as possible. This is a matter of great debate and opens up many questions regarding the authenticity of performance and the empty virtuosity that can masquerade as art. The Tokyo Quartet was always aware of these issues and made sure no individual member became a prima donna.

Apart from the music itself, there are visual aspects of a performance to interest an audience, such as the relationship between the players, but it is primarily the music that has maximum impact. As the quality and repertoire of chamber music is immense, there is also a vast choice of first-rate pieces.

The naked virtuosity of a Paganini, Liszt, or China's Lang Lang is also very appealing to an audience. People love to see conjurers or Olympic athletes perform amazing, dangerous feats, and, there is a certain applause warranted for daring virtuosity in music, too. Performance involves struggle. You might play a very difficult piece, give everything, and when you get to the end, the audience responds by going wild with enjoyment, appreciation, and wonderment. However, there are performers with charisma and some of them, like politicians, know how to work a crowd and convince an audience with their playing.

*Clive Greensmith was interviewed by the author in Sydney, Australia, in June 2009.*

# Amihai Grosz

*BRIEF BIOGRAPHY*

Amihai Grosz began studies on the viola at the age of eleven. He won first prize in the Braun Roger Siegel Competition of the University of Jerusalem, and was later awarded the Gottesman Prize for Viola in the Aviv Competition.

He joined other musicians from the University Orchestra of the Jerusalem Music Center to form the Jerusalem String Quartet in 1995, which took part in the BBC New Generation Artists scheme from 1999 to 2001. Recipient of the first Borletti-Buitoni Trust Award in 2003, the quartet has performed at all major venues in the world, including the Tonhalle Zürich, the Wigmore Hall and Queen Elizabeth Hall in London, the Concertgebouw in Amsterdam, and the Sydney Opera House.

A number of their recordings have received international prizes, including the 2010 *BBC Music Magazine* Awards and Diapason d'Or Arte for *Haydn String Quartets*, and an ECHO Klassik Award in 2009 for a CD of Schubert's *Death and the Maiden* quartet. Their 2011 recording of *Mozart String Quartets K. 157, 458 & 589* was nominated Chamber Music Choice in the *BBC Music Magazine*.

Grosz has performed with Daniel Barenboim's West-Eastern Divan Orchestra and the Jerusalem Symphony Orchestra as a soloist.

In chamber music, he has collaborated with Mitsuko Uchida, Yefim Bronfman, Janine Jansen, Julian Rachlin, Emmanuel Pahud, Oleg Maisenberg, and David Geringas. He has performed in major venues and festivals throughout the world, including the BBC Proms, Verbier, Utrecht International Chamber Music Festival, Delft Chamber

Music Festival, Salon Festival and Rolandseck-Festival, West Cork Chamber Music and Jerusalem Chamber Music Festivals, and Spectrum Concerts Berlin.

In 2010 Amihai Grosz took up the position of Principal Violist of the Berlin Philharmonic.

Grosz plays a 1570 Gasparo da Salò viola, on loan from a private collection.[140]

*In music, you surrender to the art. We are bound by many rules in society but music has no borders, hierarchy or constraints regarding interpretation, listening and response.*

—AMIHAI GROSZ

AMIHAI GROSZ ASSERTS that musicians and audiences have complete freedom of interpretation, and people from diverse cultures can react to the music in different ways, depending on their childhood, imagination, and personality. Individual members of an audience will respond idiosyncratically, with different combinations of emotions.

Musical harmony seems to be particularly powerful in evoking emotions. Perhaps music originally began with a major chord that was supposed to make people feel happier. In contrast, a minor chord was sad and darker. The Catholic Church originally forbade dissonant chords because they expressed dissension, which was considered best avoided.

Classical or serious music is a world of honesty and imagination, and one of the most sophisticated of the arts. It seems magical that black spots on a page can create music that stimulates the emotions.

Grosz believes sincerity is of the utmost importance for musicians. It requires relinquishing part of the ego and allowing the music to come first during performance. When players are on the stage, they have to lose themselves in an experience similar to meditation, or they will not have the capacity to create music at the highest level.

Most musicians accept that they have a responsibility to offer something of value to the audience and society in general. This is a daunting task, as many people who attend concerts anticipate the same sort of intense emotional experience they have come to expect from watching a movie.

Some members of the audience might have unrealistic expectations, but they should not be underestimated. They are sensitive, astute, and able to assess instinctively whether a performer is convincing or not. About half the audience might not know a great deal about the piece of music or the composer, but they are able to respond to the music alone.

When musicians open up to an audience, they can never be sure how the listeners will respond to the emotion or the "statement" they are making. Since members of the audience are searching for emotional involvement with the music, Grosz would prefer them to experience some degree of excitement, whether positive or negative, rather than nothing at all.

He is often surprised by the unpredictability of the emotional transmission. On some occasions, when the quartet appeared to be in good form, for some unknown reason they did not produce their best sound. Then, at other times, although sleep deprived and very tired, they played particularly well.

Musicians, like any professionals, can have good and bad days. The composition of the group is an important factor. When another musician is added to form a quintet, the personality of this new member can have a significant impact. If all parties don't get along well or hold conflicting ideas about the music, members of the group cannot play at their best.

Yet it is amazing how often musicians with opposing opinions on subjects such as politics can still enjoy creating music together. As music is very pure and true, there is a possibility that it might stimulate the breakdown of prejudice and hostility. Daniel Barenboim is attempting to harness music for this purpose with his West-Eastern Divan Orchestra for young people.[141]

Grosz does not focus on moral issues, as he considers himself only a servant of the music. However, he does believe that music can improve the ability to listen carefully and actively, and perhaps this skill could generalize to empathic, attentive listening during interactions with others in everyday life.

Although some people don't like the dissonance of contemporary classical music, it has an important place socially and historically, and has evolved over several hundred years from the baroque, classical, and romantic periods. It is the music of modern times and, like visual artists, composers try to experiment and push the boundaries of their art.

In the past, composers were more integrated into society. Haydn formed the string quartet as a reaction to the symphony because there was a demand for music in smaller, private settings. The aristocracy commissioned musical works, and although Beethoven depended on patronage, he fought the hierarchical society of the time through his music. Today's composers are not restricted, and their increased independence has probably led to some of the free expression found in new music.

Performing contemporary music is fascinating and exciting, especially when players can work with the composer. They are not bound by the restraints and rules they encounter when playing a work like Schubert's String Quintet in C.[142] The rules that apply to Schubert and other classical composers leave little scope for divergent views.

Like many other musicians in a chamber music group, every member of the Jerusalem String Quartet has strong opinions about interpretation and method. They used to disagree about these issues while they were traveling to rehearsals, and on arrival, they were able to settle down to more formal disputation! While trying to persuade each other to accept their individual viewpoints, they managed to construct a valid whole or unified reading, and during performance were committed to unity and full cooperation within the group.

The music always comes first, portrayed with much humanity in the works of the great composers. The string quartets of Haydn appear to be simple, humorous, and humble, yet they are also subtle and penetrating. Haydn shares hilarious jokes with the players, like giving the cello the part of the violin, or putting an accent where it is least expected. Every time Grosz plays his music, he discovers more.

The same is true of Schubert. Grosz can perform Schubert's pieces twenty times and find new feelings to express. It is unlikely that he will exhaust the mine of fresh insights when he studies these works again in the future. Perhaps the scope of interpretive possibilities is itself a reasonable criterion for judging the merit of a piece of music.

Schubert uses his music to tell the listener about his vision of the next world, as exemplified in his poignant String Quintet in C, which he wrote about two months before he died. In this work, he is not expressing a wish to die, but is focused on remembrance and affirmation of life. Reactions to this momentous piece are based on people's own experiences of longing, grief, and other highly personal memories. Grosz cannot imagine playing this work in a straightforward, earthbound manner, and his sound and phrasing is strongly influenced by his own vision of Schubert's life and death as expressed in this work.

An active imagination helps a musician during the re-creative process. When he was a student learning a new piece, his teacher would ask him to write a descriptive narrative to the music, perhaps a fairy tale or any other idea. This was not a simple childish exercise, as it served to stimulate his imagination in the development of an artistic interpretation. The physical creation of sound requires a musician to envisage the sound, the colors, and atmosphere he or she wishes to create. It is important not to analyze the music too much in case the freedom within is lost. It is also vital to leave some space for feelings or instincts that are beyond analysis.

Musicians have to take risks in performance, even if it leads to the odd mistake. There is a current fashion for very clean, perfect playing, which can be boring. Grosz loves many of the old recordings. Although often imperfect technically, the interpretations are musically interesting and full of feeling. These qualities can be absent from more recent recordings and helps to explain why live music is usually a very different emotional experience.

If everything is perfectly under control, nothing magical will happen during a performance. However, when performers play really well and the audience is connected to them through the music, the musicians become aware they are not simply playing for their own benefit. At times, they might even experience the feeling of merging with the audience. These bonds and the associated spiritual heights give Grosz the greatest pleasure imaginable.

*Amihai Grosz was interviewed by the author in Sydney, Australia, in November 2009.*

# Alison Mackay

Alison Mackay is Principal Double Bass and Artistic Director of Tafelmusik. She has been a member of the Canada-based period-instrument orchestra since 1979.

Mackay conceptualized and developed a series of novel multimedia programs for the orchestra with moving images and scripts read by actors. *The Four Seasons: A Cycle of the Sun* used the music of Vivaldi's *Four Seasons* to journey through Venice, China, north India, and northern Canada. *The Galileo Project: Music of the Spheres* featured baroque music and high-definition images from the Hubble telescope. The production was honored with a Helpmann Award, and in recognition of their contribution to the International Year of Astronomy 2009, the International Astronomical Union assigned the orchestra's name to an asteroid, which orbits between Mars and Jupiter.[143] *House of Dreams*, a project that matched baroque music to the contents of several historical homes, received a Canadian JUNO Award in 2014.

These multimedia productions have toured Canada, the United States, Mexico, China, Malaysia, Japan, South Korea, Australia, and New Zealand and were made into feature documentary films. Both *House of Dreams* and *The Galileo Project* were co-productions with The Banff Centre, Canada's foremost arts and culture organization.

Other multimedia projects include *Chariots of Fire, In the Garden of Delights, Metamorphosis,* and *J.S. Bach: The Circle of Creation.* Mackay was the artistic director of two Toronto citywide arts festivals sponsored by Tafelmusik: the 2005 Metamorphosis Festival, based on

Ovid's *Metamorphoses*, and the 2008 Sacred Spaces, Sacred Circles Arts Festival, which celebrated cross-cultural places of worship.[144]

Tafelmusik's discography of more than eighty recordings[145] includes *Baroque Adventure: The Quest for Arundo Donax*[146] on the Analekta label. Conceived and scripted by Mackay, the album received the JUNO Award for Children's Recording of the Year in 2006.

Alison Mackay was the recipient of the 2013 Betty Webster Award for her unique contribution to orchestral music in Canada.[147]

*In all multimedia projects, the music is center stage but peo-*
*ple are primarily visual, and a theatrical set with images can*
*dominate the senses. To some extent, this can be offset by a*
*more direct relationship with the audience if the orchestra is*
*freed from their music stands.*

—ALISON MACKAY

ALISON MACKAY HAS always enjoyed the baroque repertoire
played by Tafelmusik. However, she was aware that the
music was often divorced from its original social setting
in a church, or in the case of chamber music, a private
home. In order to add a historical context, she started experimenting with a combination of words and music, hoping to recreate some
of the mindset of seventeenth- and eighteenth-century listeners.

Tafelmusik performed many dance suites from baroque operas as
substantial parts of their concert programs, and Mackay was aware
that this opera repertoire contained a rich source of stories from
Ovid. These tales have been deeply etched into Western consciousness, as the education system of the West utilized Ovid's accessible
text for teaching and learning Latin. The impact of these stories is
evident throughout the culture, from plays by Shakespeare to the gardens at Versailles, where trees and bushes were clipped to represent
Ovid's characters.

Mackay decided to take these ideas in a new direction, which
reflected the great ethnic diversity in Canada. Under her artistic
direction, Tafelmusik became involved in the 2005 Metamorphosis
Festival in Toronto, a production centered on stories from *Metamorphoses*[148] about the transfiguration of a human into a bird or flower.
These tales can be understood as ancient explanations for natural

137

phenomena, but they also contain astute and timeless descriptions of human nature.

The enterprise generated about forty arts events in Toronto, including a film festival, a collection of paintings at the Art Gallery, and three operas by the Canadian Opera Company. Among the many new dance forms created for the festival, a Toronto-based south Indian dance company presented an outstanding representation of the various animal incarnations of Vishnu.

Numerous educational events involved teachers, young children, and high-school students, who studied Ovid's stories and developed arts projects such as stop-motion photography. The orchestra's contribution was a concert, incorporating several stories spoken in Latin, followed by an English translation. Exposure to the emotion and culture that supported the tales stirred a fresh and exciting communication of the music and filtered into the life of the orchestra itself. Indeed, the cultural stimulation electrified Toronto.

Another project was stimulated by the International Year of Astronomy 2009, which commemorated the four-hundredth anniversary of Galileo's groundbreaking use of the telescope. In Canada, an educational project was founded to give every child an opportunity to observe the constellations through a telescope. The organizing committee was keen to arrange events on related topics, such as the history of astronomy, and Tafelmusik was approached about creating a multimedia production. From these embryonic beginnings, *The Galileo Project: Music of the Spheres*[149] was born. It was the brainchild of Mackay, who scripted and programmed the narration, movement and music by Monteverdi, Vivaldi, Bach, and Handel.

For some time, she had wanted the orchestra to experiment with memorizing a piece of music in order to prompt a higher level of playing and audience interaction. The musicians accepted the challenge and worked hard to memorize their parts. Ultimately, they were impressed by the heightened emotional involvement of audience and performers, and an outcome that seemed much greater than the sum of its parts. This was not surprising in view of the orchestra's experience in outreach programs at schools, when it was clear that playing without the music and using the whole body to express emotion greatly increased rapport with the students. Coming together in small groups to commit the music to memory also brought an extra benefit. During this process exceptionally strong personal bonds were formed and the interaction between performers intensified. This closeness and communication could also be transmitted to the audience.

It takes Mackay about a year to develop a script and match it to the music. At a later stage, she chooses the images to weave into the production. Although the music always comes first, some knowledge of the composer, historical performance, and audience for whom the music was intended may heighten the experience of a modern audience. People can identify with others of the period through letters, diaries, and possessions recorded in state inventories. These human associations simply serve to strengthen the emotional ties to the music. Moreover, expertise in music or art is not required for satisfaction and enjoyment.

One of Mackay's projects, *House of Dreams*,[150] takes its title from Book 11 of *Metamorphoses* and moves between five houses: Handel House in London, Palazzo Smith Mangilli Valmarana in Venice, Het Gulden ABC in Delft, Netherlands, Palais-Royal in Paris, and the Bach Museum and Archive in Leipzig. These historic homes are replete with memories of the contents, in particular the art works that had filled many spaces on the walls. Mackay selected images of various pictures and other household items to complement the music of Handel, Vivaldi, Marais, J.S. Bach, and Telemann.

During her research, Mackay found a rich source of information in the estate inventories—for example, the auction catalogue of Handel's estate. It included eighty paintings and sixty-four engravings from his collection of major English and European painters, including Rembrandt, Antoine Watteau, Jan Brueghel the Elder, and Canaletto.

Jacob Dissius, a Dutch bookbinder who married Magdalena van Ruijven, occupied the tiny Het Gulden ABC house. When Magdalena died, he inherited twenty-one paintings by Johannes Vermeer, originally bought by her parents, who were friends and patrons of the artist. Magdalena's estate inventory listed all the Vermeers and their specific locations in the house.

It is a formidable task to reproduce on a stage a great work of art such as Vermeer's *Girl with a Pearl Earring*. Nevertheless, a large screen and very high-resolution images allow the audience to zoom in and see the expression in the sitter's eyes, her facial emotion, and the dab of white paint on the earring.

A subsequent production, *J.S. Bach: the Circle of Creation*, traces the origins of materials used by the composer, from the moment of inspiration to composition and performance. The presentation explores the history of Bach's writing paper, made by a family in Bohemia; his method of preparing ink; and the way he drew the lines for staves.

Apart from tracing the materials related to musical composition, the all-Bach project includes film footage of the manufacture of gut strings by a modern northern Italian factory, whose owners recovered the technology to produce resonant strings from sheep intestines.

Above all, the spotlight falls on the town of Leipzig, where the economy and social structure determined the employment of municipal musicians. Although small, Leipzig was very prosperous because of its location as a center of trade. It lay at the intersection of two famous Roman roads, the Via Regia and Via Imperii. In medieval times, these trade routes ran west to east from Santiago de Compostela to Moscow, and south to north from Rome to the Baltic.

Due to its significant location, the town received an imperial license to hold trade fairs early in the Middle Ages, and over time, three large annual fairs were established. They made Leipzig the most famous trade center in Europe and a remarkable cultural meeting place for people as far away as Siberia and Constantinople. Much of the city's prosperity revolved around the large contingent of Jewish merchants who hailed from many areas, including Russia, the Levant, and England. Although Jews were forbidden to settle in Leipzig without restrictions until the middle of the nineteenth century, they were allowed into the city during the fairs on payment of a large head tax.

Whenever a Jewish merchant, his family, or servants entered the town, their names, date of arrival, and length of stay were recorded; they were obliged to take lodgings in Brühl Street in the north of the town, and charged excise tax at a much higher rate than their gentile counterparts. All these records, meticulously kept in the town archives, have facilitated research.

In the early 1930s, Rabbi Max Freudenthal of Nuremberg examined and cross-referenced the records, making it possible for Mackay and other researchers to ascertain which merchants traveled to Leipzig during Bach's time. The town's dependence on their presence was evident following a large warehouse fire in Brody, a small town in western Ukraine. The fire kept the Jewish merchants of Brody from attending, and their absence caused the failure of the fairs during that year.

Like other musicians, Bach was hired by the municipality, which paid his salary and provided instruments, uniforms, and housing. These expenses relied on income from the fairs. Mackay is fascinated with the flowering of music in Leipzig and the way it was intertwined with the cultural, social, and economic background of the town. Bach wrote many of his works in this environment. Undoubtedly, he would have attended the fairs and met the merchants from whom he bought music books and many household items, such as the copper kettle listed in his estate.

In Bach's day, audiences varied according to socioeconomic

status, although there is a modern perception that he composed his church cantatas for the benefit of the masses. In reality, pew rentals in the congregation of Thomaskirche (St. Thomas Church) in Leipzig were only affordable to the middle class. Poorer members of society usually attended suburban churches with only limited access to music. In spite of these restrictions, there were other opportunities for the general public to enjoy music in street theaters and concerts in public gardens.

The development of street lighting proved to be the critical factor in taking serious music to a wider public. Street lamps were introduced into Leipzig around 1700, making it possible for the modest or middle class to venture out in safety at night. Previously, only the well-to-do could afford a carriage with servants and torches to brave the night. At first, town lamplighters lit large candles, and at a later stage, whale oil was used. The old lighting charts can still be found in Leipzig. They show a calendar of lighting times calculated according to sunset, moonrise, and sunrise.

Safer streets at night introduced a new phenomenon with momentous ramifications for music: the culture of the coffeehouse. From the seventeenth century onwards, coffee was imported into Vienna from Turkey and Morocco, and famous establishments sprang up in various cities, including London and Leipzig. As meeting places, they became closely linked with politics and stock exchanges—the first stock exchange in London took place in a coffeehouse.

A strong tradition of music flourished in these locales. Bach's secular music was performed in Leipzig's Zimmermannsche Kaffee-haus[151] owned by Gottfried Zimmermann. The premises had room for an audience of about one hundred fifty people, and Zimmermann owned a harpsichord, two double basses, and other strings, which were available for in-house performances.

The coffeehouse culture spurred another project for Mackay, which compares a 1740s establishment in Damascus with another in

Leipzig. Both cities were important trade centers; Damascus was the last major stop on the Silk Road to the Mediterranean after traders had journeyed in the east. The city's coffeehouses were known for storytelling and itinerant entertainers, who read about Scheherazade from *The Book of One Thousand and One Nights*.[152]

Both cities were also significant international centers of scholarship. Leipzig had a renowned university, and Damascus hosted a pluralistic community of Muslims, Christians, and Jews. In the Ottoman Empire, the rules regarding residency and freedom of worship were more liberal than those in Leipzig, even though Christians and Jews were second-class citizens. In order to reflect the social diversity, Mackay's project includes Arabic, as well as Christian music from the West, and a Jewish actor from Toronto.

Mackay is particularly interested in making global connections via history and culture. In a multimedia production of Vivaldi's *Four Seasons*,[153] she connected Toronto to the ancient Silk Road[154] and the four seasons. A local virtuoso of the *pipa*,[155] a Chinese lute descended from the Arabian *oud*,[156] played music that had been performed in the Forbidden City of Peking during the 1720s. This era coincided with the publication of the *Four Seasons* violin concertos. Like the European lute, the *pipa* was introduced through the extensive silk route, which linked China, India, and the Mediterranean, both commercially and culturally.

In Mackay's production, images of the Forbidden City during spring supplement the music of Vivaldi's "Spring." This is followed by a monsoon raga[157] for summer played on the *sarangi*,[158] an instrument reminiscent of the viola da gamba. "Winter" is represented by two north Canadian Inuit throat singers,[159] whose songs follow a custom of antiphonal, guttural voice exchanges, traditionally sung by elderly women in their winter snow houses while the men were out hunting. The rapid song dialogue often imitates winter birds. The same program features a Chinese almanac from the period, listing the days of each season and giving detailed instructions on how to celebrate them. On certain days, you might be ordered to change your ivory hatpin into one made of jade, eat a particular kind of dumpling, or shoot fireworks.

Although fascinating, the images and narration should be considered embellishments for the music, which can be conveyed independently of any visual content. Additional knowledge can, however, amplify one's experience of art. The British essayist and art lover Lord Macaulay[160] related that when he was a youth, he rushed down the Rhine on the grand tour and saw olive trees. It was only after he read the *Aeneid*[161] that he comprehended the many facets of an olive tree, and when he was old, could fully appreciate its complexity.

Similarly, musicians can raise their performance and listeners their pleasure by exploring the nuanced layers of culture linked to particular compositions and their creators.

*Alison Mackay was interviewed by the author in Sydney, Australia, in March 2015.*

# Christian-Pierre La Marca

*BRIEF BIOGRAPHY*

Christian-Pierre La Marca has performed as soloist with many orchestras, including the Philharmonia, London Chamber Orchestra, Orchestre Philharmonique du Luxembourg, Brussels Philharmonic, and Orchestre Royal Philharmonique de Liège in Brussels, and at major venues such as the Musikverein and Konzerthaus (Vienna), Concertgebouw (Amsterdam), Philharmonie Berlin, Salle Pleyel and Opéra Garnier (Paris), Wigmore Hall and Southbank Centre (London), Bozar (Brussels), Victoria Hall Geneva, Alte Oper (Frankfurt), La Fenice (Venice), Conservatory Moscow, 92nd Street Y (New York), Oji Hall Tokyo, Arts Centre Melbourne, and City Recital Hall, Sydney.

He has been a guest performer at various music festivals, including Verbier, Kissinger Sommer, Festìval Pablo Casals, Festival International d'Art Lyrique d'Aix-en-Provence, Festival de la Roque d'Anthéron, Ravinia, Festival Internacional de Santander, and Printemps des Arts de Monte-Carlo. In chamber music, he has worked with artists such as Thierry Escaich, Lawrence Power, Michel Portal, Augustin Dumay, Bernarda Fink, Jean-Frédéric Neuburger, Igor Levit, and Cédric Tiberghien.

La Marca is the cellist of Trio Dali, recipient of many international prizes, including Diapason d'Or, *BBC Music Magazine* Choice, Editor's Choice *Gramophone Magazine*, Choc de l'Année *Classica*, Scherzo Excepcional, FFFF Télérama and Clef d'or ResMusica. He has recorded CDs of Ravel and Schubert for Fuga Libera. As a soloist, La Marca's recordings of the complete cello Suites of J.S. Bach gained the awards Top Le Figaro, La Croix, Coup de cœur RTL,

Radio Classique, Europe 1, Fnac, and RCF. Other awards include the Fondation Banque Populaire and the Firmenich Cello Prize at the Verbier Festival.

From 2008 to 2010 he was Assistant Professor at the Royal Academy of Music in London and presently holds the position of artist-in-residence at the Fondation Singer-Polignac in Paris.

La Marca has played the Vaslin cello, made in 1725 by Antonio Stradivari, and now plays a cello dated 1850, made in Paris by Charles-Auguste Miremont.[162]

*If the emotions of listeners are roused, then music has done its work by whisking them away from the daily stresses of life. Then they can travel to far realms of the spirit to contemplate existence and purpose.*

—CHRISTIAN-PIERRE LA MARCA

I T IS NOT NECESSARY to be educated in music to understand or appreciate the art. However, people are more attracted to classical music as they grow older, so it would seem that life experiences affect a person's tastes. People can use music to escape from reality in times of conflict, but generally it helps them find a place where they can experience emotions safely. In such an environment, they are able to contemplate their situation and purpose in life. Christian-Pierre La Marca would like to believe that his playing, like that of other musicians, has the potential to contribute to the comfort of listeners and even their transformation, if they are inclined to ponder existential issues.

It seems miraculous that music could reflect life through the feelings in the notes, and tell an emotional story when all the notes are put together. After musicians have analyzed a piece to discover the emotions in the score, they can use their instruments to generate these emotions or "characters."

When La Marca is listening with attention, he tries to surrender to the music and, at some point in the flow, attempts to focus on an emotion that has a particular timely relevance in his life. From this moment on, though, the process is not entirely conscious.

Music can induce relaxation, transport you to the past, and give you hope for the future. Some of the listeners who respond to

La Marca's music send him online messages of thanks or come to see him after a performance. One evening, a lady came backstage to tell him his playing had left her feeling much more hopeful about the future following a very difficult and depressing year. This sort of feedback gives him enormous encouragement to practice harder and continue to improve.

These varied responses have led him to determine that music is a form of therapy for the audience. But it depends on their state of mind. There are times when listeners, including La Marca himself, are not in a receptive frame of mind when they arrive at a concert, feeling tired or preoccupied by events and difficulties during the day. Alternatively, they might be concerned with the personality of the performer and the degree of energy he or she projects on the stage.

Although artists can't force people to pay attention to their playing, La Marca believes an audience will listen and respond if musicians convey a clear message with conviction. Performers must also give of themselves emotionally, and for maximum communication, it is important, although probably not essential, to know themselves well. But no matter how much a performer offers, the listener must be receptive.

In order to perform well, an artist needs to focus completely on feelings, and this emotional state requires bursts of adrenaline. Some artists believe a considerable amount of acting is involved in expressing feelings through music, but in La Marca's experience the drama is not associated with playing. Instead, it is to be found in other aspects of performance, such as the action of walking onto the stage. The drama soon dissipates when he starts to play, and he is totally absorbed in the task of bearing the emotional narrative. Occasionally, he is so involved with the music he forgets the position of one of his fingers and makes a mistake, but an error doesn't worry him if he has been true to the spirit of the music. After all, mistakes are also part of life.

While Trio Dali generally deals with the expression of emotion in a purely abstract way, visual imagery can be useful. The group used this strategy when it played Trio II by Mauricio Kagel[163] in New York City. Although the musical language is difficult to comprehend, the piece is a powerful commemoration of the September 11 terrorist attack on the World Trade Center. Since the music was intended to be scenically descriptive, the trio discussed the possibility of using mental imagery to reinforce meaning and communication during performance.

As it happened, they found some inspiration near their hotel, which was located just outside the city. One night, as they were walking home from the bus stop after rehearsals, they passed a gas station that looked ghostly. Nearby, stood a tall building that was conspicuous by its striking illumination. The group decided to try an experiment. They would visualize how this group of buildings might appear at various times of the day and in different weather conditions while they were playing the Kagel trio. To their surprise, this strategy worked for them, and they were pleased when a music critic wrote about the "chaos" Trio Dali was able to communicate.

La Marca is convinced the study of music improves self-knowledge and may also accelerate maturity. Listening in a group helps people bond with colleagues and cultivate closer, more relaxed relationships. It also serves to unite people through shared emotion and empathy.

When he was growing up, music helped him connect with his emotions and reflect on life events, especially after he moved to Paris for further studies at the age of fourteen. He then lived on his own and was forced to mature quickly.

Even if children don't take up music professionally as he did, they can benefit significantly from music education, as the study of an instrument offers a sense of achievement and structure for everyday life. La Marca would like to see more music education for children because they won't understand and enjoy classical music without at least some familiarity. Younger musicians such as La Marca are more likely to connect with children and capture their attention. He enjoys being with them and often prompts a great deal of interest when he demonstrates the way a cello can make the "moo" sound of a cow.

All music, whether Aboriginal, African, or European, is valid and full of emotion, but in Western societies, the great composers such as Mozart have a special place. Music gave Mozart an outlet for totally free expression of emotions, sincerity, and purity. Slipping into the world of such a composer can become a treasured aspect of life for both performers and listeners.

The music of Schubert is also very rewarding emotionally. Sad themes alternate with popular folk songs, and in many of his chamber music works, the instruments play together, each one expressing a different emotion. In Schubert's Piano Trio in E-flat Major,[164] a melody based on a Swedish folk song appears in the second movement. It is in a minor key and intensely sad, tossed about, and referenced by the individual instruments. When the tune returns in the last movement, we hear it in a major key, and the whole character of the piece changes. In much of his music and notably in this piano trio, Schubert expresses his desperation and awareness of mortality, as well as a fierce desire to live. It is truly remarkable that he is able to convey so much feeling with simple themes and variations.

Many other compositions are also immensely powerful. La Marca is still haunted by a performance of Schoenberg's *Verklärte Nacht*[165] played by a sextet in Chicago. During the concert, he felt removed from reality, and immersed in a world of overwhelming emotions. When the music stopped, it took him ten minutes to recover and return to earth. Later, he spoke to the musicians, who told him they had also experienced exceptional emotional intensity during the performance.

*Christian-Pierre La Marca was interviewed by the author in Sydney, Australia, in June 2012.*

# Nina Maria Lee

*BRIEF BIOGRAPHY*

Nina Marie Lee is a renowned chamber musician who has performed at the Marlboro, Tanglewood, and El Paso International Chamber Music festivals. She has worked with many artists, including Felix Galimir, Jaime Laredo, David Soyer, Nobuko Imai, and Isidore Cohen.

As a member of the Brentano Quartet,[166] she has toured the world. The quartet has performed in major venues such as Carnegie Hall and Alice Tully Hall in New York, the Konzerthaus in Vienna, Concertgebouw in Amsterdam, Suntory Hall in Tokyo, and the Sydney Opera House. They have collaborated with many artists, including Jessye Norman, Richard Goode, and pianist Mitsuko Uchida, with whom they have a close association. The quartet has taken part in major music festivals, such as Aspen, the Edinburgh Festival, Music Academy of the West in Santa Barbara, Taos School of Music, Caramoor, and the Kuhmo Chamber Music Festival in Finland.

The Brentano Quartet received the Naumburg Chamber Music Award and the first Cleveland Quartet Award. It became the first Resident String Quartet at Princeton University, and an inaugural member of Chamber Music Society Two, Lincoln Center.

The quartet has strong interests in both early and contemporary music and has commissioned pieces by Charles Wuorinen, Bruce Adolphe, Steven Mackey, David Horne, and Gabriela Lena Frank.

Their recordings include *Mozart: String Quartet in A, K. 464; Viola Quintet in D, K. 593* with violist Hsin-Yun Huang; *Brentano Plays Haydn:*

*The Three Opus 71 Quartets, Bruce Adolphe: Turning, Returning, Chou Wen-chung: Clouds* and *Charles Wuorinen: Scherzo; String Quartet No. 1; Viola Variations; Piano Quintet No. 2* and *Wuorinen: On Alligators.*

Lee is a graduate of the Curtis Institute of Music and the Juilliard School. She is a faculty member at Princeton University and Columbia University.[167]

*It is an overwhelming, if rare, experience to feel transformed, as if all the planets are suddenly in alignment. These are the times when everyone in the group is contributing in the same way and the players are totally in the moment, connecting with the audience. The memory of these sincere moments of exchange will remain for life.*

—NINA MARIA LEE

NINA MARIA LEE describes herself as a product of the public school system in the United States. One day, a string quartet came to her school and played the Oscar Mayer Bologna commercial jingle. It started with: "My bologna has a first name; it's O-S-C-A-R."[168] The cello had the main tune, and she fell in love with the instrument. In the fourth grade, there was a free program of group lessons, which was how she started to learn the cello. She is still grateful for this opportunity, but is also concerned that these programs are disappearing. More recently, while teaching at Princeton University, Lee observed that many young people came to love chamber music when they were exposed to it.

Music is a central part of her life, not only because she plays an instrument, but also for love of the art. It can embody the human spirit in the form of a narrative, or just a feeling, and whether the music is abstract, or contains words, individuals respond differently. The ability to articulate and interpret the music is an art in itself. Serious or classical music is basically abstract, but it imparts powerful emotions. Similarly, the paintings of visual artists such as Mark Rothko are very abstract, but also deeply emotional.

Many people have told her how a piece of music resonates with them and can trigger memories. Sometimes, they recall how old they were when they heard a particular piece, where they were, who was with them, and how it affected them.

Lee has vivid memories of many wonderful performances, one of them as a music student at the Juilliard School,[169] when she heard the Brentano Quartet play with the original cellist. The occasion was Beethoven's String Quartet No. 13 in B-flat Major, Op. 130.[170] The performance was deeply moving, particularly the slow movement, which seemed surreal, as if the quartet functioned as a single entity and a higher power was playing the first violin.

The cello became a part of her inner voice, and a source of personal development and transformation. Through the music, she spends time with the composers and plays their pieces in a journey of perpetual self-realization. Beethoven taught her the struggles of life are ultimately worthwhile. Not necessarily refined, his music is incredibly beautiful, and he uses an idea as a prism, shining light through it and producing various effects. Sometimes the colors will go together, sometimes they will clash, but it all works out in the end, analogous perhaps, to his music, which is characterized by immense conflict, pain and sadness, but is also decidedly positive.

Many people think Beethoven was remarkable for composing while he was deaf, but he undoubtedly heard the music in his head, in the same way we can imagine tunes. The deafness probably served to remove him from his immediate environment and placed his spirit more directly in contact with a higher power. This connection was unfiltered and pure.

Beethoven is an important musical and humanistic influence on Lee. When she is feeling particularly vulnerable to criticism, he comes to mind, with his unapologetic demand for musicians to master all difficulties in order to further the art.

His string quartets, from Opus 18 to the late quartets, span different parts of his life. People often think the late quartets are much harder to play than the early ones because his personal struggle was more intense toward the end of his life, but the early quartets are no less difficult. The playing must be supremely clean, finely textured, and perfectly balanced, with impeccable intonation and unity of sound.

After Beethoven survived a serious illness, he expressed his thanks in the third movement of one of his late works, the Quartet in A Minor, Op. 132,[171] written in 1825. This movement of thanksgiving (mentioned earlier) is a slow hymn-like song or chorale, interspersed with faster elements, *"Neue Kraft fühlend"* ("with renewed strength"). Every time the motifs return, they are a little more integrated and enlightened.

Of all the great composers, Beethoven is the one who can best portray the triumph of the human spirit. To know him magnifies our own insights, and perhaps the world would be vastly improved if people could absorb the message he imparts through his music. Yet, the response is very personal and idiosyncratic. Two people sitting next to each other listening to the same music might experience a quite different set of emotions, often depending on events in their own lives.

Although Beethoven is a comfort, a musician's life is often solitary, with long, lonely hours of practice, trying to improve upon weaknesses, and putting right mistakes learned from previous performances. It is humbling.

Those who play in a chamber music group are inevitably taking part in a social experiment. Just sitting in a circle is significant. For artists with families or partners, considerable sacrifice is required, because they often spend more time with members of their group or practicing their instrument. The self-denial is worthwhile when communication with the audience reaches a profound level.

Playing in front of an audience unmasks the artist. People who are listening very attentively will notice if a musician is only going through the motions, without genuine commitment. Then there is compromise, which has to be settled during rehearsal. One member of the group could advocate a particular tempo to illuminate the music, whereas another might think the music should be much faster, even if it means denying some of the nuances. If the group decides to split the difference and take a tempo in between, it is often the worst decision because it fails to express either idea. And so it might be necessary to give way to another person's viewpoint.

The quartet won't play a piece in public without working on it for long hours, and the journey doesn't stop with the first interpretation. Instead, they continue with more rehearsals, some of their most productive practice taking place just after a concert. Stimulated by the performance, they are often able to inject fresh ideas into the music.

Lee believes that being a member of a string quartet improves communication skills, patience, compromise, and more. In the past, members of the group would blurt out their ideas, but they have learned to resolve differences through playing, rather than talking.

Classical musicians differ from those in jazz or pop, as their musical life is first and foremost selfless. Performance decisions aim to serve the composer. They never claim to know better, but keep asking themselves what the composers meant when the notes were jotted down, often continually soul searching, to the extent of digressing for hours about one accent. In contrast, jazz musicians are focused on finding their individual sound, and pop groups concentrate on trying to find a catchy tune.

The quartet commissions many contemporary works to focus on the modern age. A commission is always a gamble as one can't predict the music and must wait until the score is done.

Some of these commissions and other contemporary pieces would benefit from being played twice in the same concert. This could work particularly well with a number of Anton Webern's short pieces. Such a program might seem strange for modern audiences, although looking back to the time of Beethoven, musicians would play individual movements of a piece, and depending on audience reaction, repeat a section several times. A program might then contain the slow movement from an orchestral suite followed by two movements of a string quartet!

Contemporary music needs more explanation than some of the classics, as people fear the unfamiliar. Alban Berg's *Lyric Suite* is a good example. Embedded in the music is some secret notation dedicated to his mistress. When this information is communicated to the audience, they are more open to the music, and some have come backstage to tell the quartet they preferred this piece to all the others in the program. Young children generally respond more wholeheartedly to contemporary pieces, but usually become less enthusiastic as they grow older.

Lee believes music is another way for children to experience the world, and chamber music is particularly appropriate because they hear ideas being worked out in a conversational way.

The concentration required during a performance is immense, because artists are continually striving to do their utmost to connect the audience with the music, and sometimes people give the quartet feedback when they come backstage. One lady, whose husband had recently died, was in tears when she said she felt the quartet had empathy with her. She particularly wanted to know if that was the aim of performers.

Although gratifying to learn that people can respond so positively, it is not the performer's goal. Some people may feel transformed by the music while others won't. Artists simply hope to enable listeners to hear what they themselves can hear in the music.

We need music as much as spoken language, and people often gravitate to it because they are searching for someone to understand them. There might also be times when people don't want to discuss their feelings or talk to another, preferring to take comfort in a particular musical work instead.

Other cultures outside the West also find comfort and meaning in music. Chinese American composer Chou Wen-chung presented this beautifully when he explained his intentions regarding a piece he wrote for the quartet. One movement contains a soulful wedding theme based on a Chinese village folk song traditionally sung by the bride's family during the ceremony. In the past, marriage often involved moving to another village and even an hour's journey implied the family would never see the bride again. This song about the promise of newly married life also communicated love, sorrow, and longing, which helped the family deal with loss and move ahead.

Some of the great composers have used music to describe the human struggle, transmitting the very beautiful together with the wretched. Both endeavors are important. The journey that listeners can take presents a metaphor for life's passage. They might feel the despair in a theme and then follow its transmutation through many developments, until finally, when the theme returns, they have become a little older and are armed with more knowledge.

A world without this music would be a much poorer place.

*Nina Maria Lee was interviewed by the author in Sydney, Australia, in May 2011.*

# Peter Rejto

American-Australian cellist Peter Rejto has performed worldwide since winning the 1972 international Young Concert Artists award in New York. As a concerto soloist, he has toured North America, Europe, and South America with orchestras such as the Dallas Symphony, Ohio Chamber Orchestra, Rio de Janeiro Symphony, Orquesta Filarmónica de Caracas, St. Louis Symphony, and California Chamber Symphony on tour in Hong Kong. His world-premiere performance of Gerard Schurmann's cello concerto *The Gardens of Exile* with the Bournemouth Symphony UK, was broadcast live over the BBC.

He has collaborated with the Bartók, Tokyo, Colorado, American, St. Petersburg, Miró and Orion Quartets, and given solo recitals at Peking University, Beijing, and Dalian, China. He is the founder and Artistic Director of the Tucson Winter Chamber Music Festival, and frequently participates in many other festivals, including "Bravo" Colorado, Aspen, Kneisel Hall, Santa Fe, La Jolla, Sitka, and Round Top in Texas.

As founding cellist of the Los Angeles Piano Quartet, he has performed in venues such as the Concertgebouw in Amsterdam, Wigmore Hall in London, Musikhalle in Hamburg, Santa Cecilia in Rome, and Alice Tully Hall in New York.

Rejto was a juror for the fourth Melbourne International Chamber Music Competition, and returned the following year as visiting artist-in-residence at the Victorian College of the Arts, Melbourne.

Son of the late Hungarian cellist Gabor Rejto, he studied mostly with his father, former professor at the Eastman School and the

University of Southern California. He also took part in master classes with Pablo Casals, Gregor Piatigorsky, and Pierre Fournier.

He has held full-time academic positions in the United States, including California State University, Northridge, Michigan State University, and the University of Arizona, Tucson, and is currently Professor Emeritus of Cello at the Oberlin College Music Conservatory. He has given master classes in Korea, at the Central Conservatory in Beijing and the Sichuan Conservatory, Chengdu, China.

Rejto is an experienced pilot who often flies his own plane to concert appearances.[172]

*There is a unifying factor in an audience when everybody acknowledges the performance collectively. This characteristic is probably an important part of major events such as the Woodstock Festival in the United States, where in the 1960s, the anti-war campaign took on meaning through association with music and certain songs.*

—PETER REJTO

W OODSTOCK RESONATED WITH the people who took part and linked them to a cause that began a global phenomenon and counterculture. This experience, which bonded an audience of about four hundred thousand over a period of three days, is just one example of the power of music.

Such observations don't explain why we respond to music, although there are many scientific theories. Cellist Peter Rejto suggests that brains function by searching for patterns and symmetry that help us make the logical leaps from a little information to more general conclusions.

In dealing with music the brain tries to find a pattern; its recognition may give us pleasure or trigger any range of emotions. This hypothesis might explain why the return of a theme heard in the recapitulation of a piece composed in sonata form[173] may transport the listener—even induce shivers—when one becomes aware of the slight changes that have taken place since the exposition when we first heard the themes announced. Detecting these changes at a later stage implies we initially recognized the pattern.

The theories of pattern recognition have led Rejto to consider the apparent lack of patterning in some forms of contemporary music in which the mode of composition may be aleatoric, or devoid of any form. Music that is not annotated is one example—others can be an indication on the score to play a cluster of notes with a fist, or to play any number of random notes for a specified period of time, followed by a "loud bang." There was a time when such compositions were popular with composers such as Iannis Xenakis and John Cage.

Xenakis gave a lecture in Aspen[174] in which he explained his highly personal approach to composition. Most composers start with a white page and they add black notes and symbols. In a reversal of tradition, Xenakis said he preferred to start with a black page (representing an infinite number of notes) and then remove those notes by whitening them out. Music scores, he maintained, should be beautiful to the eye. In his case, architecture influenced his visual style.

Dissonance[175] has always been a powerful tool for expression, especially when resolved, as the resolution to consonance is a natural impulse. Even though we have become much more accepting of dissonant intervals, it is still difficult for many people to accept the unresolved dissonance in a great number of contemporary works. As a performing musician, one would think Rejto could tolerate unresolved discord, but he has often felt taken back on initial contact with some new works. Only after studying and rehearsing such pieces can he begin to decipher the patterns and start to bring emotional meaning to the music. Upon hearing a work for the first time an audience would not have the benefit of his expert appreciation of the piece, built on knowledge of music and identification of the patterns he has discerned. Repeated exposure would be required to help the brain cut through complexity and decode the patterns, and thereby develop familiarity. For this reason one could make a case for playing new works twice in the same program. The process could be compared with a child's "search-and-find" picture book in which the reader is tasked to find a number of objects or animals in complex and abstract images. Locating these pieces from within the whole helps the reader to make sense of the overall picture.

Giving the audience a few explanations and insights can help the natural desire to search and find patterns. Some background about the composer is another factor that can assist the audience in understanding a work and can be illustrated by a performance of the string sextet written before World War II by the Czech composer Erwin Schulhoff. The dark and foreboding character of the piece would have deterred many listeners, but they became particularly attentive during a talk about the composer's circumstances and eventual death in a concentration camp.

It is essential for performers to feel something about a piece and become emotionally invested in the music; otherwise the transmission from composer to listener may prove difficult, if not impossible. Performers need to feel there is a strong message to convey before it can be transmitted as honest expression. At that point all kinds of magic become possible. Without genuine feelings, a performance might be remembered more as a technical display. Although virtuosity itself is an exciting and important aspect of a performance, it is only one ingredient of many and not the most important.

Some musicians study the score carefully for the composer's meaning before adding their own ideas. But there are others who will disregard and sacrifice markings by the composer for a reading geared to more excitement for themselves and the audience. Would Beethoven be concerned if one played *fortissimo* where he had marked *pianissimo?* He might have been infuriated. After all, he was known to fly into a rage with his publishers when they made mistakes.

Every artist follows a highly personal path regarding the amount of attention given to the score. Whatever the outcome of that particular journey, the ultimate task is an interpretation that is convincing for the listener. This does not imply a heavily pedagogic approach; Pablo Casals' treatment of Bach illustrates this point well. On

analysis of his playing, there are possible criticisms regarding authenticity with respect to bowing, tempi, and even fingering selections,
as well as an overly romantic interpretation as viewed from our modern and supposedly more "educated" perspective. Nevertheless the
total effect is strongly personal, valid, and convincing. The enthusiasm and energy transmitted in these performances shines through.
The artist clearly has a huge role in transmitting the ideas and feelings of the composer in a way that strikes the listener as valid, real,
or even definitive.

Music is a medium for all human emotions, including grief, sadness, ecstasy, love, and reverence. In classical music one also finds
messages of truth and beauty that may not only resonate with many
people, but may in fact be one of few opportunities certain individuals
have to partake in such an experience. These ancient, timeless values
are not always apparent in our society, yet a concert is an opportunity for re-evaluation. For so many people caught up in mundane
jobs, stressful lives, or even tragedies in the family, one or two hours
of escape may be transformative. In that hour or two infused with
an honestly transmitted message, music has the potential to trigger
deep emotional response at every level. One speculates that perhaps
a beautifully turned phrase has the possibility to influence a person
to act beautifully in life. At least one hopes so.

Have the great composers given us any specific indications
regarding the sort of emotions they express through music? Rejto
is reminded of a story attributed to Beethoven. In his String Quartet No.16 in F Major, op. 135,[176] the fourth movement is marked
"*Der schwer gefaßte Entschluß*"/The difficult decision. (Grave, ma non
troppo tratto—"*Muß es sein?*"/Must it be?—Allegro—"*Es muß sein!*"/
It must be!).

Many regard that slow movement as one of the most profound,
searching, and mystical moments in the classical repertoire. Yet when
someone asked Beethoven what he meant by those instructions, he

trivialized the meaning of his composition and joked that the question was actually related to his rent. He had simply asked the landlord if he had to pay the rent that month.

This story, if indeed true, doesn't diminish the enormous emotional range in Beethoven's music and the great demands he places on performers to transmit the emotion. Most musicians are aware of their responsibility and privilege in a genuine communication of the composer's feelings to the audience. It may sound like therapy for the listeners, but it is more so for the performer, as evidenced by their enthusiasm for repeating the transmission. Some musicians have also spoken of the love they desire to extend to their audience. "All my life I wanted to play music with love to every member of the audience," said Russian cellist Mstislav Rostropovich.[177]

A very strong, intimate bond can be formed between performer and listeners. It happened unexpectedly to Rejto in a particular concert, and in a way that he has never been able to duplicate. He had just formed a friendship with a female member of the university staff in Los Angeles shortly before she was brutally murdered. The incident shocked the whole campus community, and as she was well known and liked, a large memorial service was held. Rejto offered to play some Bach during the service.

It turned out to be a harrowing experience, as he felt unexpectedly very nervous while wanting to play really well. But, instead of a powerful and emotional tribute to his friend, he was deeply disappointed with his performance. He felt he had let her down. The same night, he was due to play an important solo recital in Los Angeles. He felt driven to atone for his lackluster performance earlier during the day.

When he stepped onto the stage that night he sensed the audience was restless and he became concerned that he was in for a difficult night. A little into the performance he became aware that the audience had become very quiet. He felt strangely dislocated from the technical aspects, convinced he had complete mastery of the instrument, and could achieve anything. Nervousness was nonexistent. He was hardly aware of playing at all. Feeling free and without limitations, he sensed being released from his ego with the purpose of taking on the mission to perform. When he finished he was almost in a trance, but the audience went crazy. After the concert, some audience members came backstage with many compliments. They included a famous violin teacher, who remarked he had often heard Rejto play well but that night was very different. He was puzzled and asked for an explanation, but there was none.

In retrospect, Rejto believes he was released from the more usual feeling of trying to please the audience and of consequent judgment. That freedom allowed him to perform to his full potential, caring only about the mission to honor the memory of his brief friendship and not particularly caring about what anyone thought.

Perhaps he had tapped into a form of intense communication with the audience, something that others might refer to as a universal experience or something greater than oneself. He felt as if he facilitated the transmission as a catalyst, and this experience may tell us something about the nature of the transmission. Rejto is still mystified by the intense, emotional experience that evening and has tried in vain to recapture the essence under differing circumstances. Sometimes he approached it but never achieved it to the same degree.

In the past a great deal of music was composed for the Church. It was the vehicle for a profoundly religious message, often a depiction of Christ carrying the burden of the cross. In *St. Matthew Passion,*[178] Bach conveys Christ's great sadness and struggle to walk under the massive weight; the music is long and repetitive, seeming to echo the painful steps along the Via Dolorosa. When people hear a performance of Bach's *St. Matthew Passion,* they follow the text and absorb the message. The music functions to elevate that message and inject it with life. In this way the music empowers the story with meaning.

When music is abstract a specific or literal message is absent, leaving the listener to respond to personal emotional triggers. People might be saddened by music that is melancholic, but their reasons would vary—possibly a reminder of an event, place, or person, or just a particular mood.

The performers and the listeners are sensitive to each other. The artist is aware of the sound in the hall and whether the audience is attentive, restless, or distracted. The audience may notice how the performers are dressed and the quality of their instruments before they focus on the level of technical ability or emotional transmission.

Perceptive in their assessment of genuine feelings, the audience members can usually identify empty gestures or gimmicks. Like detectives, they can recognize a fake movement of the bow or shaking of the head. Sometimes people who are not educated listeners of classical music make negative comments about a performance without being able to explain their reasons. Perhaps they felt that something about the performance wasn't genuine.

Rejto is well aware of the mood of the audience, particularly in his role as the administrator of a music festival. When he organizes the program he starts by choosing the last piece, because it will be a lingering memory for people and he wants them to return. He looks for something unusual that will involve most of the musicians onstage. A somber piece would not be a good selection. The next choice is the start of a program, which should be engaging and positive so that one may take the audience elsewhere in the middle selection: a contemporary work, or a somber work, perhaps Mahler, or a work off the beaten path. The middle work is really the heart of the program and it is the moment that the audience is most receptive.

Variety is the key to good programming. Ideally, the audience should experience an emotional journey without repeating the same emotion too often, which could occur if there were for example, too many romantic pieces in a row. People tend to be easily bored. When they hear anything once, whether a short phrase or a lengthy section, it is "new." On second hearing, they recognize the fragment as something they have heard before (and will possibly take pleasure in the recognition), but the third time is often registered as boring.

Leonard Bernstein had a way of dealing with this problem by using a system called the "one, two, three rule" that would be familiar to composers. Comedians often take advantage of this rule by providing the punch line immediately following two introductory and similar preambles. Musical phrasing and indeed musical structure often follows this simple pattern.[179]

Rejto tries not to choose too many pieces in the same key, though at first glance with equal temperament tuning, one might think that every key should sound equal to another (except to those with perfect pitch!). However, instruments are not created equal in terms of the notes that suit them best. For example, the cello loves the open D and A strings that resonate freely. The best composers always take this acoustical phenomenon into account and will write in keys that take advantage of the natural harmonics and the open strings. When moving to other keys, the cello takes on a different color and character that can be utilized to convey a different meaning. Rejto has always loved the sound of the open string, which continues to vibrate and ring. In comparison one can pluck a violin and, although the sound is lovely, the vibration stops a lot more quickly. He was also attracted to the instrument's wide and human-like vocal range.

Many people are in awe of cellists and other performers. They look at a musician playing and the production of the sound seems almost like sleight of hand. Some listeners have asked him how he manages various sound effects, trying to fathom how the "magic tricks" are accomplished.

Is music transformative? Rejto has heard listeners say they had never known any art could be so beautiful or powerful. In the short run, music can touch them. As for the long term, he believes music could be transformative when many people are receiving the same message together and creating a synergy that takes on a life of its own. A great performance could be transformative for performers as well and could secure their reputation and future career. Musicians are not simply conduits for the music; they are affected to some degree by every performance. Perhaps their aspiration to continue playing is, to some extent, part of a constant search for personal transformation. It would be impossible to convince an audience of any feeling if the performer was not also genuinely moved.

Rejto considers himself to be an inherently rational person who looks for answers through science and logic. On the other hand, he is aware of our hunger for the spiritual and explanations that are outside normal experience. It is a driving force that motivates musicians to look for new ways to turn a phrase and organize notes that could activate emotions in themselves and thereby in others.

*Peter Rejto was interviewed by the author in Sydney, Australia, in June 2014.*

# Pieter Wispelwey

*BRIEF  BIOGRAPHY*

Pieter Wispelwey tours worldwide as a soloist with many of the greatest orchestras, including the Boston, Dallas, NHK, Sapporo, Sydney, and BBC Symphonies and St. Paul Chamber Orchestra, Yomiuri Nippon, Tokyo Philharmonic, London Philharmonic, Hallé Orchestra, BBC Scottish Symphony, Orchestra of the Age of Enlightenment, Academy of Ancient Music, Gewandhaus Orchester Leipzig, Danish National Radio Symphony, Budapest Festival Orchestra, and Camerata Salzburg.

He has worked with conductors such as Esa-Pekka Salonen, Iván Fischer, Jeffrey Tate, Sir Neville Marriner, Herbert Blomstedt, Yannick Nézet-Séguin, Kent Nagano, Philippe Herreweghe, Vassily Sinaisky, Vladimir Jurowski, Louis Langrée, Marc Minkowski, Ton Koopman, and Sir Roger Norrington.

In recital, Wispelwey appears regularly in major venues such as Lincoln Center, New York; Wigmore Hall, London; Konzerthaus Berlin; Concertgebouw and Muziekgebouw, Amsterdam; Châtelet and Louvre, Paris; Bozar, Brussels; Società del Quartetto, Milan; Walt Disney Hall, Los Angeles; Teatro Colon, Buenos Aires; and Sydney Opera House. He is renowned for performing all the Bach Cello Suites in one evening.

His more than twenty CDs have won major international awards. They include three complete sets of Bach Cello Suites. The most recent, in 2012, commemorated his fiftieth birthday.

Wispelwey studied with Dicky Boeke and Anner Bylsma in Amsterdam, and subsequently with Paul Katz in the United States and William Pleeth in the UK. Wispelwey was the first cellist to receive the Netherlands Music Prize in 1992 for the country's most promising young musician.

Wispelwey plays a 1760 Giovanni Battista Guadagnini cello and a 1710 Rombouts baroque cello.[180]

*Some concerts can be life changing. Such is the power of music.*

—PIETER WISPELWEY

F OR PIETER WISPELWEY, concerts are a time of meditation and contemplation. When two thousand people are listening and concentrating, their minds are fueled with thoughts, associations, and memories. This magical effect does not necessarily depend on the profundity of the music, nor is it more likely to occur only when the music is not too lively or energetic.

What makes music emotionally convincing? It always has some sort of an emotional story line, which a performer or listener can interpret with complete freedom. The composer conveys these emotions in melodies, motifs, counterpoint, rhythms and harmony. Purely abstract art doesn't really exist. There is always meaning, which prompts emotion. The emotional effect is created through the suggestion of conflict and tension and the release of tension, which is a process that everyone can recognize. And so, music can provide a model for coping with everyday life. If you recognize the tension and its resolution in music as beautiful, your own life with similar conflicts must also contain beauty. This is comforting.

In much eighteenth- and nineteenth-century music, the tension between contrasting themes is the lifeblood of the sonata form. For example, a bold first theme is put against a more lyrical second theme. In the development section, this leads to all kinds of tensions, conflict and some kind of resolution.

In essence, contrast is important because it accentuates characteristics of themes or details that keep the listener captivated. Performers know they should avoid playing too smoothly or evenly— otherwise emotion will be lacking. Not that emotion is always the

173

sole goal; it can also be the impact of sheer energy or revelation, stimulated by intellectual or creative genius. Experiencing great music can be a multilayered business.

Does music also have healing power? The case for music as a healing balm can be seen in Holland, where it is traditionally used during a funeral, one of the most emotionally charged events in any society. The idea behind the ritual is to start the healing process through the release of feelings. Wispelwey has played at many funerals, including those of his grandparents and cello teacher, who was a central influence in his life. At her funeral, he played the "Allemande" from the Sixth Suite for unaccompanied cello[181] by Bach, a piece of music he likens to a prayer and to feelings of eternity. A work of Bach has the capacity to put grief into perspective, he believes. It may initiate the grieving process and help people cope with their feelings of loss.

This is not to imply Bach is always mournful. Wispelwey's teacher was adamant Bach should not be played in a pedantic or overly serious manner, as one needs to keep in mind the pleasures of the dance and the joy the performer feels when playing his works. His suites written for solo cello have a special place in the repertoire for the instrument.

Although not strictly structured as question and answer, music often communicates as a conversation, with phrases answered by other phrases. The hidden harmony and polyphony is beguiling and endlessly intriguing.

The *Six Cello Suites*[182] by Bach consist of thirty-six movements, all with internal logic. Some are ambitious, like the "Allemande," while others are more modest. There are many contrasting elements, but something magical occurs as well. In a few of the movements, there is a section in which a different quality of time takes over. It leads to a sort of hypnosis, when the piece just seems to undulate. A special momentum is created, which seems unstoppable, mystical, and alludes to eternity. This effect occurs in the "Allemande" and "Sarabande" of Bach's Cello Suite No. 6. In the second half of the "Sarabande," the typical dance gestures give way to a seemingly endless series of paired notes and double stops; there is no more rhythm, but the piece does not stop. The listener, who is not necessarily conscious of the device, may suddenly grasp that the rhythm has stalled, and feel overawed. At this point during a performance, there is stillness in the auditorium, when the audience holds a collective breath. Clearly, performers are not overwhelmed when they play. Nor do they lose control. They can give that illusion, which usually works a treat.

People are probably mistaken if they believe a great deal of effort is required to appreciate classical music. It depends on previous exposure; sometimes listeners may only require one performance to develop sufficient familiarity to grasp and enjoy a work on hearing it the second time around. If people are open to the music in concerts of Bach's Six Cello Suites, they can even become experienced listeners halfway through the set.

What is the future for Western art music? Lack of support for the arts is pervasive in the West and not confined to Europe. It stems from a misdirected anti-elitism, resulting in a dominance of cannibalistic popular culture and a sad nonchalant attitude toward the power of great art. Wispelwey has found a passionate and knowledgeable young audience for classical music in Japan, Korea, and China, which has convinced him that the West is making some painful mistakes where art education is concerned. These youngsters are appropriating the music arguably being discarded by the West. Fortunately, many excellent centers for classical music still exist in the Western world. It would seem best to cherish them.

*Pieter Wispelwey was interviewed by the author in Sydney, Australia, in May 2013.*

# Diana Doherty

*BRIEF BIOGRAPHY*

Diana Doherty was Principal Oboe with the Symphony Orchestra of Lucerne from 1990 before she took up her current position as Principal Oboe with the Sydney Symphony Orchestra in 1997. As a soloist she has performed with the New York, Liverpool and Hong Kong Philharmonic Orchestras, as well as the Australian Chamber Orchestra and other leading symphony orchestras in Australia and New Zealand.

Doherty has been a guest at many international festivals, such as the Young Artist in Concert Festival in Davos, Switzerland, the Prague Spring Festival, Bratislava Music Festival, Musica Riva Festival, Italy, as well as the Australian Festival of Chamber Music in Townsville.

She was a joint winner of the Young Concert Artists International Auditions in New York, received first prize at the Prague Spring Festival Competition, and an Aria for her performance of the Ross Edwards' Oboe Concerto. While still a music student in 1985, she won an award for the Other Instruments section of the ABC Instrumental and Vocal Competition.

Her recordings include concertos by Haydn, Mozart, Bohuslav Martinů, and Bernd Alois Zimmerman with the Symphony Orchestra of Lucerne (Pan Classics); Ross Edwards' *Oboe Concerto* with the Melbourne Symphony Orchestra and Arvo Volmer; Carl Vine's *Oboe Concerto* with the Tasmanian Symphony Orchestra, *Bach: Violin Concertos* with Richard Tognetti and the Australian Chamber Orchestra, and *The Bach Album: Concertos for Oboe and Oboe d'amore* with Ironwood and Linda Kent (all for ABC Classics), *Romantic Oboe Concertos* with the Queensland Symphony Orchestra under Werner Andreas Albert; *Blues for D.D.* (a program of blues and jazz style works with pianist David Korevaar), and Graeme Koehne's *Inflight Entertainment* (Naxos 2005).[183]

*Moral values are inherent in music. For one, there is honesty,*
*in relation to self-examination, and truthful answers to ques-*
*tions, such as: "Am I giving the job my best effort? Am I real-*
*ly listening to myself play? Am I hypocritical as a teacher? How*
*did I contribute to that problem? How could I have done better?"*

—DIANA DOHERTY

USIC HAS BEEN a vital part of every culture throughout history and the production of music seems instinctive. Diana Doherty believes that classical music has the capacity to direct people toward a nobler version of themselves through dedication to high standards and the development of character. In a world full of disposable items, questionable attitudes, and intolerance, music is an honorable pursuit. It is subtle, complex, and free of dogma, and aside from many rules related to form, there is much space for freedom of expression. These qualities attest to the value of music as a most precious commodity, unquantifiable in monetary terms and difficult to articulate in words. In essence, it is intangible and greater than any individual.

Another aspect of music is the opportunity for personal development. Doherty's journey with music and the oboe has taught her a great deal about herself and others. Obviously, this type of education is not confined to music and is obtained in other disciplines as well. Her tennis teacher expressed the view that tennis was instructive in a similar way because the general lessons could be applied to life itself. Perhaps the common denominator is the perpetual pursuit of excellence that requires self-knowledge, criticism, and discipline.

These guiding principles have become Doherty's way of life. They permeate and transform everything she does, and have made it possible for her to connect with others by communicating the music in a nonthreatening way. The work is endless because there is always new music to learn and more to master in the music she already plays. As a professional musician, she feels she has a responsibility to play at her top standard all the time.

It seems that people are happiest when they live by such high values. Perhaps that is what people learn by dedicating themselves so completely to one discipline. In the process they are able to learn more about themselves, which in turn can lead them to a more tolerant and sensitive understanding of how the world functions.

Sensitivity to others is an important value, particularly when playing chamber music and having to incorporate another person's version of a work. There might be times when a performer feels very strongly about some aspect of the music. One is then faced with the challenge of maintaining awareness of other musicians' views, while defending one's own ideas with clarity and conviction.

Orchestral players must learn many interpersonal skills and some very difficult conditions can arise when they need to assert their opinions. These circumstances might occur when they are taking part in auditions or trial panels that assess other players or conductors. At these times, members of a panel are expected to express their judgments in front of others in the knowledge they might not concur with popular viewpoints. It requires courage to express an opinion honestly and risk criticism without taking it personally.

For the listener, music provides an opportunity for contemplation in a world that is busy with traffic, children, telephones, and computers. Just sitting and listening to music of great beauty can be uplifting if listeners are able to give it their full attention. It could also induce a type of meditation for the listener, with the potential to recreate this meditative state in the future. Perhaps this is the mental state that can be observed in some members of the audience who appear to be asleep or in a dreamy half sleep.

Doherty has seen powerful effects of direct interaction through music. When she was a music student, she had a moving experience at a home for children with a range of disabilities. They were sitting in a circle, some in wheelchairs and others on the floor. A roll of aluminum foil was unfurled and the children were told they were free to scrunch it up while Doherty was playing. Then the attendants asked her to play a different melody to each child. To this day, she cannot forget the reaction of one little boy who was initially very restless, but as she played the beautiful slow movement of Haydn's Oboe Concerto[184] especially for him, she looked into his eyes and became aware of his sudden, complete attention. At that moment, she was struck by the intense connection between the boy and herself.

She has also observed the transformational effects of music on the audience when maestro Vladimir Ashkenazy conducts. His personal integrity shows through, and audiences respond to his simple humanity, dedication, and wish to communicate his love for a particular piece of music.

It is unfortunate that some people feel excluded from classical music in the mistaken belief that an intellectual understanding is necessary or that the emotions expressed in music are always positive. She is reminded of an occasion when she was a child and her parents took her to an art exhibition. Afterwards, her mother asked for her reaction. She replied saying she had not liked the pictures at all because they made her feel hot, dusty, and uncomfortable. Doherty's mother accepted her response and then suggested that the artist had indeed produced effective images if he had made her feel hot and uncomfortable.

Music spans the whole spectrum of feelings and it is important to be open to the emotional effects, which can cheer, depress, or energize. Unstructured music can affect mood as well. In her yoga classes, the trainer plays soft background music containing a little harmony or dissonance, which serves to heighten the whole experience.

However, the really strong feelings are transmitted through musical harmony. Certain harmonic changes can cause goose bumps; a predictable harmony can induce feelings of calm and reassurance. Some interweaving harmonies can be moving and uplifting, as in Vaughan Williams' *Fantasia on a Theme by Thomas Tallis*.[185] In this work, the composer produces an antiphonal effect, or statement and response, by using a second orchestra that sits behind the first one. In a section of the piece, the two orchestras alternate between a loud, rich sound and a nonvibrato, other worldly sound like a church echo.

Francis Poulenc is another master of harmony, evident in his opera *Dialogues des Carmélites*[186] and the Sonata for oboe and piano.[187] In the final movement of the sonata, he uses a combination of tonalities and parallelism, so that you hear the ancient and modern at the same time, an association that produces an emotional effect.

Changing only one note of a chord can make a significant difference. In the beginning of Rachmaninov's Piano Concerto No. 2 in C Minor,[188] a half-tone dissonance has a massive impact in the eight-bar piano solo introduction. Dissonance followed by resolution is characteristic of Bach. Doherty suggests that if this paradigm were extrapolated to society, one might postulate that disagreements were a prerequisite for achieving social harmony. Ambiguity and nuance can also be expressed in music by blurring or juxtaposing keys,[189] causing the overall key to remain unresolved throughout a piece.

There is much scope for a wide range of emotional expression. Schubert is a great master of emotional changes, which he brings about through variations of key and subtlety of expression. He can even make a minor key sound happy and a major one sound sad. This emotional communication is direct, personal, and immediate. One of the characteristics of great composers like Mozart, Bach, and Brahms is the listener's instant identification with their music. People feel welcome and included, and the music seems to reflect their feelings. Then they may become aware of the architectural structure and astonishing melodic invention. For those who want to delve more intellectually, there is abundant challenge, especially in Bach, with much complexity in the voices, the way they work together, the symmetry and general construction.

There is a theory that the aesthetics of music are based on the Fibonacci numbers and the Golden Mean,[190] which would suggest that the most beautiful point occurs about two-thirds of the way through a piece. At that point of the Flute Sonata in B Minor[191] by Bach, there is indeed a dramatic climax on a trill, like a "hallelujah" moment.

Not all compositions reflect this aesthetic, and every composer presents a different sound world. Mozart expresses great elegance, poise, beauty, intellectual depth, and perfection of form; his music in minor keys contains added depth and pathos. For Doherty, one of the most sublime pieces ever written is the Violin Concerto in D Major, Op.61[192] by Beethoven. It is surely full of love and the feeling is communicated through the stable, celestial harmony, rather than inventive melody. The slow movement has Doherty tingling and awestruck by the perfection of balance, symmetry, and voicing of the chords, even though they are relatively simple.

Living without Beethoven would be a serious deprivation. It is hard to believe his everyday life was often miserable, yet this wretched state was not often reflected in his music. In fact, music probably served as an escape. Beethoven expresses his anger as if shaking a fist to heaven, but enlightenment and sparkle are never far away.

Music can be a powerful tool for invoking memories. When her daughter was very young, Doherty used to read to her from a book called *The Musical Life of Gustav Mole*.[193] The main character, Gustav Mole, plays a catchy tune on the violin. Her daughter couldn't get enough of this tune and wanted to hear it every night. At the same time, Doherty was reading *An Equal Music* by Vikram Seth,[194] but instead of hearing Bach or Schubert as she read, she heard only Gustav Mole's tune and even today, she associates this tune with *An Equal Music*.

Apart from the emotive content of the music itself, some performances have strong emotional associations. The first time Doherty played Bartók's *Concerto for Orchestra*,[195] she was only fourteen years old and it was her first attempt at playing the cor anglais. She fell in love with this music, especially the beautiful romantic melody in Movement 1V, Intermezzo Interrotto. In one section, the violas and cor anglais play the melody in canon form, with the cor anglais two quavers behind the violas. She was quite overcome by the effect and intrigued that Bartók should have thought of this device.

Around the same age, she played the oboe in a performance of Schumann's Piano Concerto[196] and remembers feeling enthralled, as the music was intensely emotional, original, and expressive. Other powerful memories continue to exhilarate: a performance of the oboe concerto by Richard Strauss[197] played by Heinz Holliger, and the Mahler Symphonies, especially when they were relatively new to her.

Music can also express love and sex, and she agrees with those who discern strong sexual associations in the overture to *Der Rosenkavalier*[198] by Richard Strauss. When the curtain opens and you see the two lovers in the Marschallin's boudoir, it is not difficult to imagine what has just preceded this scene.

The feelings associated with teenage romance are expressed in the slow movement of the Guitar Concerto by Rodrigo Aranjuez[199] and the bittersweet music by Nino Rota for Franco Zeffirelli's *Romeo and Juliet*.[200] *Fantasia on a Theme by Thomas Tallis* by Vaughan Williams conveys the yearning for a lover or the memory of a teenage crush when one was more in love with fantasy than reality. Music is a perfect vehicle for reflecting on such emotions as it offers contemplation in a secure environment.

The emotional response to music became confusing when contemporary classical music moved away from the romantic to a more intellectual form, and perhaps took itself a little too seriously. Nevertheless, Doherty enjoys much contemporary music for the technical challenges, as well as the elements of abandon and rebellion. Today, composers are less inclined to appear clever, as they have come to appreciate that music is meant to promote feelings of well-being.

There is no end to the enormous technical challenges presented by the oboe, and she often wonders why she chose such a pitiless taskmaster. There is something very soulful about the sound, but she didn't fall in love with it in the same way that she fell for her husband. It was more like an arranged marriage. She learned to love it gradually and there were many times when she felt extremely frustrated, and still does. It is a limited and unforgiving instrument at times, but she cannot imagine her life without it.

When the oboe is played, the sound seems to reside inside rather than outside the body, due to the physicality and resonance. When she plays, there is no separation between her oboe and her body. They seem to function as one entity, which is an image she encourages her students to contemplate. As in singing, visual imagery is important because most of the sound production occurs inside the body.

The task of a teacher is to encourage the right physical movement through words. It doesn't really matter what they say, as long as the desired response is achieved. There is, of course, great variability in response among individual students, and teachers need to be flexible and adapt to the needs of each student.

Methods of teaching music have changed in a single generation. Doherty's daughter learned music through its incorporation into games and body movements. The system of teaching theory has moved away from the traditional didactic approach, so that children are developing a good understanding of harmony and can imitate a song.

Doherty's major instruments were piano and oboe, but her daughter was much more curious about music and played several instruments, including piano, drums, ukulele, and guitar, some of them self-taught. She also improvised on the piano, which her mother would not have attempted at the same age. Instead of traditional studies that focused on playing piano pieces from memory, her teachers emphasized a good understanding of harmony.

Consequently, her daughter became comfortable with various styles and can play jazz in addition to classical. Her understanding of music as a craft is quite considerable. She can pick up a guitar at a campfire and play anything by ear, or sit at a piano and develop a tune someone has hummed. Besides preparing a student for music as a profession, these skills promote the integration of music as a part of everyday life.

*Diana Doherty was interviewed by the author in Sydney, Australia, in May 2012.*

VOICES

# Yvonne Kenny

Australian soprano Yvonne Kenny has performed at many great opera houses and festivals, including La Scala, Milan, Staatsoper Berlin, Wiener Staatsoper, Bayerische Staatsoper, Opéra de Paris, English National Opera, Glyndebourne, San Francisco Opera, Australian Opera, and the Salzburg Festival. Her roles have included the Marschallin in *Der Rosenkavalier* for Wiener Staatsoper, the title role in *The Merry Widow*, Dido in *Dido & Aeneas*, Blanche in *A Streetcar Named Desire* for Opera Australia, and Jocasta in *Oedipus Rex* for the Sydney Festival. She also appears regularly in recital and symphonic repertoire.

Her discography of over sixty international recordings include Mozart's *Die Entführung aus dem Serail*, *Mitridate* and *Lucio Silla* with conductor Nikolaus Harnoncourt on Teldec, Benjamin Britten's *Gloriana* with Sir Charles Mackerras on Decca, Handel's *Deborah* with Robert King on Hyperion, Strauss's *Der Rosenkavalier* with David Parry on Chandos, and *Mahler Symphony No. 2* with the London Philharmonic Orchestra under Klaus Tennstedt (LPO).

Kenny is widely acclaimed for her recordings of the bel canto operas for Opera Rara, notably the award-winning *Emilia di Liverpool*. Her recordings on ABC Classics include the Gold Disc *Simple Gifts, Handel Arias* with the Australian Brandenburg Orchestra, *Vienna City of my Dreams* with the Melbourne Symphony Orchestra and conductor Richard Bonynge, and *The Four Last Songs* of Richard Strauss with the Queensland Symphony Orchestra and conductor Johannes Fritszch.

After attaining a BSc in Biochemistry, she studied singing in London, where she won the Kathleen Ferrier Award in 1975, and was a member of the company at the Royal Opera House, Covent Garden until 1996. She is a Professor of Voice at the Guildhall School of Music and Drama London.

In 1989 Kenny was made a Member of the Order of Australia for services to music.[201]

*Music unifies all humanity. Everyone can understand this universal language, which communicates through the inner self and is more powerful than the spoken word. In fact, music may have been the original, primeval basis for communication and later evolved differently in various cultures.*

—YVONNE KENNY

THE MUSIC PEOPLE HEAR in their youth often stays with them as their most cherished memories, and for many people of Yvonne Kenny's era, the songs of The Beatles can provoke a rush of memories filtered from the life experiences at the time they first heard and loved these songs. For children, music is a great gift, providing community activity in choirs and bands and a learning experience not only in music, but also in the social skills required for cooperation and compromise. The study of music is a very cerebral and exacting process, but it also facilitates the freeing of the spirit. It has the capacity to expand our emotions and move us onto an elevated plane: a space outside everyday existence.

Perhaps such a spiritual release could be associated with anecdotal evidence that music can help or heal people who are troubled or ill. Some children and adults with autism have reportedly found an avenue of self-expression through music and, very occasionally, have shown extraordinary talent, as in the case of an autistic person, Derek Paravicini, who could play anything by ear to a high professional standard.[202]

Kenny is fascinated by the way people use music for healing. For example, The Merry Makers,[203] a group of performers with intellectual and physical disabilities, find enormous joy through inter-action with each other and communicating music and dance to an audience. It might be the only part of their lives when they can take directions, rehearse, develop self-discipline, and then fully express themselves. Their film, *The Music in Me*, has won many awards.

It is quite possible that music has some sort of healing power, although certain claims seem far-fetched. Kenny once received a let-ter from a lady who said she had been suffering from cancer, but after listening to Kenny's CD *Simple Gifts*, she went into full remission, which she attributed to the diva's voice. Kenny is convinced that a performance can ignite positivity and provide a potent way of leaving the negative behind. People turn to music for religious worship and major celebrations, such as the Olympic Games or other major sport-ing events. Music is also central to disciplined movement of parades requiring rhythmic coordination of large numbers of people, as in a military tattoo.

For Kenny, the finer aspects of classical music are the most mean-ingful and touching. Pure melodies can reverse a sad mood so that she feels uplifted and energized. They have the capacity to transport her to contemplation about the essence of existence and can melt away any little irritations. Above all, she loves harmony, especially voices singing in harmony. She is particularly moved by the plaintive qual-ity of Irish folk music, especially its harmony, rhythm, and simplicity.

She has sung Handel arias characterized by much openness in the harmony and the simple shift of a chord, which can wrench the heart. In contrast, listening to a contemporary symphony might not produce that heartfelt emotional response in spite of incredible com-plexity and density of sound and structure. Essentially, the emotional transmission depends on purity, and power of the simplest change.

Audiences are less comfortable with contemporary music, com-pared to baroque or romantic, because modern music is not often pleasing to the ear initially and the tonalities and musical language are difficult. Kenny wonders if it is only a matter of time before contemporary composers will be recognized, as happened with Benjamin Britten. However, not all audiences have been won over by Britten, during the past few decades. Kenny loves his music and believes he is the greatest operatic writer of the twentieth century. He can evoke incredibly powerful emotions in his soundscapes, particularly through the effects of chords, and especially when the chorus yells "Peter Grimes!" in the opera[204] of the same name.

The philosophical intention of a composer often depends on nationality, life events, or influential schools, such as Les Six,[205] the French group of composers in Paris. Sometimes, there is a fantastic marriage between composer and poet, such as the musical relationship between Richard Strauss and Hugo von Hofmannsthal. Kenny's favorite operatic role is the Marschallin in *Der Rosenkavalier* by Richard Strauss, and she is amazed by the composer's insights into the mental state and self-expression of a woman at the Marschallin's stage of life. Such great composers have a profound understanding of humanity, and are able to transmit these perceptions in a musical form as a message that can foster high ideals, even universal humanity.

Performers are keenly aware of the force between themselves and the audience. Kenny believes it reflects the energy level of the audience as a group and is probably related to events in people's daily lives and their capacity for concentration at the time of the concert. A performer is primarily a vessel of communication for the composer and a singer also recreates the message of the poet or librettist. In order to reproduce the music with integrity, an artist must stay true to the wishes of the composer, yet many singers take considerable liberties.

Kenny has observed how interpretation becomes broader and more relaxed as we move further in time from the point of composition, and she was very surprised when she heard the way Mahler played the piano version of his Fourth Symphony[206] on a piano roll. In this version the composer took a faster, stricter tempo, and his inter-pretation was less emotionally indulgent than she was used to hearing in modern performances. It was a fascinating insight into the vagaries of interpretation over the generations. While Herbert von Karajan[207] stretched Beethoven's tempi to the limit and pursued a huge, roman-tic, juicy sound, Roger Norrington,[208] in search of a period style, pro-duced a dry and more constricted sound.

These days, there are many fine recordings but Kenny thinks this medium of musical transmission is quite restricted when compared with live performance. The drawback was evident when soprano Felicity Lott recorded *Serenade to Music for 16 Voices* by Vaughan Wil-liams.[209] Her voice sounded lovely in the hall during the performance but the speakers used for the recording were unable to fully cap-ture her sound. Kenny admits to being frequently dissatisfied with her recording sessions. Recordings can give people a false idea of the power of a singing voice, especially when sound engineers adjust the edges of the voice and rebalance the orchestra so the vocal sound is in front and sounds immense. Later, when people hear the same voice in the theater, they are often disappointed. A live recording is often preferable to one made in a studio, as the microphone is further away.

It is important to be aware that sound is only a part of a sing-er's performance, which also involves body language, expression, and spiritual connection. Although intangible, Kenny maintains that the spiritual aspect is unmistakable. The singer must be sufficiently confident and receptive in order to allow music to resonate through his or her body and psyche without restraint. Maria Callas[210] was a good example; she became a different person when she sang with intense focus and concentration. Kenny has experienced the thrill of becoming an effective conduit for the music when her concentration and awareness are intensified. Those times are often accompanied by an expanded sense of time and drama. One aspect of the mind is centered and disciplined but another is quite mysterious, somehow capable of opening up the spirit. As the singer journeys through an aria, certain moments will focus on the voice, and others on emotion or text, enabling the audience to receive all the elements. It is the power of the mind that stimulates the artist, bringing color to the music through imagination and emotion. The mind paints the picture and the vocal mechanism responds to give the voice color. When the sound undergoes these changes, the audience reacts.

The making of a great artist requires many ingredients, including discipline, self-sacrifice, tenacity, the ability to withstand setbacks, and a love of performing. Such artists often feel more at home in performance than in real life. For an opera singer, there is the added challenge of trying to inhabit another being with unfamiliar characteristics and values.

*Yvonne Kenny was interviewed by the author in Sydney, Australia, in July 2009.*

# Daniel Knauft

Daniel Knauft, co-founder and bass of the male vocal ensemble amarcord, started his singing career as a member of the St. Thomas Boys Choir in Leipzig. In addition to his work with amarcord, he studied medicine, graduated from Leipzig University, and wrote a research dissertation on the adolescent singing voice.

The amarcord[211] ensemble has won prizes at many international competitions, including the Tolosa in Spain, Tampere in Finland and Pohlheim in Germany. In 2002 they won the German Music Competition, and in 2004, became the first group of singers to be awarded the Ensemble Prize at the Mecklenburg-West Pomerania Festival.

Amarcord appears regularly at classical music festivals and tours frequently throughout Europe and North America. In 1997, Knauft and his amarcord colleagues initiated the Festival of Vocal Music "a cappella" in Leipzig.

They have made many recordings, including *Rastlose Liebe* ('Restless Love'), released in 2009. The CD won the ECHO Klassik Award, the Luxembourgian Supersonic Award, and the CARA (Contemporary A Cappella Recording Award), the "a-cappella-Oscar." Amarcord also gained the CARA for *Nun komm, der Heiden Heiland* ('Now come, saviour of the Gentiles'), *Incessament,* and *Hear the Voice.* In 2010 they released a reconstructed version of St. Mark Passion, a lost Passion setting by J.S. Bach.[212] In 2013 the ensemble received the ICMA (International Classical Music Award) for *Zu S. Thomas, Two Gregorian Masses from the Thomas Gradual.*[213]

*The problems of political repression were dispelled in the haven of Bach's celestial concerns and the freedom intrinsic to the texts.*

—DANIEL KNAUFT

ALL THE MEMBERS of amarcord were born in East Germany and sang in St. Thomas Church Boys Choir,[214] Leipzig. They were on tour in West Germany when the Berlin Wall came down, and it was this event that provided the impetus to form a professional group. Otherwise, their singing would have remained a hobby.

When he was a child growing up in East Germany, music provided Knauft with a refuge of inner peace in an environment of political turmoil and suppression. In primary school, the teachers used to interrogate students about the appearance of the clock dial on their television screens when the news bulletin came on at eight o'clock in the evening. This was a devious attempt to establish whether their parents were watching East German state TV or a West German channel, as the clock faces were very different. Most East Germans watched Western news, and those who were out of range were dubbed "innocents."

Knauft was sixteen when the Berlin Wall came down; the youngest member of their current singing group was ten. While they were growing up, they became aware that the political system was oppressive. Many families who didn't believe the propaganda moved closer to the church, hoping to find a measure of freedom. Those from bourgeois, academic backgrounds such as his often encouraged their sons to join St. Thomas Boys Choir.

During his nine years of singing in the choir, he loved Bach, learned the music quickly, and still knows many of the pieces by heart. Even without full comprehension of the words, the young choristers found a depth of meaning in the texts, which gave comfort at times of stress, illness, or a death in the family. When his parents were ill, Knauft became aware of how much support and fortitude he could find in Bach's compositions, as well as the joy of performing music of profound emotional and spiritual power. He experienced the healing power of music much later, when his first marriage broke up and ended in divorce.

The association of music and redemption is illustrated by the story of sixteenth-century composer and nobleman Carlo Gesualdo,[215] who killed his wife and her lover. For the rest of his life, Gesualdo was haunted by guilt. Eventually, his inner turmoil found a way into musical composition, where he used his creative powers to attain healing and salvation.

Even if Knauft was unable to articulate political ideas as a young boy, he was convinced music offered an avenue of freedom, not only interpretive freedom, but also in the independence of thought that comes with analyzing the texts of songs and working with fellow musicians.

Most people in East Germany were fearful of expressing dissent because the secret police, the Stasi,[216] spied on the population at large. During 1989, however, small groups were beginning to protest following church services. Sometimes, they chanted slogans, including: "We are the people, not you up there." At the time, there was great consternation on the heels of the demonstrations at Tiananmen Square in Beijing and the Chinese government's harsh response to calls for greater transparency in the Communist Party, and appeals to rein in corrupt cadres. Many people referred to the outcome of those protests as the "Chinese solution," implying the East German government might turn on its own people the same way China had done.

Music had a part to play in the East German protests. People were keen to seek comfort from concerts at the Gewandhaus, and more and more were attending churches such as St. Thomas, where there was a regular Friday evening service with music. At least one piece by Bach was usually included. The music did not promote revolutionary fervor, but it did appear to give people respite and strength.

The same sort of music had been used for political propaganda in the early days of the German Democratic Republic, when the Communist government extolled Bach's music as a source of elevation and identity for the ascendant working class.

Unlike St. Nicholas Church, which welcomed everyone at any time, St. Thomas Church was cautious. In September 1989, when there was a protest close to the church in St. Thomas Square, some of the demonstrators sought sanctuary, but church authorities closed the doors on them.

The conductor Kurt Masur, together with other musicians and notables, cautioned all parties against the use of force. It was probably the first time cultural figures had assumed any responsibility for the social well-being of the country. Initially, the overall aim was to improve East Germany and there was no talk of unification. Several weeks later, the Berlin Wall came down.

Knauft believes music has a moral purpose in promoting the values of personal freedom, and the potential of transformation through empathy. Musicians learn about compromise and acceptance of alternative approaches regarding technique and interpretation, but the development of tolerance and compromise is not restricted to music. These qualities can be part of other activities such as sports, which has influenced the amarcord ensemble to compare itself to a football team.

The process of reaching out to move a person through music has similarities to acting, and like acting, it requires a certain level of control. One of Knauft's first teachers maintained there was always another "you" witnessing your own technique and directing you to "watch that vowel, watch the shape of your mouth, be careful, now turn right, and control your breath." This shadowy control can be helpful, yet it can hinder good performance, especially in Bach when one has to surrender some control to allow the spirituality of the music to emerge.

Bach is enormously challenging for musicians. The technical demands are great, yet virtuosity is an essential vehicle for displaying sheer enjoyment and praise of a divine power. Bach's phrases come together to form a single entity, which is greater than its parts, and the harmonic shifts are used to underline the text.

Singing complex Bach counterpoint can make singers feel as if they are taking part in the creation of life, a living music. It is not necessary to be a religious believer to perform Bach well, but listeners need open hearts and minds to allow the music to move them. It touches a wide range of people, and, even for those with no connection to the church, the music attests to the existence of a higher power. Many find themselves in awe of Bach, who was a committed believer as well as a supremely gifted musician.

His music is an emotional experience, and the *Motet BWV 225 Singet dem Herrn ein neues Lied* ('Sing a new song to the Lord')[217] is a good example of a particularly moving piece. Mozart heard it performed in St. Thomas Church in 1789 and asked for permission to make a copy. Apparently, he thought this was music from which he could learn. Mozart was probably impressed with Bach's ability to write a contrapuntal melody line for many voices, and a bass line to provide an additional melody, unlike traditional baroque bass lines that were simple and purely supportive.

Each contrapuntal voice can function independently. In the chorale from the church cantata, *Sehet, wir gehn hinauf gen Jerusalem* ('Behold, let us go up to Jerusalem'),[218] there is a line "*Meine Seel auf Rosen geht,*" ('my soul walks on roses'). The walking melody is heard in the bass and the "roses" in the alto. Usually, the harmonic shift is prepared by all the voices together, but in this case it is the alto that actually creates the harmonic modulation. This device elicits surprise and focuses attention on the roses, which appear more delicate and fragrant as a result.

Bach's music expresses powerful emotions that may reflect his own life experiences. He was orphaned at an early age and grew up with an older brother. His first wife died, as did many of his children. A great deal of sorrow is expressed in the music, as well as sections of complete joy, but even then, hints of melancholia rise to the surface. Conversely, whenever the music reflects sadness or tragedy, it is often followed by a more positive outburst.

Knauft is convinced Bach was aware of his genius, as well as an obligation and compulsion to compose. He enjoys imagining Bach sitting in his composing chamber and writing the music for next Sunday's performance. All the parts had to be copied by hand, and there was often only a day or two for rehearsal.

A work of Bach is never exhausted or irrelevant, and Knauft wishes that all children could be exposed to his music from an early age. It can be approached from many perspectives, including mathematics, harmony, and contrapuntal style. For singers in particular, the music contains invaluable instruction in the management of breathing and phrasing.

Knauft's group started a reciprocal festival that brings the rich musical heritage of Leipzig to the world and foreign cultural groups to Leipzig. Their aim is to emphasize transcultural unity in body, mind, heart and voice, drawing attention to the cross-fertilization of musical customs, such as singing styles. But Leipzig has a special historical association as the town where Bach was Cantor of St. Thomas Church and Director of Music in the main Leipzig churches for twenty-seven years until his death. If everybody could open up and listen to Bach, the world might be a better place.

*Daniel Knauft was interviewed by the author in Sydney, Australia, in July 2012.*

# Stephen Cleobury

*Choir Director, Kings College Cambridge*

*B R I E F   B I O G R A P H Y*

In his work over the past thirty years with the renowned Choir of King's College, Cambridge, Stephen Cleobury has aimed to develop its repertoire, broadcasts, tours, and recordings. These endeavors have led to collaboration with foremost orchestras and soloists, including the Academy of Ancient Music, the Philharmonia and the BBC Concert Orchestra. He also initiated the annual *Easter at King's* festival and the *Concerts at King's* series of concerts.

As a leader of choral workshops and adjudicator and conductor of international repute, he has worked in Baltimore, Salt Lake City, and Baton Rouge in the United States, as well as in Hong Kong and Sydney, Australia. He also performs widely as an organ recitalist in venues such as Bridgewater Hall in Manchester, Leeds and Birmingham Town Halls, the Hong Kong Arts Centre, Haderslev Cathedral in Denmark, and the LDS Conference Center in Salt Lake City.

His large discography of organ works includes a DVD of popular works on Priory Records.

While Chief Conductor of the BBC Singers between 1995 and 2007, he was well known for producing a unified sound and presenting new works. He remains Conductor Laureate of the group.

Stephen Cleobury is a past President of the Royal College of Organists and of the Incorporated Association of Organists. He was made a Commander of the Order of the British Empire (CBE) in 2009.[219]

*Being an avid listener of classical music won't make someone a better person. A Mozart enthusiast can still be a scoundrel, but perhaps, people who immerse themselves in classical music tend to be more thoughtful and reflective.*

—STEPHEN CLEOBURY

MUSIC IN GENERAL, and classical music in particular, is for some an indispensable activity that drives people to compose and perform. Those who believe in its value and transformative effect would like to make it available to others through performance and support for groups that can deliver the music.

Much of the choral repertoire that is the focus of Stephen Cleobury's working life is based on Christian texts. This music offers spiritual sustenance, but the mere mention of "spiritual" conjures up religion, which has negative connotations for many people. Yet a great number of those without religious convictions are devoted to this music. Even agnostics and atheists can be deeply nourished by Christian choral music and the moving story of the Passion, but as a professional who deals with technical and practical issues of music and performance, Cleobury finds these are often so absorbing that he does not always remember to reflect on the importance this music holds for so many people.

It is possible to appreciate music without direct response to the text, but the listener owes it to the composer to understand the motivation and meaning behind a work. Similarly, performers acquaint themselves with the composer's beliefs and circumstances in their attempts to enter the mind of the composer.

During a master class with young singers, the great English mez-zo-soprano Janet Baker observed that a singer must have complete belief in what they are singing in order to interpret a song and impart it with conviction. If the song is about something they reject or have never experienced, it is imperative to find some aspect of their own life that can be linked to the emotions in the text. Otherwise, the singer will not be able to convey the piece with conviction. An artist need not be a believing Christian to perform the Bach Passions, as they are full of emotion and common human situations with which any person can identify.

Mendelssohn remarked that emotions expressed in music could be too deep for adequate description in words. On the other hand, a text does offer the possibility of realizing emotions in musical form. Benjamin Britten's *War Requiem*[220] is an example that presents a dilemma. This great work includes settings of nine poems by Wilfred Owen, but some critics have declared the poetry is so exceptional that nobody should set it to music.

When performing a choral piece, the text is central, and the priority of the singer is to achieve clarity by producing a wide range of feelings in the words and musical phrases. The resulting transparency and imaginative interpretation will give the listener the best opportunity to understand the meaning and emotions inherent in the text. Compared with adult choristers, children display a very different approach as they have had much less emotional experience, but their innocence can have a powerful effect. The emotional aspect of the music can be expressed, at least in part, through changes in color. When referring to color in painting, the inference is obvious. Music is a different modality yet the terminology is valid. If Cleobury wants a brighter color, it could be achieved by brightening the vowels. Singing teachers use terminology such as "covering the sound" to produce a darker quality, but the vocabulary for description and mechanism is quite limited. In the case of stringed instruments, there could be clear technical means to achieve a darker sound by changing the position of the bow in relation to the fingerboard.

In abstract music, the emotional journey can be expressed in the development of one or more musical motifs, as in a symphonic movement. Moving through Beethoven's Symphony No. 5[221] might be difficult to describe in words, but the audience can certainly feel the composer's intentions.

Often, the journey through a piece seems to take the listener from uncertainty to certainty, a conclusion usually inconsistent with human experience and in a metaphorical sense, representative of an ideal world. However, if there is some sort of argument in a work, it is a musical one and not easily extrapolated to daily life. The musical line can be followed intellectually, but on the whole the audience approaches music through emotions rather than intellect.

Reading a score is a source of intense aesthetic and intellectual pleasure. Cleobury is fascinated by the ingenious and beautiful orchestration in a work such as, for example, Mozart's *The Marriage of Figaro*. But a listener does not require a high level of technical knowledge to appreciate the work—it could even act as a barrier. In this regard, program notes that focus on technical aspects such as musical structure and sequence are not very helpful, and it would seem more appropriate to emphasize the historical and social context.

Benjamin Britten famously referred to three vital components in the production of music: the composer, the performer, and the audience. He was mindful that music was written with the intention of its being heard. In contrast medieval music was very complex and mathematical; at that time, music was primarily an academic occupation and the small number of composers were not particularly concerned with the way listeners would respond. Most composers are, of course, mindful of their audience and yearn to have their music heard.

Cleobury sees himself as an enabler. When he reads the score, he asks himself: What does the composer want to hear? How do I achieve that technically? How do I make this composer's intentions as clear as I can? Every performance has its defects, but usually they are not large enough to divert the audience from responding to the music.

A common characteristic of composers is their compulsion to write music. Cleobury is also driven—in his case, to express himself through conducting and playing the organ and other keyboard instruments. He doesn't mind being very tough on himself, but is careful to treat his young musicians more gently.

Standards are important for Cleobury, who is continuing a superb tradition as the latest Director of Music, Choir of King's College, Cambridge. His aim is a genuine approach to the music that can reveal its complexity, beauty, and humanity. In his dealings with people, he tries to be guided by honesty and decency. These qualities are established values of his institution. They were traditionally taught through religion, but they can also be derived from music.

*Stephen Cleobury was interviewed by the author in Sydney, Australia, in July 2014.*

# COLLABORATIVE ARTISTS

# Dimity Hall and Julian Smiles

*BRIEF BIOGRAPHY: DIMITY HALL*

In 1992, violinist Dimity Hall joined the Australia Ensemble, resident at the University of New South Wales, and together with her husband Julian Smiles and ensemble colleagues Dene Olding and Irina Morozova, co-founded the Goldner String Quartet in 1995. The Australia Ensemble and Goldner String Quartet have performed throughout Australia, Europe, North and South America, and the Asia-Pacific, at major international venues and festivals, and have made over thirty recordings.

In 2002, Hall made her solo debut in a performance of Vaughan Williams' *The Lark Ascending* with the Sydney Symphony Orchestra, which she later recorded for ABC Classics. She has been a soloist with the Australian Chamber Orchestra, Canberra Symphony Orchestra, and Brisbane's Camerata of St. John's, as well as Guest Principal with the Sydney Symphony, and Guest Concertmaster with the Australian Opera and Ballet Orchestra, and both the Adelaide and Melbourne Symphony Orchestras.

After studies with Alice Waten in Sydney, she continued postgraduate studies with Herman Krebbers in Amsterdam on a Netherlands Government Scholarship. She won the Concertgebouw's Zilveren Vriendenkrans Award, and toured and recorded with the Royal Concertgebouw Orchestra of the Netherlands.

Together with Julian Smiles, she collaborated with contestants in the Chamber Music section of the Sydney International Piano Competition in 2008 and 2012.

She is a coach in chamber music for young musicians in the Australian Youth Orchestra and the Rising Stars program of the Sydney

Conservatorium. In 2003, she was a juror for the Melbourne International Chamber Music Competition.

Dimity Hall plays a Nicolò Gagliano violin on long-term loan from the Olding family.[222]

BRIEF BIOGRAPHY: JULIAN SMILES

Cellist Julian Smiles has performed as a soloist with major Australian orchestras and at many music festivals. He was Principal Cellist with the Australian Chamber Orchestra and has often performed as Guest Principal with the Sydney and Tasmanian Symphony Orchestras and the Australian Opera and Ballet Orchestra.

He and his wife, Dimity Hall, are members of the Australia Ensemble at the University of NSW and founding members of the Goldner String Quartet. He has worked with many musicians, including Stephen Kovacevich, Boris Berman, Pieter Wispelwey, Pascal Rogé, Piers Lane, Irina Schnittke, Jane Peters, and Paul Grabowsky; conductors Lorin Maazel, Charles Dutoit, Vladimir Ashkenazy, David Zinman, and Edo de Waart; and composers Arvo Pärt, Peter Sculthorpe, Ross Edwards, Nigel Westlake, Carl Vine, Brett Dean, and Matthew Hindson.

Smiles has been on the faculty of the Canberra School of Music and the Australian Institute of Music. Following an international selection procedure, he was appointed Lecturer in Cello at the Sydney Conservatorium of Music in 2013. As cellist of the Australia Ensemble and Goldner String Quartet, he has recorded over thirty CDs. He studied with Nelson Cooke in Canberra and pursued postgraduate studies with János Starker at Indiana University.

Julian Smiles plays an 1827 Lorenzo Ventapane cello.[223]

*Music is part of our cultural identity, a connection to the past and a bridge to the future. It is cathartic for the audience who takes the journey with the performers and many listeners respond with a visceral reaction.*

—DIMITY HALL AND JULIAN SMILES

FOR SOME PEOPLE, listening to music is simply a time-out from other activities. Yet interaction with culture through music or art offers an added dimension to the mundane routines of everyday life. These activities will be forgotten as societies are remembered for their cultural legacy.

Children need to learn about the importance of music as part of culture in order to perceive its potential for pleasure and achievement, and identify any aptitude they may have for the art. For many string players, the instrument feels like an integral part of their body. It was often love at first sight after "meeting" their instrument for the first time at school. When children's curiosity about music is switched on, it is self-perpetuating, but if activation is insufficient, there is a danger the art could decline, even within a generation.

Julian and Dimity want to share their love of music with young people, especially those whose preoccupation with the Internet or television deters them from taking any interest in classical music. Many who profess a dislike for the classics are not aware of the important part this music plays in the soundtrack of movies, and how often it is the music that lifts people out of their seat in a blockbuster.

Music can also stimulate mental stories and imagery. For some, simply listening to a piece can arouse the imagination. The trigger is usually a piece with a powerful emotional effect, such as the slow movement of the Ravel Piano Concerto in G Major[224] or Rachmaninov's Symphony No. 2 in E Minor, Opus 27[225] in which intense love is expressed. Shostakovich also conveys profound emotion. His Symphony No. 5,[226] which premiered in 1937, is one of the saddest pieces of music, and even when triumphant at times, the entire work expresses mourning for the terrible events in Soviet Russia. It encapsulates an emotional message of great significance, which has the power to grip future generations, surely the result the composer intended.

Conventional wisdom would suggest a composer's work is a reflection of personal circumstances, but the mission for each composer may or may not be congruous with their life. Unlike Shostakovich, who revealed the hardships of the Soviet environment in relentless, melancholy works, Beethoven produced joyous, uplifting music in spite of deep despair.

Pop music is also very moving and appealing, especially to the younger generation, so it may not be useful to separate the classics from pop. Some of the best pop songs are well-constructed pieces, written by people with good musical knowledge. Maybe the great classical composers, such as Mozart, would be writing pop or film music if they were alive today. They would certainly make a better living from pop than contemporary classical music!

Some people with little musical background may initially find chamber music to be an acquired taste. Other kinds of classical music, such as opera or large symphonic works, have much more visual interest, and are more successful in attracting a younger audience. Those who go no further than the orchestra and don't sample chamber music miss out on the most personal form of expression by the great composers. In these works, many of them communicate their "soul music" and intimacy.

The genre is undergoing changes. Groups such as the Kronos Quartet[227] are incorporating African mood and Eastern music into their performances and recordings, although, at this stage, it is difficult to know if these influences will become mainstream. At present, very strong differences between the musical styles remain.

There is enormous interest in Western-style classical music in the East, as many Asian cultures value the art and want their children to be educated in this musical tradition. But in some cultures such as Australia, sports have been dominant, and these activities are not conducive to locking oneself in a practice room for hours.

Although some people fear that interest in classical music is flagging in the West, the enthusiastic embrace of the art in the East can be seen as a triumph for Western music. It has swept China, Korea and Japan without significant reciprocal interest, at least not yet. There are some notable exceptions, such as the tango, with combined influences from Europe and Africa, and *taiko* drumming from Japan, which thrills many in the West, and seems to cross cultural boundaries easily.

Musicians are custodians of their traditions. Unlike great works of art that simply require hanging and good light, musical masterworks need constant reinterpretation for maximum impact. This doesn't imply a radical approach to performance, such as one in which a piece becomes almost unrecognizable. Being a custodian assumes a performer will present the works in a genuine way, true to the composer. An artist can add his or her own flavor to stamp their identity on a piece, but not to the point where the composer is overtaken in importance. If a musician is then able to reach the elevated stage of moving the audience emotionally, the experience can be deeply touching for the performers as well.

Sometimes an audience response can be confusing. When the Goldner String Quartet toured China for the first time, they were taken aback by the audience, which stopped clapping at the end of the performance, but didn't get up to leave. Apparently, staying in their seats was the signal for encores, unlike the Western custom of calls for encores and continuous clapping.

Acoustics are an important factor in the way the audience response can be delivered to performers. Due to a dry acoustic in the concert hall setting, an enthusiastic response could sound modest. It also peters out a lot more and seems tame. But the audience often prefers a dry acoustic because the sounds are clearer to their ears. On the other hand, a difficult, dry acoustic could lead a performer to concentrate more on the task of making an exceptionally beautiful sound to compensate for the lack of assistance coming from the acoustic in the hall. Performers need to be comfortable with the sound, so they can feel more confident to experiment and take risks.

Artists are usually aware when they are holding the attention of the audience, especially in the quiet, intimate sections of a piece, because they are alert to listeners who are distracted or fidgeting. Yet some performers, such as Julian, are too absorbed to sense the audience. Engrossed in sharing their love for music and the pleasure of playing with others, they are only conscious of the music, their own playing, nearby colleagues, and the overall sound. Consequently, they can be very surprised by the enthusiastic audience reaction at the end of a piece, at least in the West.

Performers also derive immense pleasure from producing something of quality, like craftsmen who are involved in fashioning a beautiful piece of furniture. In terms of music, the production involves many technical considerations, such as ensemble sound and intonation, as well as emotions. Feelings can be approached by interpreting the composer's emotions and what he or she is trying to impart to the listener, be it love, sorrow, jubilation, or reverence. Hopefully, a synthesis can be reached between the emotions of the composer and the performers.

How does the composer accomplish the magic of emotional transmission? The impact of harmony is an important mechanism. Some chords are very stable and controlled, like the tonic chord of a piece. This is a very straightforward chord. In the baroque era, composers understood that chords leading back to the home key often contained harmonic tension, there to be resolved. This concept was vital to the way music was written and performed.

Understanding harmonic language and its impact gradually increased, but in the early twentieth century, the rules appeared to relax to the point of disappearing. In reality, the music was bound by rules but harmonies had become very complex with some notes in the chord only a semitone apart. This dissonance created extreme tension and therefore corresponding power in the resolution.

The leaps between notes are also relevant to emotion. There might be a small progression, like a major second or minor third; however, if you go up an octave, it creates a lifting feeling. Going down an octave produces the opposite effect. A major seventh interval can also bring immense emotional power. All the great composers understand the impact of these chords and use them for maximum effect. Other parameters involved in producing emotions are also open to composers. These include volume, orchestration, tempo, and a whole palette of colors. Performers can change some of these parameters, so that the same work can sound very different, depending on the individual interpretation. Such differences are apparent in the recordings of sixty or seventy years ago compared with those of today.

Tempos have a marked effect on sound. Playing with a livelier tempo and cleaner sound creates an impression of increased energy. Another factor is the fundamental consequence of major versus minor. Even people who have never heard music before can appreciate the difference between a happy and a sad key, which is a characteristic central to Western-style music. A poignant example can be heard in the slow movement of the Piano Concerto No. 2 in F Major, Opus 102 by Dmitri Shostakovich.[228] The beautiful plaintive tune is initially presented in a major key, and the second time it emerges in the minor key, with extraordinary effect.

In some pieces, the emotion arises in large blocks, and at other times, as gradations. An observer can almost hear the conversation taking place in the composer's head: an internal dialogue turning into musical sound.

Complexity grew as an evolution of harmonic language in contemporary music, particularly that of Richard Strauss and early Arnold Schoenberg. Strauss used collisions of harmonies where one part of the orchestra plays in one key while another part plays in a different key. Due to his immense skill in the use of harmonic language, the great tone poems by Strauss are very powerful. Mahler and Stravinsky also experimented very successfully with harmonic language.

Listening to Anton Webern and the Second Viennese School,[229] one is aware of remarkable tension and resolution. The ability to progress from something that sounds completely wrong—clashing—to moments of resolution, holds great dramatic power. Contemporary Russian composer Alfred Schnittke[230] achieves this effect repeatedly. Australian composer Peter Sculthorpe[231] endorses his message regarding asylum seekers in detention centers or the plight of the planet through the uses of harmonic tension and timber to color the sound, especially in the viola and cello parts.

Resolving the tension acts like a blurred lens coming back into focus. The return of tonality is not registered as a simple relief, but as increased power and value of the tonality, which also becomes very beautiful because it was derived from great tension. In the progression of music to modern times the tension has become much more potent.

Today, some arts promoters and festival organizers are looking for multimedia experiences, fancy lighting, projections, or smoke and mirror effects, so there can be a certain resistance to presenting a string quartet, which is a very pure art form. It would be inappropriate to superimpose props on a string quartet unless they really suited the music or added to a particular theme. Music itself is the essence; if it is dressed up in too many clothes, the audience may be distracted from the composer's objectives.

For many in the audience, concert programs are a gateway to the music. When planning a program, it is helpful to start with the final piece. The best program is like a meal with a balanced menu of large and small, heavy and light items. If the program features two massive pieces of music at opposite ends, the audience won't know when they have had their main course. The ending is also important. A quiet finish invariably leads to a muted audience response. Occasionally, a successful program could be based on a theme or a group of composers who were connected to each other in some way. In any case, it is ideal to aim for variety in tonal language and mood.

Working with living composers can be rewarding because it gives performers an opportunity to identify the composer's overall vision and their wishes regarding mood and technical issues. If the composer is unhappy with an interpretation that does not match the version in his imagination, he might ask for suggestions from the performers or they could rework a passage together. In personality, composers are just like other people; some are very fussy about an artist's approach to the work, while others leave performers free to insert their own ideas.

Using imagery in the preparation of a new work can be useful. A member of the quartet might say, "This piece sounds like someone saying goodbye"; or at another point in the score, "This part sounds like a steam engine coming my way." These descriptions, although simplistic, can be helpful for musicians who are sensitive to imagery. Finding evocative images are also important in teaching young artists.

Students are often preoccupied with technical issues, and they need to be reminded about emotions, the mechanism of stimulation by a particular movement or phrase, and how they can project feelings in a personal way to the audience. The emotional communication also involves body language. String players move in certain ways to produce a particular effect on the instrument, but empty mannerisms without genuine commitment don't often fool an audience.

Chamber music is intimate and exposed, and performers can be very moved as the composer takes them on a journey through the score. *Quartet for the End of Time*[232] by Olivier Messiaen is one of these pieces. Fulfilling the potential of this work requires considerable energy and complete immersion during preparation. The extremes of sound contribute to the feeling of otherworldliness and sense of wonderment. In the last movement, the chords in the piano hint at a cosmic heartbeat in the form of a pulsar. While traveling into infinity, it beams back to earth like a ripple in time and space.

*Dimity Hall and Julian Smiles were interviewed by the author in Sydney, Australia, in June 2014.*

# Stefan Heinemeyer
# and Thomas Hoppe

Atos Trio cellist Stefan Heinemeyer has performed as a soloist with many orchestras, including the Berliner Symphoniker and the Vogtland Philharmonie, and he frequently performs as Principal Cellist in the Münchner Rundfunkorchester and Orchester der KlangVerwaltung, among others.

Heinemeyer won many prizes from an early age, including first prize at the International Instrumental Competition Markneukirchen in 2001, and prizes and special awards at the International Cello Competition Roberto Caruana in Milan, the Domenico Gabrielli Competition, and the Concorso Internazionale di Esecuzione Musicale Provincia di Caltanisseta.[233]

Heinemeyer was a foundation member of the Atos Trio together with Annette von Hehn, violin, and Thomas Hoppe, piano. The trio won first prize for best interpretation of a work by Schubert at the 2006 International Competition, Franz Schubert and Modern Music in Graz, Austria. In 2007 they were awarded the Kalichstein-Laredo-Robinson International Trio Award. At the Fifth Melbourne International Chamber Music Competition in the same year, the Atos Trio won first prize, Grand Prize, Musica Viva Australia Special Prize, and Audience Prize.

They have performed in major venues, including Wigmore Hall in London, Carnegie Hall in New York, and the Concertgebouw in Amsterdam, as well as festivals such as Schwetzingen, Schleswig-Holstein, Budapest Spring, George Enescu, and City of London.

The trio was chosen as a BBC Radio 3 New Generations Artist in 2009 and 2011, and was awarded a Borletti-Buitoni Trust Award 2012.[234]

*BRIEF BIOGRAPHY: THOMAS HOPPE*

Atos Trio pianist Thomas Hoppe has performed in many venues, including Carnegie Hall and Alice Tully Hall in New York, the Louvre in Paris, Tsuda Hall and Oji Hall in Tokyo, Wigmore Hall in London, Concertgebouw in Amsterdam, and City Recital Hall in Angel Place, Sydney.

Hoppe has collaborated with artists such as Itzhak Perlman, Joshua Bell, Jens Peter Maintz, Stefan Milenkovich, Antje Weithaas, Mihaela Martin, Alban Gerhardt, Frans Helmerson, and Tabea Zimmermann and is a foundation member of the Atos Trio.

Hoppe has taught master classes in collaborative piano and chamber music in his native Germany and around the world and is an official pianist for many international competitions, including the Queen Elisabeth Competition, Brussels; Joseph Joachim International Violin Competition, Hannover, Germany; International Violin Competition of Indianapolis; Grand Prix Emanuel Feuermann, Berlin; and ARD Munich. At the invitation of Itzhak Perlman, he served for many years as a faculty member and staff accompanist at the Perlman Music Program, Juilliard School of Music.

Hoppe was the first recipient of the Samuel Sanders Memorial Award at the Juilliard School, where he worked for the studio of violin pedagogue, Dorothy DeLay. Currently he is on the academic staff of the Hochschule für Musik Hanns Eisler in Berlin.[235]

*Even though many members of an audience come to a concert simply for enjoyment or entertainment, they have an opportunity to use the concert time for reflection or problem solving, with the same aims of truth and sincerity as the performers.*

—STEFAN HEINEMEYER AND THOMAS HOPPE

A S CLASSICAL MUSICIANS, Stefan Heinemeyer and Thomas Hoppe have a mission to try to make sense of musical sounds and put them together according to the wishes of the composer. In order to achieve these aims, they need to approach a piece of music on many levels and bring about the coordination of brain and fingers. Although challenging, this intellectual process is immensely satisfying. The task involves understanding the composer's message, and the clearer their concept of his or her meaning, the more convincing and effortless it will be for the listener to follow. Like painters or chefs planning a work of art or a new dish, musicians have to conceptualize what they want to achieve before they embark on the production with the ultimate aim of performance.

The basic requirements involve learning the notes and playing with dynamics and phrasing. After these essentials are mastered, musicians can enter the artistic phase, and open themselves to some sort of divine inspiration. This cannot be forced or contrived and it is not predictable, but they are always ready in case it should happen. To some extent, the process depends on the depth of their concentration on the piece, how they are feeling, and the way they are listening during the performance. At some point, if they are fortunate, a special bond with the audience could emerge, and a moment when they can truly connect with the work and with their listeners. Achieving such a high level of communication is one of their greatest pleasures, but such heights are not easy to achieve.

Sometimes, a performance can be particularly exhilarating for the audience. This effect is not necessarily associated with beautiful sounds, but often with the message of the music, played with powerful conviction, even if the interpretation is individualistic or eccentric.

The message conveyed by the composer is usually conjectural and often personal. It might portray a love letter or perhaps point the way to overcoming a problem. In the Piano Concerto No. 1 in D Minor by Brahms,[236] the first movement is full of turmoil, and the second, slow movement is very intimate. Some interpret this movement as religious, but it could also be perceived as a love letter to Clara Schumann, pianist, composer, and wife of the composer Robert Schumann. The third movement is uplifting and triumphant, changing from a minor to major key. If the performance is convincing, it should trigger many personal associations for the listener.

During a performance, it is important for musicians to take maximum risks, in order to generate interest, a unique approach, and an element of unpredictability. If musicians try to play perfectly, and with too much control, the end product risks sounding more like a recording. Due to the lack of spontaneity and interaction, recordings can defeat the bonding between artist and audience, and there is a case to be made for recordings to function mainly as encouragement for listeners to attend live concerts.

When people are listening to music, the vibrations can be felt on the body, but there is some anecdotal evidence of healing power as well. When Hoppe was a student pianist, he visited a hospital for severely mentally and physically handicapped teenagers with the aim of learning to communicate through music. While listening to one of the classical pieces, he held the hand of a Turkish girl who was unable to move or speak. She grasped his hand quite firmly and Hoppe mentioned this to the doctor, who was very surprised to hear about the girl's response, as she had not moved her hands in years.

Most musicians are aware of their responsibility to society, and how privileged they are for the good fortune of doing what they love while getting paid for it. Some people criticize professional musicians for merely developing a born talent and not doing enough to ease the numerous ills of humanity. They hold that such people could do a lot more for society if they worked as doctors and treated the sick instead of devoting themselves to music.

Although it is difficult to refute these arguments, a concert can help listeners escape from the tensions of everyday life. And music does make people happy, at least for the duration of the performance, and perhaps afterwards as well, if listeners are able to reminisce about the experience. There are times when performers also manage to give the audience a glimpse of magnificent, even ethereal, beauty, especially when the interaction between the two is powerful.

Heinemeyer and Hoppe have tried taking friends with no background in classical music to concerts. Prior to the performance, these prospective concertgoers often expressed concern about having insufficient knowledge to appreciate the classics, which were also too serious and difficult to enjoy. Invariably however, they left the concert feeling spiritually elevated.

Such a response is not always related to the excitement of virtuoso passages, although a piece that ends loud and fast usually invites more applause. A calm finale, tinged with sadness, could also leave the audience with a strong emotional reaction that listeners carry with them after they have left the concert.

Many people are unaware music arouses fantasy, creativity and imagination, qualities that are an important part of everyday life, relationships and business. No doubt, any music, whether classical, jazz, or pop can stimulate the brain in similar ways. Another important aspect of music is its intrinsic moral value, as it represents a force for good that is an integral part of composition and performance. Whatever the religion or ideological background of the composer, a great work is powerful enough to touch each person in a distinctive way. Also, music does no harm; it is free from ideology, and can only bring joy to people. Wielders of evil, like the Nazis, misused music, but such exploitation does not diminish its beauty and positive function. A bread knife can cut or kill, but that does not vilify the knife. What matters is how you use it.

As for the character of a composer or performer, it may have little influence on the quality of the music. Personal integrity seems to be irrelevant as well. Nasty people have been known to produce beautiful, sincerely felt compositions and performances. Wagner is a case in point, for in spite of his abhorrent ideology, his music is beautiful and it became influential in the development of orchestration. Irrespective of their personal views or ideologies, composers have tried to channel into music what it feels to be human, and in the process evoked powerful, fundamental emotions in masterworks full of interest and color. People are still enjoying the enormous gifts of the great composers hundreds of years after their works were written.

When it comes to twentieth-century music, many listeners complain about the dissonance. This is understandable, as our ears are conditioned by harmony and we are not used to some of the sounds in contemporary works. However, it is possible to become familiar with new tones so that they sound quite regular. It can be problematic to judge the quality of some modern works and there are good and bad pieces, the latter more associated with an emphasis on music as a fascinating intellectual idea rather than an art form.

How modern composition will evolve is difficult to predict, but it appears people are longing for more harmonious music. In the future, we might see pieces for a combination of different mediums, such as string quartet, together with radio and video installations. Appreciation of classical music is much easier for people who used to play an instrument or sang when they were young. It also requires time and effort. Sadly, many schools in Europe have been cutting down on music curricula, and it is likely that future listeners will have little knowledge about historical compositions, let alone contemporary ones.

*Stefan Heinemeyer and Thomas Hoppe were interviewed by the author in Sydney, Australia, in November 2010.*

# Dene Olding and Irina Morozova

BRIEF BIOGRAPHY: DENE OLDING

Violinist Dene Olding is an eminent soloist with a repertoire of over forty concertos and Concertmaster of the Sydney Symphony Orchestra. He has performed in the United States, UK, Europe, Australia, and New Zealand, was soloist with the Sydney Symphony and Vladimir Ashkenazy at the Edinburgh Festival in 2010, and gave the world premiere of Carl Vine's Violin Concerto with the Australian Youth Orchestra. Together with his wife, violist Irina Morozova, he premiered *The Double Concerto*, written for them by Richard Mills. He is a member of the Australia Ensemble and was leader of the Australian Chamber Orchestra.

He has recorded sonatas of Beethoven, Brahms, and Mozart with his father, pianist Max Olding, as well as the premiere recording of Ross Edwards's violin concerto, *Maninyas*, which won the 1994 ARIA award for best classical recording and the Cannes award. With pianist Vladimir Ashkenazy, he recorded Rachmaninov chamber music, and as first violinist of the Goldner String Quartet has recorded the complete Beethoven string quartets.

He trained at the Juilliard School in New York and won a Winston Churchill Memorial Trust Fellowship for higher studies.

Olding has served as a juror on international competitions and is Artistic Advisor to the Michael Hill International Violin Competition.

He plays a Joseph Guarnerius violin made in 1720.[237]

Violist Irina Morozova is a member of the Goldner String Quartet and the Australia Ensemble. She has often performed as a soloist with the major Australian and New Zealand orchestras and is a frequent Guest Principal with the Hong Kong Philharmonic Orchestra.

Morozova was Principal Viola in the Australian Chamber Orchestra, Guest Principal of the Sydney Symphony Orchestra and Principal Viola of the Elizabethan Trust Orchestra. As a member of the Australia Ensemble and Goldner String Quartet, she has performed throughout the world and made many recordings.

She studied with Richard Goldner and Robert Pikler at the NSW State Conservatorium of Music and furthered her music studies in Europe and the United States.

Morozova has served on the juries of the Shostakovich International String Quartet Competition in Russia, the Melbourne International Chamber Music Competition and the Lionel Tertis International Viola Competition, Isle of Man.[238]

She plays a 1947 viola made by A.E. Smith of Sydney, especially for Richard Goldner.

Consisting of two husband-and-wife teams (Dene Olding, violin, and Irina Morozova, viola; Julian Smiles, cello, and Dimity Hall, violin), the Goldner String Quartet was launched in 1995. The quartet is named after Richard Goldner, founder of Musica Viva Australia. It has established an international career since its debut at Wigmore Hall in London in 1997, and regularly returns to London and many major European, UK and Asian music festivals. It has performed at the 92nd St Y in New York and in Washington DC, as well as South Korea, Singapore, Brunei and New Zealand. In the

2011 City of London Festival, it attracted capacity audiences and enthusiastic acclaim by critics.

The quartet has worked with numerous international artists, including pianists Boris Berman, Philippe Cassard, Daniel Adni, Irina Schnittke, fortepianist Malcolm Bilson, violinists James Buswell and Oleh Krysa, violists Rainer Moog and Brett Dean, cellists, Alexander Ivashkin, Robert Cohen, Torleif Thedéen, Young-Chang Cho, Philippe Muller, Yehuda Hanani, and guitarist Slava Grigoryan.[239]

Since 1991, they have appeared annually at the Music in the Hunter chamber music festival and are regular guests at the Australian Festival of Chamber Music in Townsville. They performed at the inaugural season of the Melbourne Recital Centre, the Coriole Festival in South Australia, the Aurora Festival and the Huntington Estate Festival in New South Wales. In 2000 they presented a major retrospective of twentieth-century string quartets at the Adelaide Festival, and in 2004 they played the complete Beethoven string quartet cycle for Musica Viva, which was recorded live on ABC Classics and went on to win the 2009 Limelight Award for Best Classical Recording.

On Hyperion, the quartet, together with pianist Piers Lane, has recorded discs that highlight string quartets and piano quintets of Bloch, Bridge, Dvořák, Elgar, Harty, Taneyev, Arensky, Vierne, and Pierné. These recordings have received great praise, including Editor's Choice in *Gramophone* magazine and *BBC Music Magazine*, and in 2009, finalist for the *BBC Music Magazine's* Chamber Music Award. The GSQ has recorded the complete quartets of Szymanowski and Stravinsky (Naxos), String Quartets by Peter Sculthorpe (Tall Poppies) and the complete quartets of Carl Vine (ABC Classics).[240]

*"Why fund the arts?" This is a question musicians often face and should not be approached simply from a financial perspective. Our society would be much poorer without music, and future generations are more likely to judge us by our cultural legacy than a particular year's budget deficit or profit.*

—DENE OLDING AND IRINA MOROZOVA

WHEN DENE AND IRINA think of the purpose of music, particularly classical music, they reflect on the possible impact on society if music were lost. Every culture has some kind of folk tradition, so it must be fundamentally important to people. This music often evolved from certain speech patterns or rhythms. Eventually, it developed into a particular style of music that reflects a national character, yet is universally understood.

Music is intrinsic to society. It provides a sense of unity in times of war or stress. It often serves to bring people together, whether they are singing their national anthem or simply enjoying the same music. It marks significant social events like birthdays and weddings, and more than the other arts, has the capacity to change one's mood. Many people who want to feel happy turn the radio on to easy listening and sing along or dance. It is a vital part of ceremonial and religious occasions. The use of music in a religious context increases devotion during prayer and acts as a vehicle to uplift and provide comfort in difficult times.

Even if music has a disturbing message such as war or death, listening to it can help people experience some tranquility. Troubling themes are integral to the human experience and facing them through music adds meaning and helps to accept loss and handle distress. People are often looking for meaning in life, and sometimes it can be found by listening to the great works of classical music that stimulate the recognition of emotions or situations in their own lives—indeed a reflection of the human condition. Exactly how this comes about is a mystery. Why does the note G followed by C (dominant to tonic) create a sense of finality? It is simply a mixing of sounds, yet something magical emerges and tugs you emotionally. Structures such as sonata form, passacaglia, and fugue contain themes and keys, which take a musical journey and return home, generating a sense of inevitability and order. This process holds equally true for a pop song or a Mahler symphony.

Some people experience music as a form of meditation. When a friend of Dene and Irina brought a Tibetan monk to one of their concerts, he claimed the quartet was surrounded by a golden purple aura while they played and declared they had no need to meditate, as the music itself held meditative power accessible to the artists. The members of the Goldner String Quartet (GSQ) were a little skeptical about this suggestion, since it seemed a rather stressful way to meditate!

Music is like a drug that can alter the listener's state of consciousness; time can seem to stop. Some musicians have described a distorted sense of time during the performance of a great piece of music. Even if the work is very long, players may not notice the passing of time. After such an experience, it is often difficult for musicians to calm down. If a similar state could be induced in listeners, their heightened awareness might be therapeutic—all without the unwanted side effects of a drug-induced mental state!

There is also some evidence for the healing effect of music. Physical changes have been observed in listeners, and some studies show that daily sessions of music-guided slow breathing[241] or live piano music[242] can reduce blood pressure. Studies in neonatal care suggest that singing or instrumental music may assist in calming newborn babies, managing their pain during procedures, and improving weight gain. In one study, a group of healthy premature babies were exposed to a half-hour of Mozart on two consecutive days. Results showed that while the music was playing, the energy expenditure of these babies decreased compared with another group that did not hear the same music.[243]

Music can stimulate emotions, even those we have not experienced before. We are limited by language, and there are many gradations in emotions that are difficult to label. Music can help people recognize emotions that are difficult to verbalize.

Re-experiencing a broad range of emotions does seem beneficial for listeners. The process could be considered a form of therapy. In order to transmit emotions to the audience, performers need to be able to access their feelings in the same way as a great actor. As people mature, they usually develop greater breadth of feeling and a more complex personality, but these characteristics may or may not influence interpretation or performance. Music making is not necessarily driven by intellect or a general education, even though we find most great artists are highly intelligent and sophisticated people.

Whether people have come to hear a rock band, symphony, orchestra, or opera, they are attending a concert for the same reasons—they want to experience pleasure, be transported, or simply put aside everyday anxieties. The opportunity to escape briefly from the concerns of everyday life could explain why Broadway musicals and the entertainment industry generally do well during an economic downturn.

Music was not always a vehicle for the composers' personal expression. The wide spectrum of emotion observed today was more limited in the seventeenth and eighteenth centuries. When Mozart was faced with a personal tragedy, his reaction was not often reflected in his work directly. Music was more of a pure art form at the time, and while the capacity for emotional expression existed, many of the cheerful pieces of that era were divorced from personal life events.

The wide emotional spectrum conveyed in the music of Beethoven reaches deep within the listener and touches what might be called the soul. Whenever the GSQ performs his music, all members of the quartet are profoundly moved, no matter how many times they have played the same piece. He generates joy even when the music is melancholic, which is an interesting paradox.

Beethoven is undoubtedly an elemental force in Western music. He uses simple melodies and rhythms that people can identify. In his *Pastoral Symphony*,[244] thunder and lightning come alive. Professional musicians are continually amazed by his simple language, inventiveness, and surprises. It is hard to believe that today, the late string quartets still sound so modern, and that much of the music Beethoven wrote was created after his deafness became apparent. His music is particularly exciting and satisfying for the GSQ and other chamber music groups to play because of the perfect integration of all the instruments and the equal importance given to each player.

Despite explanations, many listeners are not fully attuned to the dissonance in contemporary works. Modern audiences are more accepting of dissonance, but the currently tolerated levels of dissonance would have sounded cacophonous to audiences one or two hundred years ago. It is not surprising that some of Beethoven's last works, which sound quite atonal, were so shocking to listeners at the time. In contrast to adult audiences, children and even teenagers often have no preconceived ideas about music. They seem to accept any music, including dissonant and atonal, and respond with refreshing honesty and enthusiasm.

Learning music can benefit children. Using both sides of the brain helps them organize sound and space and develop physical coordination. From the educational perspective, there is some data to show that a music-based math program may significantly assist children to master fraction concepts.[245] Playing an orchestral instrument in orchestras and chamber groups is also a good tool for socializing constructively; children learn to cooperate with others and assert themselves in discussions based on reasoned argument and knowledge of music. Even if they give up music later, they have gained from the learning process.

Professional musicians play for love of the music, and while the applause is gratifying, the main aim is communication. When the audience takes the musical journey together with the performers, the mutual involvement is palpable. It is especially gratifying for musicians to play for people who are deeply moved and open to the possibility of being transformed by the experience. But there is even more for performers in this interaction because they feed from their listeners' attentiveness and are able to experiment and improve in the future. In this never-ending process of experimentation, there is always something for performers to learn and try out. It is part of the reinterpretation of music and makes it possible to hear the same piece without feeling bored. Every interpretation by diverse performers, or even the same artist, is different. In this way music is unlike art or literature, although it is, of course, possible to have different impressions of the same literary work or painting on subsequent contact.

Do life events affect performance? The GSQ members have experienced much drama and tragedy in their lives and sometimes they are asked if these harrowing life events have affected their playing. Perhaps their sound and interpretation have altered slightly, though it is difficult to be specific. However, they feel certain that the process of facing and overcoming hardships has made them a lot more resilient.

Strength of character and hard musical training doesn't prepare artists for sorting out the ills of the world. However, many musicians would like to believe they could make a difference, at least for some people, even if they can't change the world. A first-time listener might be overwhelmed by the beauty of a piece of music and will be persuaded to start attending concerts. No one can predict when the interest and enthusiasm of a member of the audience might be sparked. On many occasions, the GSQ has learned (often years later) how a particular performance of the quartet had affected listeners, and even motivated some of them to become professional musicians.

One of the current problems in classical music is terminology. The word *classical* itself suggests an elite or esoteric branch of the art, but it is worth remembering that some of the compositions played today might have been top of the pops back in the nineteenth century. In the twentieth century, a disjunction developed between audience, performers, and composers. It has taken a long time to get back on track and now there is a real desire by composers to reconnect with their audience, rather than impress their colleagues.

Writers of film music have continued to relate to listeners in the vast quantity of classical music composed for movies, but many are not aware of the legacy of classical music traditions in film scores and also pop music, and how these genres follow musical rules and patterns that were established centuries ago. Often a full orchestra had been used to play the music of a film score. This became fashionable again after the success of *Star Wars*, which probably made the sound of an orchestra more accessible for the many people who saw the film.

Great composers are still relevant many centuries after their death. It makes one wonder why some music is more enduring. Most probably, this music survives because it is unique. The Beatles are an interesting example of an inimitable group, whose sound is instantly recognizable. They could be compared with Schubert, as they wrote over 270 songs with beautiful lyrics and tunes.

One of the features of good music is an instantly distinctive quality. This may take the form of a rhythmic pattern, harmonic language, melodies of great power or beauty, and many other factors which combine for a satisfying whole. However, a great piece of music is not easily categorized and contains secrets that are only divulged to those who are sufficiently patient to delve into the score and mind of the composer over many years. The GSQ might play a piece of music many times, but on repeated examination they notice new, unexpected details and insights, such as a previously overlooked secondary melodic line in one of the instruments.

The fine qualities of Western music are increasingly recognized in the East. The GSQ has often toured China, Korea, and Japan, where they are always very impressed by the number of youngsters and parents in the audience. Many parents expect their child to learn to play an instrument. Today, the fashionable instruments are piano and strings, although wind, brass, and others will probably follow quite soon. There is a huge market for music in the East; audiences are becoming much more sophisticated not only in the large cities, but in the provinces as well. For many listeners in the East, Western music is exotic and adds value to society. It uses harmonic development, sophisticated rhythm, melodic invention, and counterpoint differently than Eastern music. Musicians trained in Western music should be proud of their tradition; classical music is one of the greatest artistic creations of Western culture.

A major argument in favor of fine music is its great beauty in the face of much ugliness in the world. It can also serve an important social function by inducing people to come together as a group for a few hours.

Some regular classical music radio broadcasters have chosen to play only sections of more popular pieces. In this type of programming, they are following the style of popular radio channels such as Classic FM (UK). Although people may label such simplification as a "dumbing down" of music, it serves as a means of exposing this superb art form to greater numbers of people. Is it not better for people to hear one movement of a Bach, Mozart, or Beethoven work than none at all?

*Dene Olding and Irina Morozova were interviewed by the author in Sydney, Australia, in May 2012.*

# Michael Powell and Kevin Cobb

*BRIEF BIOGRAPHY: MICHAEL POWELL*

Trombonist Michael Powell joined the American Brass Quintet in 1983 after four years with the Kansas City Philharmonic as Principal Trombone. He has performed solo with the Orchestra of St. Luke's, Kansas City Philharmonic, the Aspen Music Festival, the New Hampshire Music Festival, and appeared on Broadway. He frequently performs and records with the Orpheus Chamber Orchestra, Little Orchestra Society, and Orchestra of St. Luke's. He has also worked with a variety of groups, such as the Chamber Music Society of Lincoln Center, New York Chamber Symphony, Zankel Band of Carnegie Hall, Speculum Musicae, Musical Elements, Classical Band, Tidewater Quintet, and Professor Peter Schickele's New York Pick-Up Ensemble.

Powell is a member of faculty at the Juilliard School, SUNY at Stony Brook, Mason Gross School of the Arts at Rutgers University, and the Aspen Music Festival School, and has taught classes in trombone and chamber music throughout the world.

He records for radio, television, and cinema, and has promoted new works through his commissions, first performances, and recordings of solo works by Eric Ewazen, Robert Martin, Steven Sacco, and David Sampson. [246]

*The American Brass Quintet* (ABQ) regularly tours all over world. They have released almost sixty recordings and premiered more than one hundred-fifty contemporary brass works, including ABQ commissions for composers such as Elliott Carter, Gunther Schuller, and Joan Tower. The ABQ is also committed to expanding education in brass chamber music, offering mini-residencies in chamber music to young musicians from the United States and abroad. In 2013 the ABQ was the recipient of Chamber Music America's highest honor, the Richard J. Bogomolny National Service Award.[247]

*BRIEF BIOGRAPHY: KEVIN COBB*

Trumpet player Kevin Cobb joined the ABQ in 1998. He performs regularly with the Metropolitan Opera, New York Philharmonic, and New York City Ballet; he is Co-Principal Trumpet of the Aspen Festival Orchestra and has played with Metallica, Peter Gabriel, and James Taylor.

He has recorded many television commercials, and a collection of all-American unaccompanied trumpet solos on *One*, a CD for Summit Records.

Cobb teaches at the Juilliard School, Aspen Music School, The Hartt School, SUNY Stony Brook, and the Colorado College Summer Music Festival.

At age fifteen, Cobb performed solo with the Toledo Symphony. He is a graduate of the Curtis Institute of Music and The Juilliard School, and was a member of the Manhattan Brass Quintet and Meridian Arts Ensemble.[248]

*Pieces that contain anger and hatred might provoke those emotions in a listener, but there is an overwhelming redemptive quality to much of the great Western art music tradition. A good example can be found in Beethoven's Ninth Symphony, a piece that speaks with universal appeal about love and humanity.*

—MICHAEL POWELL AND KEVIN COBB

MUSIC IS REALLY an extension of speech, taken to the level of great poetry or the grand epics of literature. When children start speaking, their singsong "Mom-my" or "Dad-dy" is usually identifiable as a minor third interval, and their parents' responses are often musical as well.

In any art form, the highest order illustrates the human condition, and most songs, especially love songs, bear this out. Many people credit the Western tradition with the highest form of artistic expression. The demands on musicians are also boundless. As Russian pianist and composer Sergei Rachmaninov mused: "Music is enough for a lifetime, but a lifetime is not enough for music."[249] The returns for performers and listeners are immense and commensurate with the level of commitment and depth of study. Many people who take an interest in classical music are eager to intensify their exploration, which exemplifies one of the attributes of great art.

In the modern world, the classical music audience suffers from a lack of knowledge about the art, and how much is involved in its re-creation. In contrast, those who have devoted many years to music, or studied an instrument, can appreciate its subtleties and the infinite involvement of musicians with the art.

241

The delicacy of a phrase is such that musicians may continue to fine-tune it innumerable times until they are satisfied with the result. When successful, such concentrated practice is very fulfilling for the performers, who hope listeners will be gratified as well. However, music is much more than technique and execution of phrases, as the masterful composers can take us on a new journey every time we listen to an old favorite or a new work. No matter how many times one returns to the same piece, one will find new ideas. For musicians, too, there might be a particular phrase, passage, or counterpoint they have played many times, yet on every hearing, they are captivated and their body responds with goose bumps.

On the other hand, people are quick to notice repetition and are easily bored. Milliseconds before a phrase is actually heard, we can register what is about to come, and if some detail in a piece of music is very predictable—and we like predictability at times—there might be a certain point at which we start to lose interest. If such a detail or section is repeated with a difference, even one that is very slight, our interest peaks again.

The variables of change are legion, and could involve chords, rhythm, timing or words within a song. Sometimes, a composer introduces a strange modulation that takes the piece to an unexpected place. Most people have a basic sense of chord progression and where they would like chords to go, but the way a composer like Mozart is able to use chords for emotional impact is truly astonishing, and even somewhat addictive for the listener who returns time and again to the same modulation and source of pleasure.

Live performance is characterized by marked or marginal differences in interpretation of pieces we have heard repeatedly, and these deliberate or spontaneous modifications make concerts more interesting and exciting than recordings.

For the audience, music works simultaneously on the intellectual and the visceral level. Intellectually, listeners might be intrigued by the interaction between the players on the stage, the instruments and how they are being played, or they may take an interest in the ensemble itself. On the emotional level, people could be uplifted for a short period and be transported to a meditative state, although such an experience requires active surrender to the musical journey.

Simple enjoyment of the music is passive, but some people who are not regular concertgoers, or have never been to a classical music concert, feel they should come armed with more knowledge. This is unnecessary. The most important aspect of listening should be pleasure, and any soporific effect of music during a concert is acceptable.

Like food, literature, or other interests, there is a baseline for those who want more information. Perhaps some aspects of the music will motivate a new listener to buy a recording or read about the history of a piece. As the repertoire is so large, there is an area of interest for most people. Compared with chamber music, opera has a greater following because it is three-dimensional, the storylines are fanciful, the costumes fantastic, and the experience is immediately arresting.

Such props are not part of a brass quintet or symphony orchestra concert, but there are other advantages for the audience. Concerts of abstract music without outside supports leave the imagination time to construct an individual response based on one's own mental associations in the form of storylines, pictures, or movies. Everyone is capable of this feat of imagination, which is facilitated by frequent listening. Even those who shun contemporary music for years may embrace it ultimately, as they develop an aural palate.

People might be uncomfortable with unfamiliar contemporary music in the same way they could be apprehensive about approaching a new or difficult subject, or attending a play by Shakespeare, because they are unaccustomed to the language. Whenever we don't understand something, our natural reaction is to withdraw rather than engage. This applies to new pieces of music, too, but it is worth making the effort to invest some time and attention to a new work, not only by reading about it, but also by listening in an active way. This process could involve being open to the surprising and humorous parts of a work and asking oneself questions such as, "What might come next?" or "What would I do next if I were the composer?"

Sometimes, composers like Dmitri Shostakovich and Alban Berg aim to disturb the listener. Berg's opera *Wozzeck*[250] is a masterpiece that tugs at the heart and perturbs us with its treatment of mental instability and oppression of the weak and poor. When people see this opera they may feel very uncomfortable, but the work is a genuine expression of the human condition with a strong story line and emotions all of us can recognize. Such a work helps people gain perspective on life, gives them more insights, and promotes contemplation.

Apart from the narrative, there is magic in the music itself. Some of the most beautiful melodies are tiny snippets that are fleeting. At the very end of the opera, in a heartbreaking scene, the little boy on a pogo stick sings a simple song while he jumps about without his mother. It is extraordinary that Berg manages to illustrate this scene and the accompanying emotion so vividly in music, not unlike a painting that captures one's attention simply because it is magnificent.

The composer wrote deep feelings into this last scene of *Wozzeck*, but listeners can implant their own emotional experiences. Those feelings may shift throughout life, so that a marriage, which began as puppy love, is a very different entity after forty years. Because of changes in feelings, performers may also alter their approach as they age. When Leonard Bernstein was a young conductor, he was well known for taking fast tempi, but when he was much older, his tempo in the same piece was often very slow.

Interpretations of pieces by the American Brass Quintet have also altered over the years. Members of the group have noticed these changes, especially in some of the works they played for several seasons or maintained as staple repertoire. The *Monteverdi Madrigals*[251] are a good example. When they first started performing these pieces, their tempo was much faster than the one they settled on much later. The reasons for this change could be attributed to improved knowledge of the madrigal texts and more familiarity with accepted performance practice by erudite players.

Listeners are not only stimulated to respond emotionally; they could be transformed by the music as well. The Verdi *Requiem*[252] is a potentially transformative piece for the audience and all the more so for performers. The techniques used by Verdi in the *Requiem* are operatic, and on a textual level are an expression of great religious devotion. But there is much more. The power of Verdi's dedication and respect for the novelist Alessandro Manzoni, in whose memory it was written, appeals to something very deep within us, something spiritual, such as Michelangelo's fresco of *The Last Judgment* on the ceiling of the Sistine Chapel in Vatican City. The final movement, "Libera me," is ardent, and almost frantic. This is only one example of the many powerful works by composers such as Aaron Copland, Frank Martin, Tchaikovsky, Beethoven, and Monteverdi.

Like many other brass players, Michael Powell started playing the trombone when he was in school. He chose the instrument, or perhaps it chose him. Much later, he came to the realization that the trombone could sing as beautifully as a cello, violin, or the human voice, and was simply trying to imitate this voice through the extension of song and language.

Kevin Cobb started playing guitar when he was seven. He wanted to join the school band and ended up with the trumpet. To some extent it was a love affair, because he was hugely attracted to the sound his teacher made on the instrument and the sounds of trumpet virtuosi in recordings. He also loved the brass parts in orchestral works.

For brass players, the instruments are virtually an extension of themselves. The hall is an extension of the instruments, so the acoustic is vitally important. Prior to a concert, American Brass Quintet players test the acoustic to discover the best place to sit and direct the sound. They also need to adjust relative volume so that one instrument is not favored over another.

Clearly, good sound is dependent on teamwork, and in their group, all the players get on well. They are allies on the stage, there to support and assist each other. In bringing the score of a composer to life, they also resemble actors in the theater who read their lines from the same work and take instructions from the playwright.

There is enormous subtlety in the colors of the sounds produced by brass instruments, so they spend time listening carefully to their own sounds and those of their colleagues. Some musicians like Alexander Scriabin advocated the association of pitch with color.[253] In brass instruments, the "color" of the sound might be heard as fine gradations between bright or dark, lugubrious or crystal clear, soft or loud, legato or detached. Pitch can also render color for brass.

Like all musicians, brass players are craftspeople and the objective of their study is performance. Their first task is to energize and support their colleagues in the group through good playing and teamwork. At the same time, they perform their magic on the audience.

*Michael Powell and Kevin Cobb were interviewed by the author in Sydney, Australia, in May 2014.*

# Alina Ibragimova
# and Cédric Tiberghien

Violinist Alina Ibragimova has appeared as soloist with many orchestras, including the London Symphony Orchestra, Deutsche Kammerphilharmonie Bremen, Konzerthausorchester Berlin, Stuttgart Radio Symphony, Orchestre Philharmonique de Radio France, The Hallé, Philharmonia, Orchestra of the Age of Enlightenment, all the BBC orchestras, Seattle Symphony, Mariinsky Theatre Orchestra, and the Australian Chamber Orchestra. She has worked with many conductors, including Sir Charles Mackerras, Valery Gergiev, Sir John Eliot Gardiner, Sir Mark Elder, Paavo Järvi, Vladimir Jurowski, Rafael Frühbeck de Burgos, Philippe Herreweghe, Richard Hickox, Yannick Nézet-Séguin, Tugan Sokhiev, Edward Gardner, Gianandrea Noseda, and Osmo Vänskä.

Ibragimova has also toured with the Academy of Ancient Music, the Australian Chamber Orchestra, Kremerata Baltica, and the Britten Sinfonia as soloist and director.

With Cédric Tiberghien, Ibragimova has performed at international venues such as Carnegie Hall, Wigmore Hall, Concertgebouw, Mozarteum, Musikverein, Theatre des Champs-Élysées, and at various festivals including Salzburg, Verbier, Lockenhaus, MDR Musiksommer, Manchester International, and Aldeburgh. Her discography includes many chamber works and concertos.

Ibragimova studied at the Gnessin State Musical College in Moscow and at the Yehudi Menuhin School and Royal College of Music in the UK.

Her list of awards includes the Royal Philharmonic Society Young Artist Award 2010, the Borletti-Buitoni Trust Award 2008, and the Classical BRIT Young Performer of the Year Award 2009. She was a member of the BBC New Generation Artists Scheme from 2005 to 2007.

She plays a circa-1775 Anselmo Bellosio violin kindly provided by Georg von Opel.[254]

## BRIEF BIOGRAPHY: CÉDRIC TIBERGHIEN

Pianist Cédric Tiberghien has performed concertos with many of the major orchestras of the world, including the Boston Symphony, Washington National Symphony, Orchestre de la Suisse Romande, Tonhalle Orchestra Zurich, BBC Symphony, The Hallé, Stuttgart Staatsorchester, Hamburg, Dresden, Czech, Arnhem, Tokyo and New Japan Philharmonic, Budapest Festival Orchestra, Orchestre Philharmonique de Radio-France, Orchestre de Paris, Orchestre National de France, and the Sydney Symphony.

Conductors Tiberghien has worked with include Kurt Masur, Christoph Eschenbach, Myung-Whun Chung, Simone Young, Iván Fischer, Yannick Nézet-Séguin, Robin Ticciati, Jiří Bělohlávek, Lionel Bringuier, Leif Segerstam, and Louis Langrée.

In chamber music, he often collaborates with violinist Alina Ibragimova, as well as cellist Pieter Wispelwey and soprano Sophie Karthäuser. His discography together with Ibragimova includes *Beethoven: Violin Sonatas* on Wigmore Hall Live, and the music of Schubert, Ravel, Lekeu, and Szymanowski on Hyperion.

He has recorded César Franck's *Symphonic Variations* and *Les Djinns* with the Liège Philharmonic under François-Xavier Roth, Brahms's Concerto No.1 with the BBC Symphony and Jiří Bělohlávek, and six recital discs of Debussy, Beethoven, Bach, Chopin, and Brahms for Harmonia Mundi; and he recorded *Karol Szymanowski: Masques, Métopes & Études* for Hyperion.

Tiberghien studied at the Paris Conservatoire. He has won prizes at major piano competitions, including the Paris Conservatoire Premier Prix at the age of seventeen, and first prize and other awards at the Long-Thibaud Competition in Paris.[255]

*When you listen to music, you receive the meaning communicated by the composer and interpreted intellectually by the brain. The process can induce a spectrum of emotions including raw, negative feelings like aggression and anger, which should not be seen as a drawback; it is important to be in touch with the whole range of human emotions, not only peace and tranquility.*

—ALINA IBRAGIMOVA AND CÉDRIC TIBERGHIEN

ALINA IBRAGIMOVA AND Cédric Tiberghien, who perform as a violin and piano duo, believe music is an art that is vital for everyone. It seems there is an innate human trait to use music to express feelings and ideas. The music[256] they play together is beautiful and powerful, and listeners have told them how it seems to connect with very early memories and also the rhythm of the heartbeat. In some ways music can be healing; people turn to it when they are upset, and even if it is melancholy, it helps them release tension.

Music such as heavy metal has been criticized for promoting violence, and indeed studies have shown some evidence for a correlation between antisocial behavior and a preference for rock music with destructive themes.[257] However, life is not beautiful all the time, and art explores life, so it would not be logical to focus solely on pleasant or appealing music.

People are able to connect with the emotions in a piece of music, even though the composer's intentions are generally unknown. Listening to great music, like that of Beethoven, helps people experience more about living and for want of a better expression, it feeds the soul. A similar experience might come about through literature, philosophy, observing a beautiful, memorable landscape, or meeting an outstanding person.

Although musicians have a deep respect for the composer, their role is not simply that of a messenger. They express themselves too, and as they mature, a multitude of new and diverse feelings mold their characters with the potential to enlighten their interpretations. Musicians need to experience a wide spectrum of emotions in order to enrich their art. Going to the ballet or seeing pictures in a gallery can stimulate new thoughts about beauty and feelings. Like writers who need to meet many people in their search for fascinating stories and individuals, musicians can benefit from a multitude of experiences in their quest for genuine self-expression.

Everyday life also affects the way people play. There are times when musicians have to perform a happy program full of lightness and major keys, despite feeling miserable. Such conflict could present difficulties in accessing the right emotion to match the piece they are about to play.

Apart from the stress associated with traveling, musicians are saved from the humdrum existence associated with many everyday occupations. In contrast, they deal with the intense emotions they wish to express and share through their music. The love they feel for their art is profound, and they often regret that vast numbers of people have never been adequately exposed to its emotional and intellectual pleasures.

Classical music belongs to everybody. It is a great social leveler and also very personal. The whole spectrum of emotions can be found in the great compositions. Schubert's music is enchanting, but it also contains pain, anger and hatred. Many people falsely idealize composers such as Mozart and Schubert with their fanciful notions about the fragility and sweetness of their music and personalities. In this respect, the play and film *Amadeus*[258] shattered many romantic, commonly held views of Mozart as a paragon or divine being.

Similarly, a performer might not be a person of integrity but can play brilliantly. In chamber music, however, a fellow member of the group can affect a musician's mood and musical relationship, so it is often difficult to perform with those who don't appear to share the same values.

Music conveys emotion when a player's feelings are stimulated, but quite often the emotional impact is not planned. If they don't have feelings for the piece or connect with it, a performer might devise a way of playing with feeling, but feigned emotion is undesirable and stressful. Fortunately, Ibragimova, and Tiberghien are able to choose and perform the music they love.

Musicians who play chamber music must find ways to express feelings through the music. On the stage, other members of the group and any sounds coming from the audience can influence a performance. Such stimuli can affect the way the next note is played, and therefore chamber music is not simply conversation between instruments, but also an interactive relationship with other musicians and the audience. Even when all the performers in a group are in agreement about a piece, these stimuli and responses produce surprises that may enhance a performance. A definite energy is produced when hundreds of people are focused without distraction on the music and players. These conditions also create a dynamic that allows for unscripted variations in performance. Mistakes occur too, and they add a human element.

This spontaneity is absent from a recording, in which the goals include capturing fine points often missed in a live performance. While making a recording, artists are aware that some people will listen very carefully to the details in the final product. The slow process of recording affords much time for experimentation and preoccupation with minutiae, and it is possible to try out various ideas and decide when the performance is sufficiently polished. In contrast, whatever happens in a concert is instantaneous. It has a finite life and then it is over. After a concert, there is also a social dimension, as relationships among members of the audience can alter and deepen.

Sometimes particular works speak to the listener in a personal way and seem to provide a mirror. At those times, the emotional experience moves up to another level. The reaction is also physical as the heart speeds up and people hold their breath. It varies between people and also depends on mood, thoughts, and occasion, but when it happens it can seem miraculous.

Contemporary art music is not really very different from the music of the past. Young people often prefer it to the classical symphony, possibly because it relates more closely to the modern world. Many listeners are apprehensive about new music, but it is worth remembering that some of Beethoven's quartets and symphonies were difficult for his audiences to comprehend, and some people thought he was crazy, rather than thinking he was ahead of his time.

Classical or serious music is not the only high-quality genre, but one among many, including musicals, pop, tango, and jazz. Some of this music, particularly jazz, also offers great freedom of expression.

Composers and performers are mutually interdependent, and meeting the composer of a work can enlighten musicians. Sometimes it is simply the personality, energy, and strong presence of a composer that leaves an impression capable of changing the way a performer will play the music. Usually composers talk about the ideas behind a certain work, which encourages new ways of reading the music.

Much of the re-creative musician's work involves searching and finding, followed by more searching. This evolution is an integral, exciting part of the duo's work. They are always probing the music for new emotions, colors, and avenues for expression in a journey that can take them far into the unknown. This process can improve self-knowledge, expand the freedom to explore new ideas, and even generalize into other aspects of life, increasing sensitivity to emotions, mental, and physical states.

People don't usually delve into music for philosophical answers, nor do they require extensive knowledge to derive enjoyment. Occasionally they love something they heard as a background to a movie and then feel motivated to listen and learn more about that particular piece. Even the seasoned concert-going audience doesn't intellectualize a great deal and simply receives pleasure from the music.

The duo's collaboration is happy and creative. They understand each other musically and work together constructively, trying to take the pieces to a new level with each performance.

*Alina Ibragimova and Cédric Tiberghien were interviewed by the author in Sydney, Australia, in October 2010.*

# MORE ON BACH AND BEETHOVEN

# Andreas Loewe
# and Katherine Firth on Bach

BRIEF BIOGRAPHIES

Dr. Andreas Loewe and Dr. Katherine Firth have collaborated on musical projects for over a decade, most recently, in Loewe's *Johann Sebastian Bach's St. John Passion (BWV 245): A Theological Commentary: With a new Study Translation by Katherine Firth and a Preface by N. T. Wright* (Brill, 2014). The translation and commentary have informed performances of Bach's *St. John Passion*. Previous collaborations between Loewe and Firth include projects such as a children's opera, and sacred music performed in the UK and Australia.

Loewe is Dean of Melbourne, leading St. Paul's Cathedral in the Anglican Diocese of Melbourne, Australia. His academic research centers on theology, as well as ecclesiastical and music history, in particular the way in which Scripture can be communicated through music. He has published widely in the fields of ecclesiastical history and music, including recent research on Martin Luther's philosophical theory of music in *Music and Letters*. He is a Fellow and Lecturer at the Melbourne Conservatorium of Music and a Fellow of the Royal Historical Society (UK).

Firth is Head of Academic Programs at Trinity College, University of Melbourne, and Adjunct Faculty at Trinity College Theological School, Australia. She is an award-winning educator who lectures at the University of Melbourne on graduate research and communication skills. Her research focuses on the relationships between music and poetry, including the collaboration in composition and performance for art song in the twentieth century and the influence of music on the poetic avant-garde in English. Firth is a lyricist, and the Choir of Trinity College Cambridge (UK), the Choir of Trinity College Melbourne, and the Oriana Chorale in Canberra (Australia) have performed works containing her lyrics.[259]

*Like Bach, many performing musicians are attuned to the tran-*
*scendent, and mindful of the possibilities of existence beyond*
*the range of ordinary human experience. Painters and sculptors*
*are also aware of a creativity that is not generated entirely from*
*within. Some describe it as a muse or a spirit, and most have an*
*awareness of a source of inspiration beyond their rational control.*

—ANDREAS LOEWE AND KATHERINE FIRTH

BACH IS PIVOTAL in the development of religious and secular classical music. He showed how freedom could be obtained through experimentation, and also demonstrated that a piece of music, like the *Art of Fugue* (BWV 1080), could be imagined as a mathematical and musical exercise, rather than performed. This concept helps us understand how Beethoven was able to compose in spite of his deafness. Bach would have composed most of his work in his head before he wrote the music, delegating the copying to members of his own family. When he lost his sight at the end of his life, he was still able to compose by dictating his music. Unlike the conventional style of composing from a melodic line with the harmony below, Bach began with the *basso continuo* line to build up his composition.

Bach's position as a composer has occupied a central role in new trends and developments in modern music. The early music revivals and forward leaps in avant-garde music (from the late nineteenth century to the present day) have often featured Bach in the forefront, his presence conferring legitimacy to the movement. This was evident when Mendelssohn popularized Bach alongside new mid- to late-romantic music, and during the first English early music revival from around 1900 to the 1940s. Bach's role was influential in the incorporation of jazz and the early music revival of the 1970s. He very likely stimulated the mathematical thinking that influenced Schoenberg, in the 1920s, to develop the atonal twelve-note scale from the eight-note, enabling the advance of modern music.

Bach left a huge musical legacy, of which many works were written specifically for performance in the Lutheran church. We cannot always be fully certain about his sources for his libretto texts beyond the obvious Biblical texts and chorales, but it is clear that he was an avid collector of books and attended book auctions. Before buying a book, he may well have used a lending library or the library at St. Thomas School to further his reading. Over the years he acquired multiple copies of books and hymnals, including many of Luther's works in several different editions. Bach's large library contained the Calov Bible, a three-volume Old and New Testament with commentary by Martin Luther and the great Lutheran theologian, Abraham Calov.[260]

From 1717 to 1723, Bach was Capellmeister to Leopold, Prince of Anhalt-Köthen, a Calvinist prince. When he became Cantor of the Lutheran St. Thomas Church in Leipzig his knowledge of Lutheran theology was formally tested before his appointment was finalized. Bach would have been aware of Luther's vision of music as the perfect vehicle for understanding and communicating scripture through psalms and hymns, with the ultimate purpose of illuminating God's wisdom and well-ordered kingdom.

In his work as a church cantor, Bach looked to role models from Scripture to explain his craft and calling. He found his role models in the Temple musicians described in the Chronicles of the Old Testament. He felt that church musicians should emulate their example by expressing the worship of Christ in music and singing. Furthermore, Bach believed the service should be a reflection of the divine order, and therefore well organized.

During his mature years, Bach annotated his *Calov Bible*, under-lining key Lutheran concepts and ideas about music in the text. These included references to the doctrines of salvation and justification, and to the role and function of music and song. Compared with the many entries alongside descriptions of the dedication of the temple in Jeru-salem described in the books of the Chronicles, he made relatively few annotations in the margins of the Psalms. His annotations show he was interested in the Biblical text as a guide for church musicians. His markings focused on the "appointment, training, and setting apart of Temple musicians in 1 Chr 25:6-end; the ordering of their divisions and specification of service in 1 Chr 28:21; and the musical spectacle of the dedication of the Temple in 2 Chr 5:11-14."

In Bach's *Calov Bible*, the psalmist Asaph is described as King David's *Capellmeister*, and the annotations in the margins of Bach's Bible indicate Bach's identification with Asaph in this Jewish narra-tive. Whenever the Levite musicians Asaph, Heman and their sons were given the title "Capellmeister," Bach underlined the term.

The story of the dedication of the Temple from Chronicles attests to the care that was taken in the preparation of the music for the dedication ceremony. This process involved training musicians in cohorts, with the aim of making beautiful music in honor of God, and singing from the Hallel, the great Psalms of praise. The music had to be properly organized and directed, in order to serve, praise, and glorify God. In Chronicles it was stated that such music, when offered in praise, brought forth God's resplendence in the form of a cloud that filled the Temple.

In Bach's view, the offerings of Temple musicians had glorified God, who then favored them with His presence during their perfor-mance. Indeed, in the margin next to the account of the dedication of the Temple in 2 Chronicles 5:13, he affirmed one of his funda-mental beliefs when he wrote: "in sacred music, God is always pres-ent in his grace—*Bey einer andächtigen Musique ist allezeit Gott mit seiner Gnaden-Gegenwart.*" Bach was not claiming that God was actually present in some physical form of the divine, but suggesting that music provided listeners with a means of accessing God's glory and experiencing grace.

Bach was probably attracted to several aspects of the descriptions in the biblical story from Chronicles. Like the Levites' music, his own church music was carefully planned. Where in Chronicles, God's presence was experienced in the form of the descending cloud, Bach believed that in his music God could be experienced through grace. Like his own family, the musicians who served in the Temple were also members of a large family: Levite instrumentalists, who had been selected to train, prepare and perform sacred music that was pleasing to the Almighty. Like the Levites, the large Bach family was a clan of musicians. They included generations of prominent composers, organists, town pipers, and directors of town orchestras. Some were cantors in Lutheran churches: Bach's father, Johann Ambrosius Bach, had been the town piper of Eisenach and had organized music for the parish church as well as formal council occasions. Bach would have been excited by the idea that a single family of musicians like his own had been elevated to serve in the Israelite Temple and commissioned to produce music that had the capacity to convey the divine presence.

Apart from liturgical work, Bach wrote dance music for general enjoyment and entertainment. His secular music, written for his student orchestra, the *Collegium Musicum*, would have been performed at a local coffee house, Zimmermann's: it was often centered on dance rhythms, and therefore has quite a different feel from the compositions written for St. Thomas Church Leipzig.

Bach's music is also operatic, a quality occasionally used with dramatic effect in staged versions of *St. Matthew Passion*. When deconstructed, his music contains much disharmony, and if you stopped on a certain chord, it could sound dissonant. At the same time, the disharmony lends great character and richness—it is there to be resolved. This method was part of the baroque aesthetic, or affect: through the brokenness in his music, Bach reflected on the story of the death of Jesus, who was broken on a cross and who thus symbolized the brokenness of the world.

In conveying such messages through music, Bach followed the baroque theories on affects (*Affekte*)—affections such as admiration, love, hatred, desire, joy, and sadness. Much of his music theory followed the concepts outlined in *Der vollkommene Capellmeister*, 1739,[261] a book on musicology that associated intervals, keys and pitch with specific emotions. The author, Johann Mattheson, was one of the great writers on baroque aesthetics. His book, which was commonplace at the time, was accepted as a standard authority.

Particularly in his choral music, Bach makes good use of affects to express a certain message through word and music. His sacred works are often based on a Biblical text—the recitatives—as well as reflections on that text through poetry: the arias, verses, and chorales. Whether Bach here intentionally follows the well-known rabbinic tradition of Midrash is unknown. Although other composers, such as Telemann and Buxtehude use the same method of elucidating text, Bach perfected the technique. Unlike Bach, Handel tended to follow the biblical text in a more straightforward way, without such Midrashic commentary.

Contemporary performances of operas and concerts are far removed from the experience of an audience in baroque times. In the concert hall, convention dictates that members of the audience refrain from talking, yet in the baroque era, people chatted and enjoyed a meal during an opera. Today, there are many excellent chamber music groups that play baroque music in concerts that anybody can attend. Regardless of whether the music is played in a grand house, a concert hall, or church, audiences will sit quietly and not applaud between movements. We have Mendelssohn to thank for the metamorphosis of the concert into a sort of church service, where people sit still, silent and reverential, storing up any excitement until the very end of the performance. Mendelssohn introduced these changes in Germany, and as Queen Victoria was one of his great admirers, the innovation became part of English custom.

In Bach's time, however, the music played would be specific to the venue. The religious music would be listened to in church, where the congregation would join in the chorales and the music would sit between prayers and sermons. The secular music might be played at court for an aristocratic audience. Alternatively, it might be played in a concert hall or coffee house, where the emerging middle classes and townsfolk would be in the audience.

Often twenty-first century music lovers experience concerts through recordings, film versions, or via livestream. This means they miss the experience of sitting in an audience and responding to a piece of music as a group. What's more, few home speakers are able to produce the same range of tones and sound vibrations experienced in a live concert. In Richard Strauss's famous *Also Sprach Zarathustra,* listeners in a concert hall begin to feel the vibrations, before the music is audible. These vibrations build up, so that the listener is already at a high pitch of excitement by the time the timpani and trumpets sound out in that famous opening. Bach's listeners would have experienced such vibrations through the deep bass pipes of the organ in St. Thomas Church, contrasted with the higher notes of other instruments and human voices.

Although composers can learn the craft of choosing the correct tone, tempo, and so on, the art of music demands internalizing this skill before connecting it with any transcendent quality. After much study and practice, musicians may then find their own voice coming through in a rather mysterious way. This process was probably very familiar to Bach, whose music has a distinctive sound that can be immediately differentiated from his close contemporaries and his sons (two of whom became composers in their own right). Bach marked all of his music *Soli Deo gloria* ('To God alone be the glory'), perhaps suggesting he believed his music was inspired by God, and the purpose of his craft, skill, and inspiration was to direct people's minds to the divine.

*Source for all references to Bach's Calov Bible marginalia and Bach's religious beliefs: Andreas Loewe, Johann Sebastian Bach's St John Passion (BWV 245): A Theological Commentary (Leiden: Brill 2014).*

*Dr. Andreas Loewe and Dr. Katherine Firth were interviewed by the author in Sydney, Australia, in April 2012.*

# Gerard Willems on Beethoven

*BRIEF BIOGRAPHY*

Gerard Willems is Associate Professor in Piano at the Sydney Conservatorium of Music and has performed in the United States, United Kingdom, Europe, Asia, Australia, New Zealand, and Israel, including live broadcasts for Dutch, French, Austrian, Australian, and Israeli radio stations. During a tour of Norway in 2010, he gave a concert in the Grieg Museum in Bergen.

Willems teaches and lectures worldwide, and is regarded as a specialist in the first Viennese School. He gives master classes and is invited on juries of national and international competitions.

His recordings include *Mozart: Complete Piano Trios*, *Reflections on Mozart*, *Beethoven: Complete Piano Sonatas Vols. 1–3*, and *Beethoven: Complete Piano Concertos* and *Diabelli Variations*. They have received worldwide tributes, with two ARIA awards for his Beethoven Sonatas and the World Music DVD prize in New York for his 2005 recording of Beethoven's *Emperor Concerto*. The Australian Elizabethan Theatre Trust awarded him the inaugural Queen Elizabeth II prize in 2001 for research into Early Music Performance Practice in Europe and the United States.

Willems is an insightful communicator on music who broadcasts frequently on ABC FM. He covered the Sydney International Piano Competition in 2004 and 2008 as the ABCs special critic and as a contributor to *The Australian* newspaper. He was Artistic Director of the Southern Highlands International Piano Competition in 2013.

Born in Holland, Willems graduated from the Sydney Conservatorium of Music and continued piano and conducting studies in

Amsterdam and Munich. In 2008 he held a position for six months as Guest Professor at the Hochschule für Musik Freiburg, Germany, and in 2000 held the Hephzibah Menuhin Piano Chair at the Rubin Academy in Jerusalem. He was appointed artist in residence at the Yong Siew Toh Conservatory of Music in Singapore in 2012.

In 2012 Willems was awarded an Order of Australia (AM) for his services to the arts.[262]

*Ludwig van Beethoven's music approaches our purpose on earth through its reflection of nature and intense awareness of values important to humanity: beauty, intensity, diversity, and complexity. These concepts, built into his works, give us pleasure because we love structure. Just as children organize blocks by lining them up or building a tower, so Beethoven uses a similar process in composing his music.*

— GERARD WILLEMS

GERARD WILLEMS IS CERTAIN Beethoven will remain a driving force in the world because of his immense contribution to mankind.

Beethoven is relevant today because his music is emotionally powerful. It is played all over the world in a great many concert programs, and piano students usually study his sonatas at every stage of their musical development. Every part of one's personality can be expressed through the music of Beethoven—love, sadness, joy, and reverence. His music can attract some people almost like a drug, as they feel connected to his music on a deep, spiritual level and are able to experience immensely pleasurable rewards from listening to various pieces.

The fundamental characteristic of his music is its structure, and although the music is complex, the clarity of its architecture removes any doubt as to the general musical path and one's location in the score.

One of the interesting features of Beethoven's music is the way it can blend with almost any other composer in a concert program. In this respect, Beethoven is perhaps unique among composers, and it is possible to feature his works with Brahms, Bartók, Shostakovich, and many others.

The organic quality of his music is one of its most distinctive aspects. Like sowing a seed, he can plant a simple phrase with the capacity to propagate sections of a musical work. These sections are structurally connected and grow into a mighty symphony. In nature, each blade of grass is a discernable part of a greater organism; in Beethoven's music, any small segment can reveal something about the overall work. Moreover, every bar belongs to a particular work and could not be transferred to another. Unlike Beethoven's work, one could remove part of a piece by Mozart, such as a section of a piano concerto, insert it into another of his compositions, and it would fit reasonably well.

In a sense, Beethoven's creativity reflects the fundamental process of alternating tension and relaxation in the natural world. This can be seen in the flowers that open in the morning and close at night, in the tightening and expansion of muscles, and the contrast of a storm followed by calm. When Beethoven was tense, his music was tight and he was motivated to compose. Tension and relaxation are also part of the structure in his music. The first movement of the *Moonlight Sonata* is a statement of love and a stark contrast to the third and last movement, which erupts like a volcano and should be played with great intensity, although not loudly.

Apart from the contrast of tension and relaxation, Beethoven expresses another dichotomy in the opposition of ugliness and beauty. He loved humanity but wanted to focus on the clash of these attributes as a true mirror of life. These opposing forces can be found in the *Hammerklavier Sonata*.[263] The fugue is an ugly piece of music, but the slow second movement is a testament to loveliness and serenity.

Beethoven also provides a personal example in his heroic response to his disability. Once he accepted that he was becoming deaf, he renounced depression, enabling his sublime creativity and life-affirming perspective to strengthen. In spite of the immense daily hardship caused by his deafness, this impairment probably intensified his imagination, and by overcoming the calamity, he strengthened his resolve and developed an inner calm. Consequently, he was able to rise to his full potential. Many of his works exemplify the defeat of despair.

Piano Sonata No. 26 (*Les Adieux*)[264] is a farewell to his friend and patron, the Archduke Rudolf, who had left Vienna. The first movement is filled with the pain of loss and the stringent chords of the slow movement reflect the inner struggle concerned with adjustment to loss and the uncertainty of his friend's return. In this sad and dramatic movement, the chords of ninths need to be resolved; yet their resolution is postponed until the end of the third movement, when the beloved friend returns and happiness erupts with much celebration and pealing of church bells. It is an autobiographical picture, a historical statement, and a work of great artistic depth and meaning. Ultimately, the music celebrates life and the human capacity to master loss.

Beethoven helps us to reflect. Most people have some tendency for contemplation. He appeals to this inclination by compelling one to listen and concentrate on his music, particularly during the slow movement of a sonata. A good example is the first movement of the *Moonlight Sonata*,[265] when time seems to stop.

The works of Beethoven, written centuries ago, continue to be intimate, relevant, and touching throughout the generations. The listener needs little explanation to appreciate his music, and due to its power and creativity, it is often chosen to showcase diverse politics. When the Berlin Wall came down, the last movement of Symphony No. 9 (*Choral*)[266] was played, and Symphony No. 5[267] was often performed in Nazi Germany. Beethoven himself was politically aware as he lived through Napoleon's invasion of Austria and the bombardment of Vienna. Much of his music is driven by a passion that is easily appropriated during wartime.

The music can also stimulate strong feelings in children. Willems has powerful memories of his first response to the *Triple Concerto*.[268]

He was seven years old when he heard a recording of the piece and instinctively treasured this music, although he didn't know the name of the composer until he was fourteen.

Beethoven was a man of extremes, and his music achieves a compelling dramatic effect that probably mirrors his own personality. In his thirty-two piano sonatas, there are only two markings for *mezzo forte* (halfway between loud and soft). Elsewhere, the markings are *forte* (loud) or *piano* (soft). These dramatic qualities allow performers to be outrageous, which excites the audience and stimulates enjoyment. Mozart, on the other hand, never aimed for drama, even though there are thrilling moments in his operas, symphonies, and chamber music. These moments are an integral part of a work by Mozart, whereas Beethoven often sets out to shock the audience.

He liked to challenge listeners, which may explain why much of his music, such as the *Große Fuge*,[269] remains difficult to follow even to this day. It is very complicated, perhaps resembling Beethoven's own character. His personal complexity might have originated in his relationship with his father, Johann van Beethoven. A professional court musician, Johann was an alcoholic and cruel authoritarian. He would return from work in a drunken state and wake young Ludwig late at night to make him demonstrate what he had learned to play on the piano that day. Johann criticized his son for not matching up to Mozart, but unlike Mozart, whose music might be considered celestial, Beethoven was earthy.

He saw himself as something of an aristocrat, at least in the field of music. Socially, he desired equality but had to accept the patronage of aristocrats and titled students—countesses and princesses. He shunned the control of a single patron and was the first composer who openly aspired for the freedom to compose as he wished. In these objectives, he even had some aristocrats on side. Given Beethoven's fierce individuality and freedom of spirit, it is no surprise he refused to compromise regarding his works or employment or that he was the first composer who wanted to do away with patronage. Unlike Haydn, who wrote music according to the specifications set out for the entertainment of the Esterházy [270] family, Beethoven could not adjust to conformity or control by patrons. In Beethoven's rebellion against authority, he is occasionally compared to Shostakovich, who stood up to Stalin and the Soviet regime through the mockery he expressed in his compositions.

Beethoven accepted the tonality of the period, though toward the end of his life, he was already proceeding in a direction far removed from his contemporaries and was beginning to think in terms of atonality in his late works. Sections of the *Große Fuge*, the last string quartets, the *Hammerklavier Sonata* and the last piano sonata, Opus 111, sound quite atonal in parts. He was experimenting in these pieces and aimed to expand musical possibilities. This new path opened ideas for later composers, who would experiment with his atonal ideas, and develop music beyond the chromaticism that had been exhausted in the romantic age.

Although Beethoven was probably brought up with the spiritual values of his Belgian Catholic grandfather, it seems unlikely that organized religion played a major role in his life. Undoubtedly, some of his most profound feelings were expressed in musical form, but not all of his works are overly serious. They often include humor as well. When heard out of context, some of his music, such as the first theme of Symphony No. 5, might be considered cheap and even a little reminiscent of a German military march, yet as part of the whole symphony it fits in very well.

At the time of his death in 1827 at the age of fifty-seven, Beethoven was considered one of the greatest composers. Among the successors profoundly influenced by his music were Schubert and Brahms. Many considered Brahms to be Beethoven's heir and his Symphony No. 1 [271] was often hailed as Beethoven's Tenth.

A cultured audience does not need technical information about the piano or a high level of musicianship to appreciate and enjoy Beethoven's music, though it helps if one wants a deeper understanding. His music can affect the listener in a transformational yet subtle way, like eating a piece of chocolate or being in love leads to states of mind when the whole world seems to be a better place. One can feel transported by almost every piece, whether it is a sonata for piano, violin, cello, or his song cycle *An die ferne Geliebte*.[272] His house in Bonn is reportedly one of the town's most popular tourist destinations, and there are usually fresh flowers on his grave in Vienna.

Alfred Brendel's [273] interpretations of the sonatas are particularly insightful. Brendel has retired from the concert platform, but remains a prominent authority on music. He expresses great respect for Beethoven's serious intent, but also draws attention to the composer's sense of humor.[274] An example can be heard in the first movement of the Piano Sonata No. 16,[275] when both hands play in a disunited manner—the effect is rather comical.

As a pianist, Willems was drawn to the Beethoven sonatas and intrigued by the vast individual differences between these works. Some are jaunty, humorous, and more like folk songs. Others are exceptionally spiritual and mystical. It is difficult to define the spiritual or mystical, yet the properties of a particular chord or musical phrase can trigger such descriptions from the listener. Similarly, it would be a formidable task to describe precisely how one felt about the various touches and strokes of a massage.

These issues have continued to fascinate Willems, and Beethoven's piano works have been a major influence during his life as a performer and teacher. The project of recording all the sonatas, concertos and the *Diabelli Variations*[276] took the better part of ten years, and throughout this time, Willems was completely immersed in this repertoire, almost to the exclusion of everything else in his life. Studying the thirty-two piano sonatas brings one close to their diverse personalities, each with a separate emotional story, and often connected to the dedicatee. The *Moonlight Sonata*[277] was inscribed to Countess Giulietta Guicciardi, and she seems to stand before the listener when the music is played. In writing a slow first movement to this sonata, Beethoven's composition was revolutionary.

Very occasionally, Beethoven expresses love; the first movement of the same sonata is an example. The slow movement of the *Hammerklavier Sonata*[278] is also full of love and tenderness, but later, he goes into a fury when he seems to be fighting the elements and the people around him. Nevertheless, Willems is convinced that Beethoven had an immense capacity for love.

*Gerard Willems was interviewed by the author in Sydney, Australia, in May 2012.*

# Administrators
## OF MUSIC
## ORGANIZATIONS

# Berenika

*Concert Pianist and Artistic and Executive Director*

Berenika is a concert pianist who has performed worldwide with many orchestras, including the Pittsburgh, Penderecki Festival Orchestra, Boston Civic Symphony, Oxford Philomusica, Winnipeg Symphony Orchestra, Sinfonia Varsovia, Camerata New York, Beethoven Academy Orchestra, and the Aspen Sinfonia. She has toured South America, performed at Rock Hotel Pianofest in New York, Jazz at Lincoln Center, and Wigmore Hall, London.

She is the Executive Director of Casa Romantica Cultural Center and Gardens in San Clemente, CA, Artistic Director of the Dana Point Symphony and Executive Producer of the Symphony Spectacular Aboard the Pilgrim. She also serves as Vice Chairman of the Arts & Culture Commission for the City of Dana Point, California.

Her academic background from Harvard University and Oxford University, and the Julliard School and Royal Academy of Music, encompasses cultural policy, piano performance, public-private partnerships, and American government. She was awarded the Leonard Bernstein Scholarship at Harvard, the Arthur W. Foote prize of the Harvard Musical Association, and a DeVos Fellowship at the DeVos Institute of Arts Management, Kennedy Center for the Performing Arts in Washington DC.[279]

*Music itself might not have the potential to civilize those who com-
pose, perform, or listen to it, but the discussion can have a human-
izing effect if we are open to it. Simply listening to music doesn't
make us any better or worse. In this respect, concert halls can provide a forum for conversations about classical music, including
interpretation, culture, history and new music by a living composer.*

—BERENIKA

T HE CONCERT HALL should not promote elitist views or
stifle any type of discussion, as all individual emotional
responses to music are acceptable. Discussion should
focus on the way the performer reads the compos-
er's message for our times. There is no need to accept a particular
orchestral or soloist's version as sacrosanct; however, a performer
should make a piece of music by Beethoven sound like Beethoven. If
performers want a very different sound from another's version, it is
their choice, and provided their approach is honest and convincing,
the interpretation will have validity. After all, who is to say how
Beethoven should be performed?

Berenika's dedication to the arts and music rests on the belief that
music can move people. When she gets up in the morning and hears a
piece she loves, the emotion is overwhelming. Perhaps she just experiences music differently or more intensely than others. In any case,
she feels compelled to share this enthusiasm because it celebrates life
and the excitement of being alive. Music also has the advantage of
being available to a large number of people at the same time.

Is there a moral component in music? Being able to value a composer's creative work is a significant step in appreciating the human

capacity for greatness and could, conceivably, help one strive to be a better person. Such concepts might not direct people toward improved morality or excellence, but Berenika is convinced they have changed her.

She started her career as a concert pianist when she was nine years old. Later she studied music and government at Harvard University and became the school's first graduate with a dual degree. Her thesis was a case study involving the municipal politics and funding required for building a concert hall. Berenika analyzed the project in terms of relevance and success for a community and discussed aesthetics as well as musicology theory and urban planning. In her thesis she argued that concert halls are a part of civilized societies and their heritage, but only sustainable if they reflect, involve, and serve a community.

Some of the knowledge gained in her dissertation is being put to use in her work as Artistic Director of the Dana Point Symphony, Chairman of the Arts Commission, and Executive Director of Casa Romantica Cultural Center and Gardens, Orange County, California.

There is a current trend to make concert programs more interesting, affordable, and relevant to everyday life. In keeping with this aim, Berenika has managed to keep the price of concert tickets down to the same price as movie tickets, at least for first-time concertgoers. The local population in Dana Point is mostly middle class and Dana Point Symphony could have charged much more for tickets, but she wanted to make the concerts as accessible as movies. It may seem impossible to pay all expenses with such low ticket prices, but she succeeds by setting a budget beforehand and keeping to it without deviation. For an administrator who wants to maintain very high artistic quality, keeping costs down is not an easy task.

Her organization aims to contribute to the life of the community. Free passes are sent to all schools in the surrounding area. Some members of the community have offered to do voluntary work. One nine-year-old girl wrote to say she plays the cello and would like to volunteer, so she was allowed to work as an usher and hand out programs. Youngsters from the local arts high school, where Berenika used to run a piano program, often volunteer and can obtain credits for their work.

Performances incorporate a visual arts exhibition and post-concert reception for the whole audience, not just the major donors, and people are invited to discuss the concert and meet the musicians, who usually stay and mingle. As Executive Director, Berenika is there to talk to everyone and, together with the musicians, takes note of all feedback. Involvement of the city is an important aspect, so the mayor and some of the council members are usually present at the post-concert receptions.

These events also help the musicians wind down. Performers share a great deal of emotion and personal experience in a very public way, and after concerts the adrenaline level is still high. When they finish playing, performers are expected to go home or to their hotel room and switch off, but an artist does not have a nine-to-five job.

Meeting the audience can also assist performers who want a more personal connection with their listeners. When musicians are on the stage, they only feel the presence of the audience in the dark hall.

As a performer, Berenika always appreciated the opportunity to attend a reception where some of this pent-up energy could be diffused, and where she could meet members of the audience, not only for social interaction but also to receive feedback.

One of her initiatives is a visual arts exhibition run in parallel with the concerts. The art works, which are all for sale, are not necessarily related to music, but they reflect her love of the visual arts and offer an avenue for communication after a concert. In order to promote social cohesion and common interests, she likes to select the exhibitors from the artists who live in her city. Unlike a regular art gallery where visitors filter through gradually over time, the concerts offer an instant seven-hundred–person audience.

Berenika decided to get involved in the arts in Dana Point and San Clemente because the cities had no consistent classical concert series. In the past the municipality had supported a symphony orchestra, but it experienced financial difficulties. When she came to Dana Point, most of the music in the community revolved around summer-oriented bands, and she thought there was room for a classical program in winter and spring.[280]

The project and its inaugural season in 2012 created a great deal of civic pride in Dana Point. A survey of the audience showed that the post-concert reception is an important part of the evening experience. In spite of the late hour, people want to stay, join the conversation, share their feelings about the concert, and express their sense of ownership of the orchestra. One of the questions in the survey asked people to rate the importance of a symphony to a city. Almost everyone gave it a very high rank, in some cases off the rating scale!

In the survey, the audience ranked the choice of programs just as highly as customer service and accessibility. Future surveys will assess what aspects of the concerts have greatest value for the audience, in order to determine where resources need to be directed.

Dana Point Symphony puts on four concerts each season, which is standard for a mid-range symphony, and they usually fill the seven-hundred–seat auditorium. The success of Berenika's program depends on securing passionate people who will play high-quality music. The audience responds to the enthusiasm of the performers and they gravitate toward the music. She started with that concept in mind and then focused on the most important task: finding the right musicians.

The artists she hires are usually in the early stages of their careers because she wants the principal sections to go to players who need the experience. Watching them give their all is immensely pleasurable, and the happiness she observes among the musicians and audience is her reward. Most of the revenue goes to pay the musicians, but she is careful to avoid the pitfall of hiring expensive soloists who are expected to fill a hall, as they don't always cover their costs.

A vast number of hopeful applicants contact her organization regarding solo work. It is important to be as objective as possible about soloists, so she doesn't take recommendations. Berenika is one of three judges who hold the auditions, which take place behind a screen to avoid gender bias. In order to prevent a conflict of interest she forgoes playing as a soloist with the orchestra.

Her relationship with the conductor, Dean Anderson, is vitally important. Anderson is an excellent musician who is young, enthusiastic, and particularly skilled at maintaining a high morale in the orchestra. They work together on the program. He sends her a list of ideas, and they discuss all the possibilities until they come to a consensus.

The arts program has included some high order performances such as the Brahms Double Concerto for violin and piano[281] and the Naval Academy Women's choir, as well as the Christ Church Cathedral Choir from Oxford, England. To inaugurate the first season an award-winning composer, Juan Colomer, wrote a work about Dana Point. This composition has stimulated unity and focus in the community and made people aware of their orchestra's value. The first page of the composition was framed and now hangs in City Hall.

One of the recent seasons began with a blending of the arts on board a tall ship docked in Dana Point Harbor. Entitled "A Symphony Spectacular Aboard the Pilgrim," the show charted the journey of Dana Point's namesake, Richard Henry Dana Jr., from Massachusetts to California. The ship was lit up in blue, green, and purple, and it served as a backdrop for a combination of orchestral music and film scores, opera, musical theater, and aerial ballet. The music ranged from Wagner's *Ride of the Valkyries* and Gilbert and Sullivan's *Pirates of Penzance* to music from the *Pirates of the Caribbean* movies. It engaged performers from the Los Angeles and San Diego operas, Luminario Ballet of Los Angeles, and Dana Point's South Orange County School of the Arts. Berenika was the show's executive producer and writer, which was extremely rewarding.

The performance was a sellout. Six hundred people saw the show from the pier and another sixty without tickets watched from the side. Berenika conceived the spectacle as a new frontier for orchestras in the United States and she hopes to introduce more people to the idea of a re-imagined traditional symphony orchestra.

Such arts projects require devotion and hard work by the chief executive if they are to be successful. The CEO does not have to be a musician or professional administrator, but should be passionate about the job. Capable managers understand that the characteristics of an effective administrator are in direct contrast to those of an artist. The latter deals with emotions, whereas the former needs to seek entrepreneurial opportunities and make cool-headed, savvy decisions. Good leadership is crucial as well. In Berenika's case, she is driven by love for the art, though she could have devoted herself enthusiastically to other projects if she didn't have such an avid interest in music.

In the United States, arts organizations are generally public-private partnerships so raising revenue is always an issue, but she likes to emphasize the "fun" part of funding. Public-private partnerships are a good way of doing things, as there can be much wasteful spending in large organizations. Moreover, they often lack good business models that aim to avoid accumulation of debt.

The project is a personal challenge and a test of Berenika's ability in management. After the first concert, members of the audience came to her and made donations without being asked. Consequently, she decided to have envelopes ready at future concerts in case people felt inclined to donate. There was a good response. Another initiative to raise funds involved sponsoring the salary of a member of the orchestra. In this way, donors had a personal relationship with individual players.

She runs a very tight ship, and although the city helps with funding, her organization has almost paid its way from ticket sales alone and then moved toward using some of the surplus for the purpose of attracting funds.

Marketing is expensive and arts groups don't often assess whether their marketing methods are productive. Her organization's survey was helpful in showing that most people attended concerts via word of mouth, rather than advertisements.

Berenika was very pleased to be running on surplus and made plans to grow the project in a slow and steady manner. When arts organizations have too much money there is a tendency to waste it on projects that don't have a good return. Instead, she looks for steady growth, building on successes, while avoiding the temptation to create outlandish ventures that would threaten stability.

Currently, as Chairman of the Arts and Culture Commission for the City, she is creating an annual celebration of the arts that is in line with a national directive. October will be a celebration of the arts, and she will include all arts and humanities nonprofits in the city to participate and showcase their valuable work. Often giving nonprofits a collective platform is what they need to publicize and effectively market their work.

Establishing strong boards is essential for every arts organization. Boards should include those who are passionate about every aspect of the mission, have a selfless approach to philanthropy, and are committed to see the organization thrive.

Following a fellowship at the DeVos Institute of Arts Management, Kennedy Center, Washington, DC, Berenika was appointed Executive Director of Casa Romantica Cultural Center and Gardens. She now manages a ten-person staff and a million-dollar budget, and works in all genres—history, cultural tours, wellness, visual arts, music, drama, dance, education, gardens, and horticulture. Pianist Garrick Ohlsson[282] was a featured performer in 2015.

Her work is a growing passion and she has also come to love the historic location upon the bluff in San Clemente. The experience gained at the Dana Point Symphony and the skills she developed at the Kennedy Center Fellowship have helped to make her an effective and innovative leader. The appointment at Casa Romantica is another step forward in her cultural work.

*Berenika was interviewed by the author in Sydney, Australia, in June 2012.*

# Mary Jo Capps  *CEO, Musica Viva Australia*

Mary Jo Capps was appointed CEO of Musica Viva Australia in 1999, and has aimed to widen community education and access in fine music. Previously, she worked in various Australian arts companies and was Deputy Managing Director and Director of Development for the Sydney Symphony Orchestra.

Canadian born, Capps graduated with an MA in Musicology from the University of Toronto, and has worked in Australian arts organizations for over thirty years. She established her own consultancy practice in 1987, incorporating planning and development for several major Australian arts companies, including the Sydney Symphony Orchestra, Company B Belvoir Theatre, Bangarra Dance Theatre, National Institute of Dramatic Arts (NIDA), and the Museum of Contemporary Art.

In 2010 Capps became the first female President of the Sydney Business Chamber. She chairs the Advisory Board of the Faculty of the Victorian College of the Arts and Melbourne Conservatorium of Music, University of Melbourne. She is also a Board Director of the Community Council for Australia, Green Music Australia, and a Council member of the Centre for Social Impact.

She has an interest in supporting young talents, especially in the field of arts administration. In a related capacity, she works as a professional mentor.

Mary Jo Capps has served as a Board Director of the NSW Business Chamber, Deputy Chair of the Australian Music Centre, Board Director of the Pascall Foundation, and The Orchestras of Australia Network.[283]

*Connecting people through chamber music is the basic philosophy of Musica Viva. The way this is done has changed over time, but the original vision of Richard Goldner has remained central. Goldner and other refugees from Nazi Germany found solace in chamber music during hard times in prewar and wartime Europe, and they wanted to share this music as a gift to their new country.*

— MARY JO CAPPS

MARY JO CAPPS maintains that the founders' choice of chamber music was particularly appropriate because of its intimacy and depth. It is not surprising that their first concerts featured late Beethoven quartets, which are such profound expressions of humanity and spirituality. They also promoted live music as a medium with the potential to transport people out of their everyday life and a tool to remind listeners about important issues.

In the 1940s, Australia was a country of great opportunity but lacking in culture. An arts organization like Musica Viva had the capacity to form bonds between the community and the artists. Since those early days, the organization has evolved and expanded into regional touring, education programs, and development for young artists, while staying focused on the shared experience of audience and artists in live performance.

All the founders were extraordinary people, especially Richard Goldner, who was an inventor as well as a musician. In Vienna, he played the viola in the renowned Simon Pullman Ensemble and became a close associate of Pullman. Playing chamber music was an activity eagerly anticipated by musicians performing in the orchestra.

Pullman and other members of his orchestral group later died in a Nazi extermination camp.

Goldner escaped Vienna and arrived in Australia in 1939, where he auditioned for the Sydney Symphony. As a foreign national, he was denied the post and instead worked as a jeweler. Known for his inventive skills, he was approached by the War Office to design a zipper for parachutes. The design brought in some money, which he used to establish the Musica Viva Society with its own chamber music ensemble, in collaboration with Charles Berg, Alfred Dullo, Fred Wenkart, Gaston Bauer, Paul Morawetz, and other refugees.

Why were they so enthused by chamber music? Capps believes the reason can be found in the genre itself—the music can only be realized with full consensus, reached through close partnership and intense listening to one another. It is music stripped bare: the pinnacle of musical expression. As a paradigm of cooperation, it is also a model for humanity.

These concepts were central to the founders, who often referred to chamber music as a conversation among intelligent friends, in which no member of the group is a leader or follower, and everyone must contribute to achieve results. Orchestral musicians find themselves in a very different situation because they are under the instruction of the conductor and follow a regimen of rehearsals and breaks, without much input into the choice of pieces or their interpretation.

Coming from an orchestral background, Capps immediately noticed differences when she started working at Musica Viva. It was clear the relationship between the musicians and the administration was entirely different from that of an orchestra. The chamber musicians appeared to be more satisfied with their work, at peace with themselves, and happy for the opportunity to play for people, despite the downside of spending much time traveling.

The repertoire for chamber music is also very powerful, with heroic role models such as Beethoven, who overcame the struggle against deafness, and Shostakovich, who asserted his feelings about Soviet oppression most openly in his quartets. Although there are many other styles of chamber music, the quartet repertoire is a unique vehicle of expression for composers and performers.

One of the interesting features of Musica Viva is the passion for chamber music among subscribers, many of whom share a strong cultural alignment with European musical traditions. The organization grew from grassroots support, unlike an opera house, ballet company, or art gallery, which are often decreed into existence as symbols of a cultured society. In contrast, Musica Viva developed in the living rooms of private homes before graduating to the public concert stage. It became a significant force because people willed it into existence and, for a long time, was run by volunteers. The administration was professionalized more recently, although it remained small in number. The scope of Musica Viva was greatly enlarged with the development of the schools education program in 1981. In relation to its output, the management is still small and relies quite heavily on volunteer support.

Globally, it is one of a kind. Arts organizations in other countries focus on the main cities and provinces are often ignored. In contrast, Musica Viva is dedicated to bringing live concerts of uniformly high standard to centers all over Australia. In carrying out this mission, it has built up a countrywide network to deliver tours of major soloists from Australia and overseas. Tours limited to the major cities would be more profitable, but this consideration has never been part of Musica Viva's philosophy.

A considerable effort is made to look after visiting musicians and ensure they have an enjoyable time. They are usually pleased to be guaranteed many concerts, in spite of a heavy work schedule and touring huge distances. During the first tour of the original Takács String Quartet from Hungary, the group played twenty-eight concerts, and after each performance, the local Hungarian community offered them a goulash meal. Even when they played in the mining town of Mount Isa, they were welcomed by about fifty Hungarians and yet another goulash!

Sometimes, unexpected bonuses arise, thanks to Musica Viva's connections that stretch from emerging new artists to the established international titans of the field. One such relationship developed between the Takács Quartet, who were the tutors, and the young Orava Quartet, who were participants during master classes at the Musica Viva Festival in 2008. The Takács were sufficiently impressed to offer the Oravas their biennial scholarship in Denver, Colorado. Musica Viva then stepped in to help raise the extra funds required. The Oravas have now completed their studies with leading ensembles in the United States as well as the Takács, and have secured a position as ensemble-in-residence at an Australian university. They will perform in various Musica Viva programs as fully-fledged professionals.

Capps has no wish to dictate the way listeners should think and feel, but hopes they could be transported to a high level of reflection and awareness through the music. The greatest performances can achieve this state of mind, but the recipient should be active rather than passive. Performers are sensitive to listeners who are responsive and actively processing the music, an observation they often make about Musica Viva audiences.

Capps would also hope that listening thoughtfully to a chamber music concert might encourage more attentive conversation and increased awareness and responsiveness to others. The very fact of coming together for a live performance instead of listening to music in one's living room is already meaningful. A choice has been made to share the experience in the expectation it will be worthwhile—not necessarily perfect, but touched with a little magic.

Sharing the music is an important aspect of the total experience and involves reaching out and bonding with others. Some might even consider it therapy. Capps feels deeply gratified when she sees audience members talking with like-minded people of all ages and discussing new works. People are very mistaken if they believe that chamber music is elitist, as subscribers come from all socioeconomic groups.

Emotions in the music cover the full range from exhilaration to despair. Even music that makes one very sad can elevate and fortify. Occasionally, performers themselves are deeply affected and emboldened to risk all. Capps recalled a particularly forceful and thrilling rendition of a trio by Shostakovich, which had the audience on the edge of their seats. Afterwards, the performers talked about the risk they were prepared to take because they felt the audience was with them, helping and willing them to do it. On another occasion, a cellist who was performing the Bach cello suites was so immersed in the music that he seemed to vanish. The audience was very moved and many were in tears.

It is interesting to contemplate why people cry in response to music. Perhaps the music touches very personal memories or the human condition in general. Capps is reminded of the pathos of Violetta's lonely death in Puccini's opera, *La Traviata,* or the poem "Spring and Fall" by Gerard Manley Hopkins,[284] which expresses mourning for mortality.

Although many enjoy the intellectual pleasure of music, the audience wants to be moved. The three overlapping circles of the Venn diagram can be useful to explain how the emotional transmission is effected. One circle represents the composer's creation and intention, the second one the artist's interpretation, and the third the participation of the audience. When the three combine to form the overlapping sweet spot in the middle, the emotional transmission is realized. Arts administrators try to make the circles overlap by presenting the best compositions, artists, and environment. But an exciting outcome is not predictable. It can happen even if a work is mediocre, the performance imperfect, or the environment not conducive. However, there is no doubt when it does occur because the effect is magical. Music is not the only art that can move people, but it can stimulate emotions without words or images.

There is a trend to include multimedia in concert performances. Capps is not averse to this development, but she believes it should always complement the music. When multimedia presentations are used to tell a story, as in Tafelmusik's *The Galileo Project: Music of the Spheres*, the performance might resemble a chamber music version of an opera. Tafelmusik's production featured poetic narration, choreography, and music by contemporaneous baroque composers, which deepened the story of Galileo and made it more meaningful.

Most arts organizations are very responsive to fresh ideas. A new generation of listeners is showing more interest in the type of chamber music concerts that Musica Viva started early on, when a few people got together in a small venue or in someone's home. The current obstacle for a concert audience may not be the music, but the idea of sitting in a darkened hall for two hours without knowing much about the other members of the audience. If this trend to smaller venues continues, it will throw into question the future of large auditoriums. It would make more sense to alter the venue than throw out the music, says Capps; she believes it is the music that has greater value and will survive.

Like all organizations, those in the arts have budgets to balance. Musica Viva had no government support for many years and was run by volunteers. Today, over 50 percent of its revenue comes from tickets purchased for concerts and school programs. Government support is secured for unprofitable tours to regional areas, education development programs, and artistic ventures, while private sector support has risen to 25 percent of the annual turnover. Even as costs have risen, the organization has managed to balance the budget and build reserves to support future risk-taking projects that will extend artistic vibrancy.

One of the largest items is the Live Performance Plus schools program,[285] partnered with international mining company Rio Tinto Ltd. The education program involves up to one thousand schools across Australia every year, as well as twenty-seven professional music groups, spanning classical, world, jazz, improvisation, a capella, and folk music. Musica Viva recognized that performers had a vital role to play in education, as most primary school teachers were either ill-equipped to teach music in the classroom or were skilled but only knew about a particular aspect and were open to extension activities into other genres of music.

The program consists of three stages. The first involves instruction for schoolteachers, including the interactive educational resource kits linked to the curriculum for kindergarten to year eight. Digital activities are an adjunct to those resources. In the next stage, teachers follow the plan as best suits their classes. Finally, professional music groups come to the school for an interactive performance. Linking the musicians and classroom educators gives the children the richest possible experience.

Performers who work with children in schools are trained to ask students to listen for the melodies, as well as the structural and harmonic components. They then play a passage and request children to raise their hands when they hear a change, such as a transition from major to minor key in the melody. This exercise develops listening with intent. Rather than judging children's capacity for playing a particular instrument, the organizers of the project measure the ability to understand, create, and participate in music as an activity. In a survey[286] by the University of Western Australia, all teachers agreed that the program helped students develop a positive attitude to music and influenced creativity, imagination, and self-expression. An overwhelming number of teachers and students also gave high ratings for enjoyment and learning.

Although the educational program began with classical music, other genres are included, provided the music has the depth and quality to withstand scrutiny and deconstruction. Capps is concerned about the trend of lowering intellectual content, as well as confining listening material to familiar music, which disregards new compositions and ideas. She contends that it is listening to unfamiliar music that stretches the aural and musical imagination.

The program overlaps with that of El Sistema,[287] the successful music program for disadvantaged children, and a reminder of music's potential to help build communities, self-esteem, and many skills. As in sports, the program demands self-discipline, constant repetition, and the strength to recover from mistakes and failure. Those lessons are often lost in current education. Capps points out that her son probably learned more from his band training at school than from writing essays. Many essays could be written the night before they were due for submission (and forgotten just as quickly), but the preparation of a piece of music requires consistent piecemeal work and multiple rehearsals prior to performance—and even if disaster strikes on performance day, the way one recovers becomes essential training in resilience.

Music education is vitally important for the next generation audience, as the future will probably involve more listener participation. This trend is exemplified by the Elias Quartet and their Beethoven Project, which aims for greater interaction with the audience not only musically through concerts, but also experientially via the Internet and social media.

People are becoming more eclectic in their tastes, and might wish to listen to the Kronos Quartet playing a contemporary piece followed by a Bach cello suite or an experimental sound artist. Arts organizations could think about following the Amazon.com model, which aims to multiply sales by drawing attention to additional items of interest for people who bought a particular book. This approach would widen the field for new works and exchange of ideas. In opposition to this trend are those companies that analyze a customer's favorite pieces of music based on their browsing history on the Internet and continually produce variations of the same.

Research has shown that concert attendance increases exponentially for those who have studied an instrument. These days, children are less likely to follow through with practice and self-discipline and after starting to play an instrument, tend to give up after several lessons. Attitudes are very different in the emerging nations, where thousands of children attend classical concerts and some performing musicians are treated like rock stars. Fine music has always been associated with an aspirational society, like the one Richard Goldner saw in Australia when he arrived as a refugee in 1939. Today, such aspirational societies can be found in China, India, and Brazil.

What caused interest in classical music to slide in the West? Capps believes that poor teaching methods in the 1960s and 1970s resulted in unhappy memories for many students, and when they had children, they decided against putting them through a similar experience. It was preferable to let children have fun, an easy life, and immediate gratification. Perhaps the present generation will reverse this trend when they have their own offspring. They may recognize good reasons for learning to play an instrument, such as the development of persistence and diligence. Educators also need to accept some responsibility for ensuring that music is relevant to students and could be rated as a valuable skill.

Arts presenters have obligations to the community as well; they must choose exciting performers and engage the audience to think about the program before a concert, become enthusiastically involved in the performance, and muse about it later.

Capps thinks there is a real danger of losing classical music as an art form. People point to the rediscovery of Bach by Mendelssohn as an example of safeguarding traditions, but this revival was fortuitous and may not have occurred without the championship of Mendelssohn.

Arts companies have a responsibility to grow and develop new approaches to presentation. They must plan strategically, advocate for classical music, and encourage adherents among the audience. If the organizations don't change, they will become victims of their legacy and their long-term future could be in jeopardy.

There is an exciting blossoming of young performers. The music is excellent and speaks to people in every generation. However, the way it is conveyed, enjoyed, and kept alive needs to be constantly reassessed.

*Mary Jo Capps was interviewed by the author in Sydney, Australia, in August 2014.*

# William Lyne, CBE, AM

*BRIEF BIOGRAPHY*

William Lyne joined Wigmore Hall as Director in 1966 and built the venue into one of the finest recital and chamber music halls in the world. He was the first to present a themed concert series, which achieved great popularity. The series included Chamber Music, Song Recitals, Early Music, Pianoforte, Young Masters, BBC Radio 3 Lunchtime Concerts, and Sunday Morning Coffee Concerts. He added festivals of music, and brought some to the UK from France, Sweden, and Norway. He also presented music from his native Australia.

Lyne's flair for discerning new talents assisted the careers of artists such as Ian Bostridge, Matthias Goerne, Wolfgang Holzmair, and the Belcea and Takács Quartets. He offered residencies for outstanding musicians, established a successful education program and commissioned new works. For some years from 1997, he was also Artistic Director of Musica Viva Australia.[288]

In recognition of his contribution to the arts, he has received many awards, notably the CBE in the 2002 Queen's Golden Jubilee Birthday Honors list, an AM by the Australian government, the International Artist Managers' Association Special Award 2003, the Austrian Grand Cross of Honor for Science and the Arts, First Class 2001, the 2001 Cobbett Medal for services to the Art of Chamber Music, the Evening Standard Award for Outstanding Artistic Achievement for Classical Music 1997, the Ambassador for London Award: Lifetime Achievement 1997, Chevalier dans l'Ordre des Arts et des Lettres in 1996, and an MBE in 1986.

He is also an Honorary Member of the Royal Academy of Music and the Royal College of Music, the Guildhall School of Music and Drama, and was awarded an Honorary Fellowship of Trinity College of Music. In order to improve the Wigmore Hall and its services, he added a recording studio, restaurant, reception room, and extra office space to the premises.

His retirement in 2002 was celebrated with a Director's Festival of forty-three concerts, and closed with a gala concert starring thirty-three international artists. He is still involved with the Hall as Director Emeritus, as well as serving as a juror on international competitions.

Lyne is a member of the Music Committee for Her Majesty the Queen's Medal for Music.[289]

*What does the audience need? They want to be moved by something outside their experience of everyday life. There are times when listeners can be moved to tears because of an artist's interpretation and involvement with the music.*

—WILLIAM LYNE

GREAT MUSIC CAN take you to another world, depending on the composer and the listener. Schubert is pure genius and, for William Lyne, Schubert's music comes straight from heaven. The spirituality of such music has nurtured him and became part of his life; he would be very depressed without it. He loves song, whether German, French, British, Russian, or Scandinavian; he also loves opera and the great chamber music repertoire. The latter is particularly intimate, moving, and more satisfying for him than many symphonic works.

Lyne often tells people to try to listen to a Haydn quartet or symphony when they feel troubled, as Haydn is a very good doctor with a great sense of humor. Moreover, he is highly original, completely unpredictable, and offers listeners the choice of a huge variety of superb string quartets.

The emotional component is foremost for Lyne. In this respect, he draws attention to the Lindsay Quartet, who might have been a little off-key at times, yet managed to capture the spirit of Beethoven. The minor imperfections were unimportant. Of course, the finest performing musicians have both technical perfection and emotional communication, and for Lyne, one of the greatest living artists is the Hungarian pianist András Schiff.

Legendary pianist Artur Schnabel demonstrates emotional versus technical considerations in his recordings of Beethoven's sonatas. Although Schnabel makes a few mistakes, Lyne doesn't hear them; such is the performer's involvement with the music. Apparently, the recording producer Fred Gaisberg (who discovered Caruso for HMV) asked Schnabel if he would like to repeat a movement to correct the mistakes. Schnabel said he would be happy to play it again, but it wouldn't be as good, meaning the music might be note-perfect but not realized as well.

Today, there are many piano competitions and many contestants who tend to concentrate on the technical aspects of virtuoso pieces rather than works demonstrating their range of abilities. However, the jury is usually looking for insights into the music rather than emphasis on virtuosity.

Lyne's early experience taught him the advantage of a good background in music. To this end, he believes it is particularly important to start listening when young, curious, and receptive to new experiences. He can remember nearly everything he heard in his youth, especially the concerts organized by the great conductor Eugene Goossens. In Finland, he has seen many attentive young people at the Kuhmo Chamber Music Festival,[290] and it is probably relevant that at a very young age those children would have had music as part of their education. No doubt, the middle-aged people who regularly attend concerts in New York or London also had some musical education at an early age.

Perhaps there is something deeply personal that leads people to music. In his family, Lyne was the only aficionado. His parents and sister weren't interested in music, although his grandfather loved opera. However, he believes most people can develop an interest in music through their own searching, and it is up to them to become inquisitive and listen.

As it may require a little familiarity to appreciate the classics, Lyne ran an education program for adults and children at Wigmore Hall. If people are exposed to music when young, they won't feel daunted about stepping into a concert hall. Music education at school is also vital. British clarinetist Michael Collins has expressed deep gratitude for his state school education in music, but deplores the cuts in funding that would deny today's youngsters the opportunity he received.

Memories can be powerfully coupled with music, and Lyne can recall powerful associations with a particular piece. He was a young boy when he first heard a radio broadcast of Beethoven's *Eroica Symphony*[291] conducted by Wilhelm Furtwängler, and still today, he can picture the room and the old radio during that memorable experience.

Conductors have strongly influenced Lyne's appreciation of music. He used to enjoy some of Wagner's operas, performed by splendid casts, but it wasn't until he heard Reginald Goodall[292] conduct Wagner that everything fell into place, as Goodall seemed to understand the feeling and spirit of the music.

The interpretation of the composer's message is crucial, but other factors also come into play. Some performers, such as the Jerusalem String Quartet, have a definite charisma. The first time they walked onto the stage at Wigmore Hall, Lyne knew they were different, and when they played, it was apparent they had something special.

The stage itself can have a strange effect on performers. Lyne has seen singers come in looking old and worn out, but when they walk onto the stage they can be transformed, especially in the second half of a performance. On one occasion, Dame Sybil Thorndike, who was taking part in a poetry and music recital, had to take Lyne's arm to walk down the aisle of the hall because she could hardly move due to severe arthritis. The moment she got onto the stage, however, she was striding about!

It is vital for performers to present themselves well. Lyne recalls hearing a wonderful artist who came on stage looking miserable, and only at the end managed to carve a smile at the audience. Some of the Russian artists can look forbidding on the stage, but this is only because they take music so seriously. Backstage, they are warm and friendly.

Lyne has known some wonderful chamber music groups who performed at the hall. The Beaux Arts Trio had an extraordinary pianist, Menahem Pressler, who always played with remarkable freshness. Now in his nineties, he still has a flourishing career.

Sometimes musicians acquire something remarkable in their later years. When Mieczysław Horszowski gave a recital just before his one-hundredth birthday, one heard the distillation of a lifetime's piano playing and the essence of the music. Today there are many young groups competing for performance work, but the good ones, like the Doric Quartet and Sitkovetsky Trio, are doing very well. Lyne is often asked to recommend an agent, as it can be difficult to find the right person within an agency. Some of the larger classical music organizations can be very commission-oriented, but smaller ones often give personal attention and are committed to finding engagements.

Quartets with a mellifluous, warm sound appeal most to Lyne, and these qualities do not necessarily demand superior instruments. Some Polish and Czech artists don't have good instruments, but if they are really committed musicians, they can still move the listener. A good instrument can, of course, make a huge difference and there are some excellent modern instrument makers.

When he was director of Wigmore Hall, Lyne encouraged famous artists to make music there. He also wanted to discover and nurture new artists and experiment with new programs for people's enjoyment. Taking the audience on a musical journey of discovery was one of his major aims when he embarked on a series of Gabriel Fauré concerts. At the time, a music critic remarked that no one would attend, but the venture proved to be extremely successful.

From that experience, he learned it was possible to succeed in presenting a series with well-known artists together with some good performers whose names were less familiar. In the first festival of Haydn concerts, the hall tried to show that Haydn was a very great composer and not just the "starter before the main course." Devised by András Schiff, each concert presented trios, piano solos, Haydn songs, and a quartet to finish. A subsequent Haydn series featured the Lindsay String Quartet, who also spoke to the audience about the significance of Haydn. In the next series, when the hall presented all the Haydn Quartets from Opus 20 onwards, attendance was excellent.

It can be difficult to engage great artists, and this was a problem for Lyne in his early days at Wigmore Hall. The turning point came on the occasion of its seventy-fifth anniversary. Celebratory concerts included performances by Arthur Rubinstein, Elisabeth Schwarzkopf, Peter Pears, and Murray Perahia. Before his piano recital on May 31, 1976, the producer of NBC television asked Rubinstein if he could film the first few moments of his performance. "You can film me wherever you like," Rubinstein allegedly replied, "even in the bath if you wish, but the moment I put my hands on the keys, it will cost you $10,000."

Rubinstein refused to accept a fee for the Wigmore concert because he wanted to help the hall. When the performance ended, he announced it was his farewell recital. Lyne feels deeply indebted to Rubinstein, as many great artists were engaged following Rubinstein's farewell recital.

Lyne is not sure what advice he would give to administrators these days. Funding is always a concern, and it is inevitable that economic difficulties in the West will cause funding problems for music education and performance. In spite of the many financial cuts, he always thought it preferable to lower ticket prices in favor of larger audiences at more concerts, rather than higher-priced tickets and smaller audiences.

In hiring musicians, he simply followed his instinct. That was how he engaged artists like the original Takács Quartet and German baritone Matthias Goerne. If he believed in an artist, he took no notice of negative opinions in the press and his assessments always worked out well.

Many arts administrators in the UK have university degrees but insufficient experience in performance, handling artists and staff, and other facets of music production. Lyne believes in the value of choosing employees with a long-term commitment to their work and strong motivation to support the artists. Some members of the staff at Wigmore Hall have worked there for well over twenty years. Consequently musicians who perform at the hall often feel as if they are among family.

Arts organizations need to know how to market a concert. It is not just the artist who is responsible for the success of a performance. The program is also an important factor. Contemporary music often requires some explanation, which the Brentano Quartet has done with notable success. If one is putting on an unknown work, it is essential to be aware that the audience needs to know your reasons for choosing to present this piece and what makes it special. The same would apply to an unknown artist. An administrator must be perfectly honest about these issues in order to build trust with the public.

Lyne likes to remind arts organizations they would be making a great mistake if they underestimated the intelligence of the public. Listeners can be very sophisticated and they often stay loyal to a favorite venue. Some of the regulars at Wigmore Hall know each other by their seat numbers and have been known to remark, for example, that they saw B7 at the Barbican last week!

The composition of audiences for different types of music can vary considerably. The early music audience tends to be younger but this group can be attracted by a wide variety of music. When the hall presented all the Shostakovich quartets, Lyne was surprised so many young people came to the concerts.

Musical taste is very personal and changes with age. In their younger years people often listen to pop music, but as they mature they may want to discover something deeper. Radio broadcasts are very helpful in this regard. In the UK, people from a wide cross section of society are listening to more classical music on air. This development challenges accusations of elitism, as people from all classes appreciate this music. Today, people may also learn a great deal from the Internet, where they can hear the same piece played on YouTube by a number of different artists.

Does music have any morality? András Schiff has adopted a strong moral stance. He refuses to play in his native Hungary in protest against the right-wing, anti-Semitic elements in the government, and the way some musicians have been treated.[293] Similarly, he declined to play in Austria when Jörg Haider's Freedom Party was part of the coalition. Schiff has also spoken out about the Hungarian authorities that collaborated with the Nazis in persecuting the Jewish population. Lyne certainly admires people who stand firm on their beliefs and morals, but asserts that such individual attitudes have nothing to do with music.

Does music have an influence on performers themselves and the way they balance their lives? Lyne's own observation is that musicians have separate personal and music sides, and usually don't want to talk about music, except perhaps to other musicians.

Many artists have a difficult family life because they travel a great deal. Manuel Fischer-Dieskau, the cellist from the Cherubini Quartet, now disbanded, was the son of the late German baritone,

Dietrich Fischer-Dieskau. He told Lyne he hardly ever saw his father when he was growing up and eventually decided to give up quartet playing to avoid repeating the same mistake with his own children.

For people who are fairly new to the art, Lyne would suggest they read about music and attend concerts. Despite the proliferation on the Internet and a massive number of compact discs, live concerts are a different experience. Special, impromptu inventiveness can occur, encouraged by rapport with the audience and the stimulation of a great concert hall.

Listeners need to concentrate on what they are hearing and try to remain focused. When people are sitting in a concert hall after working all day, they are inclined to think about their problems. As they begin to listen carefully, they might then become aware of the different sound colors, become immersed, and enjoy the full impact of the music.

*William Lyne CBE, AM was interviewed by the author in Sydney, Australia, in August 2013.*

# Fanny Waterman, DBE, DMus, FRCM

*BRIEF BIOGRAPHY*

Dame Fanny Waterman is a legendary piano teacher and arts administrator. A native of Leeds, she studied with Tobias Matthay, and later with Cyril Smith as a Scholar at the Royal College of Music in London. Following a distinguished career as a pianist, she gave up performance to focus on her great love of teaching.[294] Some of her students have won prizes in the Leeds, Tchaikovsky, Rubinstein, Busoni, London, and Geneva competitions. Her instruction books for beginners, *Me and my Piano*, co-authored with pianist Marion Thorpe, sold over two million copies.[295] She has given master classes all over the world.

Together with the Countess of Harewood (later Marion Thorpe), and her late husband, Dr. Geoffrey de Keyser, Dame Fanny founded the Leeds International Pianoforte Competition in 1963, regarded by many as the foremost piano contest. The competition offers winners many UK and international engagements. Prize winners include some of the greatest living pianists, such as Murray Perahia, András Schiff, Mitsuko Uchida, Radu Lupu, Louis Lortie, Piotr Anderszewski, and Peter Donohoe.[296] Now in her nineties, Dame Fanny is still very active as Artistic Director of the competition and chairman of the jury.

As a jury member of international competitions, she is in great demand, and has served on the Tchaikovsky, Dublin, Beethoven, Horowitz, Hamamatsu, Chopin, Bach, Viña del Mar, and UNISA juries, among others. Future engagements as a jury member include the China and Leipzig piano competitions.

In 2001, she received the Distinguished Musician Award conferred by the Incorporated Society of Musicians in the UK. She has received honorary doctorates from the Universities of Leeds, Leeds Metropolitan, and York. She is a Fellow of the Royal College of Music and was Director of the Postgraduate Certificate in Advanced Piano Performance at Leeds College of Music until 2006. In the same year, she was given the Freedom of the City of Leeds in recognition of her contributions.

In the 2005 New Year Honors, she was appointed Dame Commander of the British Empire (DBE).[297] She is President of the Harrogate International Festivals.

*The Leeds International Piano Competition starts with the adjudicators listening to an overwhelming number of entrants. Many will have to be excluded, but the judges are guided by the motto: "when in doubt, never leave out."*

— FANNY WATERMAN

S TARTING OFF AS a cottage industry with a budget of £12,000, the Leeds International Piano Competition has grown to a million-pound operation. Dame Fanny Waterman, founder, Chairman, and Artistic Director of the competition, is also involved with another project to present classical music to some of the poorest children in British schools. In this initiative, she was spurred on by her own background as an impoverished child who won a scholarship to the Royal College of Music. Perhaps a few of the children who hear classical music in her new program will be fired with the same enthusiasm for music she had as a child.

Due to World War II, Dame Fanny was forced to give up a career as a concert pianist and decided to devote her life to music education, in the belief that music is a unifying force against the divisiveness of politics and religion. She believes great music is a source of hope and comfort in times of sadness, and happiness in times of joy. A concert of unaccompanied Bach played by a great cellist or violinist can be a sacred experience, a time when nothing else seems to exist. Schubert's music is also transcendental, concerned with reflections on life and death, and often encapsulated in the miniature form of song.

All the great compositions are emotional representations in sound. Mozart can make you supremely happy, yet within a few bars, the music could be tinged with sadness. His trios and quartets

313

present a vast landscape of feelings, and an avenue for contemplation and self-knowledge.

Today, many children are only interested in pop. In contrast, a great number of Asian children, particularly Chinese, are eager to study the piano or another instrument. The parents, who are heavily involved in their children's education, always attend the music lessons, and they pay close attention to Dame Fanny's instructions. At the end of the lesson she gives the children a mark for their achievements. Then she awards the parents with their own mark! The attitude and assistance of parents is so important that she tends to "choose the parents" rather than the pupils![298]

In her lessons, she likes to emphasize that every note in music is meaningful and students need to listen very carefully. In order to develop this skill, she allocates specific "listening time." One day she noticed a young pupil who was sitting quietly with his mother and younger brother, and staring pensively out of the window. When she asked him what was going on, he announced that he was giving himself listening time.

One of Dame Fanny's students, who became a top barrister, then a judge, and later, Master of the Rolls, attributed much of his success to the skills he learned at the piano, especially the ability to read a music score with precision. Studying music helped him develop good judgment, an eye for detail, and the aspiration for excellence. Many of her pupils are highly gifted even though they are not prodigies. An important part of the talent includes the drive to practice for the sake of the music, not simply to please parents. Such students need supportive parents and fine teaching at an early age.

An extraordinary talent can be recognized immediately. She recalled such an occasion. She had a phone call from an acquaintance, who insisted he was bringing the winner of the forthcoming Leeds competition. The pianist was Murray Perahia,[299] now recognized as one of the greatest living pianists. What were the special characteristics of his playing and indeed, those of other great pianists? The shape of Perahia's phrasing was subtle. Each phrase was slightly different, though related to the previous one, and all of them followed sequentially. Then there was the nuanced method of building a climax, taking into account timing and dynamic range to reflect moods. If a performer only uses three dynamics, such as *mezzo piano* (moderately soft), *mezzo forte* (moderately loud) and *forte* (loud), they are not reaching the soul of the composer.

The acclaimed Russian pianist Sviatoslav Richter[300] was able to produce many dynamic shades between *pianissimo* (very soft) and *piano* (soft). The effect was enticing for the audience, and they often leaned forward, as if to listen more attentively. When he played loudly, it was thunderous but it never sounded hard. Great artists understand that loud and soft are relative, and, like Richter, they have a brilliant conception of the miniscule differences within the dynamic spectrum. A music score is little more than dots and dashes, but their full realization as beautiful music requires great interpreters who can shed light on these symbols. Performers need listeners, but audience numbers have been dropping, and the prospect for classical music in the West looks uncertain. Perhaps the future rests with China.

*Dame Fanny Waterman was interviewed by the author in Sydney, Australia, in November 2012.*

# CONCLUSION

*Classical music could be envisaged as a package of cosmic
DNA coded for human intellect, emotions, and movement.*

M USIC IS AN IMPORTANT PART of cultures as a nonverbal language of emotions, but classical or art music developed complexity and became central to the high arts of Western civilization and, to some extent, an auditory recollection of social history. It may have been elitist in the Christian Church, aristocracy, and salons of Europe, but today appreciation of music is open to everyone, despite reduced funding for music education in many schools.

While most musicians are not activists, many realize they must uphold their tradition as custodians of an art that communicates with immediacy and great emotional and intellectual power. Generally, however, the audience approaches music through emotions rather than intellectual evaluations.

On a micro level, the creative interface between performer and audience involves a reciprocal transfer of emotion, which is most potent during live performance, and stimulated by group electricity in a concert hall. Most of the artists I interviewed felt that a live audience is required for maximum inspiration and communication.

With so much current emphasis on the material side of life, this transmission serves as a reminder of one's inner world. Composers are able to translate sounds into emotional stimuli and when the performer as conduit successfully transmits the energy, a sensitive listener can enjoy a deeply personal, and at times shared, experience of pleasure and excitement, relaxation, reverie, and the safe release of negative or painful emotions. Being in touch with the whole range of emotions, even melancholic, seems beneficial. Much research remains to be done in this field.

The alchemic space between performer and listener also offers a meditative sanctuary for the contemplation of our profound desire for sincerity, love, beauty, freedom, self-knowledge, and spirituality. Not everyone is inclined to transcendental wonder, but many can appreciate the philosophical meaning in the resolution of tension, voyage of a theme, natural world revealed in sound, heroic struggle of Beethoven, or celestial concern of Bach. Journeys with the great compositions are much more than entertainment, relaxation, and simple comfort. As with all great art, participants encounter confrontation, sorrow, and loss. At the same time, art music injects hope and a sense of empowerment, with boundless room for individual response. The contemplative, reflective approach requires active rather than passive listening but can ultimately offer nourishment, and perhaps revelation.

On a macro level, classical music is a positive humanistic force that unifies people in a language intelligible to all, through notation given magical life and reinterpretation by successive generations of performers. A concert is a meaningful, shared experience that promotes group bonding and attentive listening.

Of all genres, chamber music has a special place due to audience intimacy with the composers and performers. As an exercise in freedom, cooperation, and compromise, it is a paradigm for social tolerance and inclusion.

Beneficial aspects of classical music continue to be recognized. Its physiological effects are the basis of use in therapies such as drug and alcohol rehabilitation, and healing for premature babies. Memory for music can be surprisingly well retained and used to stimulate mental capacity and communication in degenerative neurological conditions. Through music, children gain from the development of brain function, dexterity, self-discipline, and social skills. The brilliant El Sistema education project in Venezuela has shown the value of music as a social agent in some of the most impoverished communities, and is emulated in many countries.

When I embarked on this project several years ago, I was seeking answers to questions about music's association with emotions, spirituality, health, social function, and its contribution to civilization. In the past, such a quest would have taken for granted that music was a secure aesthetic that only required reinforcing the current audience base and revealing music to new listeners who might come to love and value the art. But today, classical music is under some threat.

The ideology of relativism, although well intentioned, has contributed to a shift in values and led to the view that all disciplines and ideas can be considered equally valid. This ideology puts art music on a par with other categories of music and therefore the great classical compositions and re-creative musicians have no claim to preeminence.

It is not beyond the realm of possibility that the study and performance of art music could be seriously crushed in two or three generations if it is not protected and given special status. This requires some funding, but above all, the will to promote education and live performance.

There are still a number of excellent music schools, orchestras, conductors, performers, and arts organizations in the West that are prepared to try new ideas, such as incorporation of other arts and music genres. No culture is absolutely pure, and outside influences can be a source of strength, but rather than level all music and neglect the classics, opportunities should be found to appreciate the great masters, past and present.

New possibilities have opened. Some countries in the East, and particularly China, have embraced classical music with enthusiasm and are finding great value in the art, taking up the baton that seems to be languishing in the West.

Modern composers have begun to focus less on intellectual exercises and more on writing for the pleasure and well-being of an audience. Vast networks for rapid dissemination of information and music have also developed through the Internet, especially social media. However, it is not sufficient to promote simple listening; the philosophical aspects of art music need to be aired together with arguments for its defense.

# NOTES

1. "Ludwig van Beethoven Quotes," EQUOTES, accessed February 12, 2015, http://equotes.wikifoundry.com/page/Ludwig+van+Beethoven+Quotes.

2. Philip Ball, *The Music Instinct: How Music Works and Why We Can't Do Without It* (London: Vintage, 2011), p.5.

3. Steven Pinker, *How the Mind Works* (New York: W. W. Norton, 1997), p.528.

4. Joseph Carroll, "Steven Pinker's Cheesecake For The Mind," *Philosophy and Literature* 22 (1998): 478–85.

5. Lambert Zuidervaart, "Theodor W. Adorno," *Stanford Encyclopedia of Philosophy*, ed. Edward N. Zalta (2011), accessed February 12, 2015, http://plato.stanford.edu/entries/adorno.

6. The thesis that there is no absolute truth, only subjective validity, and that all points of view are equally valid.

7. John Carey, *What Good are the Arts?* (NY: Oxford, 2006).

8. Blake Morrison, "What Good Are the Arts?," *The Guardian,* June 11, 2005, accessed February 12, 2015, http://www.guardian.co.uk/books/2005/jun/11/highereducation.news.

9. Music has been banned in Mali (Manuel Toledo, "World stars of Africa Express seek to revive Mali's music industry," *BBC News,* October 14, 2013, accessed February 26, 2015, http://www.bbc.com/news/entertainment-arts-24334791), Syria ("Syria jihadists say music and singing is bad for God," *AFP*, January 20, 2014, accessed February 26, 2015, http://www.your-middleeast.com/news/syria-jihadists-say-music-and-singing-is-bad-for-god_20980), Somalia ("Al-Shabaab bans music like the Taliban," *Freemuse.org*, August 23, 2010, accessed February 26, 2015, http://freemuse.org/archives/1625), Gaza ("Gaza Voices," *BBC News*, August 3, 2007, accessed February 26, 2015, http://news.bbc.co.uk/2/hi/talking_point/6929360.stm) and the Taliban in Afghanistan and Pakistan ("Report: Religious extremism disastrous to music in Pakistan," *Freemuse.org*, March 17, 2014, accessed February 26, 2015, http://freemuse.org/archives/7322). In the UK, radicals are determined to ban music in their own enclaves (Rebecca Camber, "'No porn or prostitution': Islamic extremists set up Sharia law controlled zones in British cities," *Daily Mail*, July 28, 2011, accessed February 26, 2015, http://www.dailymail.co.uk/news/article-2019547/Anjem-Choudary-Islamic-extremists-set-Sharia-law-zones-UK-cities.html) and in some UK schools (Tom Warden, "Private school chief linked to Islam Trojan Horse plot says: Stone all adulterers to death," *Daily Mail*, April 20, 2014, accessed February 12, 2015, http://www.dailymail.co.uk/news/article-2608662/Private-school-chief-linked-Islam-Trojan-Horse-plot-says-Stone-adulterers-death.html).

10. Quoted by Ricardo Muti in *Carlos Kleiber: I am Lost to the World*, directed by Georg Wübbolt (Berlin: C Major Entertainment, 2010).

11. Marcia Adair, "Turning trash into musical instruments for Paraguay's children," *Los Angeles Times*, December 19, 2012, accessed February 12, 2015, http://articles.latimes.com/2012/dec/19/entertainment/la-et-cm-turning-trash-into-musical-instruments-20121214.

12. El Sistema, *El Sistema USA*, accessed February 12, 2015, http://elsistemausa.org/el-sistema/venezuela.

13. "SDYS Community Opus Project to Receive Getty Grant from the League of American Orchestras," *San Diego Youth Symphony and Conservatory*, accessed February 12, 2015, http://archive.constantcontact.com/fs116/1101930228760/archive/1116004977763.html.

14. H. Petsche quoted in Kerstin Wartberg, "What influence does music education have on your child's development?," *www.docstoc.com*, accessed February 12, 2015, http://www.docstoc.com/docs/28258962/What-influence-does-music-education-have-on-your-childs-development.

15. Frances H. Rauscher, Gordon L. Shaw, and Katherine N. Ky, "Listening to Mozart enhances spatial-temporal reasoning: s a neurophysiological basis," *Neuroscience Letters* 185:1 (1995): 44-47.

16. Emily Sohn, "Why Music Makes You Happy," *Discovery News*, January 10, 2011, accessed February 12, 2015, http://news.discovery.com/human/psychology/music-dopamine-happiness-brain-110110.htm.

17. Ibid.

18. Liila Taruffi, Stefan Koelsch, "The Paradox of Music-Evoked Sadness: An Online Survey," *PLoS ONE* 9(10) (2014): e110490, accessed March 27, 2015, doi:10.1371/journal.pone.0110490.

19. "Vladimir Ashkenazy Conductor/Piano," Harrison Parrott, accessed February 12, 2015, http://www.harrisonparrott.com/artist/profile/vladimir-ashkenazy.

20. "Vladimir Ashkenazy," *Prominent Figures in History*, accessed February 12, 2015, http://promfih.com/vladimir-ashkenazy.html.

21. "Chief Conductor & Artistic Director Alexander Briger," Australian World Orchestra, accessed February 12, 2015, http://www.australianworldorchestra.com.au/about-us/artistic-direction-chief-conductor.

22. "Mozart—Sinfonia Concertante in E flat for violin and viola," *Classic FM*, http://www.classicfm.com/composers/mozart/music/wolfgang-amadeus-mozart-sinfonia-concertante-e-fla/.

23. Richard Wagner, The Ring of the Nibelung, Suite arranged by Alexander Briger.

24. The Ring Cycle, accessed February 12, 2015, http://theringcycle.com.

25. "Ride of the Valkyries," *last.fm*, accessed February 12, 2015, http://www.last.fm/music/Richard+Wagner/_/Ride+of+the+Valkyries.

26. Roger Dettmer, "Dmitry Shostakovich, Symphony No. 9 in E flat Major, Op. 70," *ALLMUSIC*, accessed February 12, 2015, http://www.allmusic.com/composition/symphony-no-9-in-e-flat-major-op-70-mc0002366978.

27. "Sir Charles Mackerras," *last.fm*, accessed February 12, 2015, http://www. last.fm/music/Sir+Charles+Mackerras/+wiki.

28. "Beethoven's Symphony No. 5, The Destiny Symphony," *All About Ludwig van Beethoven*, accessed February 22, 2015, http://all-about-beethoven.com/symphony5.html.

29. "Mozart – Symphony No. 40 in G Minor," Classic FM, accessed February 12, 2015, http://www.classicfm.com/composers/mozart/music/symphony-no-40-g-minor.

30. Scott Gordon, "Schiller – Freedom's Hymn" *Harper's Magazine*, November 9, 2008, accessed February 12, 2015, http://harpers.org/blog/2008/11/schiller-freedoms-hymn/.

31. "Madama Butterfly," metopera, accessed February 12, http://www.metoperafamily.org/metopera/history/stories/synopsis.aspx?customid=8.

32. "Sergei Rachmaninoff plays his Piano Concerto No. 2," YouTube video, 9:34, posted by "bwv1064," August 30, 2008, accessed February 12, 2015, http://www.youtube.com/watch?v=x8l37utZxMQ.

33. Tony Duggan, "The Mahler Symphonies," *MusicWeb International*, accessed February 13, 2015, http://www.musicweb-international.com/Mahler/mahler9.htm.

34. *Live Music Now*, accessed February 13, 2015, http://www.livemusicnow.org.uk.

35. George Dvorsky, "Can Music Be More Effective Than Drugs?" *www.io9.com*, accessed February 13, 2015, http://io9.com/can-music-be-more-effective-than-drugs-465249779.

36. "Mass in B Minor – Johann Sebastian Bach," www.choirs.org.uk, accessed February 13, 2015, http://www.choirs.org.uk/prognotes/Bach%20B%20minor%20mass.htm.

37. James Harley, "Luigi Nono," *ALLMUSIC*, accessed February 13, 2015, http://www.allmusic.com/artist/luigi-nono-mn0001196376.

38. Maev Kennedy "Embellished Mozart manuscript uncovered," *The Guardian*, October 1, 2011, accessed February 13, 2015, http://www.guardian.co.uk/music/2011/sep/30/embellished-mozart-manuscript-uncovered.

39. "Guy Noble," *Adelaide Symphony Orchestra Plays James Bond*, accessed February 15, 2015, http://www.aso.com.au/__files/f/219091/Click_here_to_download_or_read_the_program_notes.pdf.

40. "Nabucco," The Metropolitan Opera, accessed February 15, 2015, http://www.metopera.org/metopera/season/synopsis/nabucco?customid=17.

41. Gerard McBurney, "Dmitri Shostakovich—Symphony No.7 in C Major 'Leningrad,'" Boosey & Hawkes, accessed February 29, 2015, http://www.boosey.com/cr/music/Dmitri-Shostakovich-Symphony-No-7-in-C-major-Leningrad/7103.

42. "Schroeder," *Peanuts*, http://www.peanuts.com/characters/schroeder/#.VOCaNVOOG8h, accessed February 16, 2015.

43. Linda Cantoni, "The Marriage of Figaro," Regina Opera, accessed February 16, 2015, http://www.reginaopera.org/figaro.htm.

44. "Alexander Gavrylyuk," Askonas Holt, accessed February 16, 2015, http://www.askonasholt.co.uk/artists/instrumentalists/piano/alexander-gavrylyuk.

45. Konstantin Stanislavski, *My Life in Art* (London: Taylor & Francis, 1952).

46. Quartet No. 13 in B-Flat Minor for Strings, Op. 138, *Shostakovich Quartets,* accessed February 16, 2015, http://www.shostakovichquartets.com/quartets/page/quartet-no-13.

47. "New Research Provides the First Solid Evidence That the Study of Music Promotes Intellectual Development," *sciencedaily.com,* accessed February 16, 2015, http://www.sciencedaily.com/releases/2004/08/040820082332.htm.

48. "How Classical Music Can Reduce Crime, Benefit Your Mood and Increase Your Spending," *SixWise.com,* accessed February 16, 2015, http://www.sixwise.com/newsletters/06/10/05/how-classical-music-can-reduce-crime-benefit-your-mood-and-increase-your-spending.htm.

49. "Angela Hewitt," Harrison Parrott, accessed February 16, 2015, http://www.harrisonparrott.com/artist/profile/angela-hewitt.

50. The independent musical lines or melodies that move relative to each other in counterpoint.

51. "Ludwig van Beethoven, Sonata No. 31 in A-Flat Major, Op. 110," Freebase, accessed February 16, 2015, http://www.freebase.com/m/085ypw.

52. "El Sistema," El Sistema USA, accessed March 8, 2015, http://www.elsistemausa.org/about-el-sistema.htm.

53. "Polymaths: 20 Living Examples," Intelligent Life, accessed March 8, 2015, http://moreintelligentlife.com/blog/ed-cumming/hunting-modern-polymaths.

54. "Stephen Hough," Harrison Parrott, accessed February 16, 2015, http://www.harrisonparrott.co.uk/artist/profile/stephen-hough.

55. Evgeny Kissin, accessed February 16, 2015, http://evgenykissinfansite.co.uk/biography.

56. "Sviatoslav Richter," arkivmusic.com, accessed February 16, 2015, http://www.arkivmusic.com/classical/Name/Sviatoslav-Richter/Performer/18855-2.

57. Robert Cummings, "Ludwig van Beethoven Piano Sonata No. 32 in C Minor, Op. 111," *ALLMUSIC,* accessed February 16, 2015, http://www.allmusic.com/composition/piano-sonata-no-32-in-c-minor-op-111-mc0002365634.

58. "Beethoven's Moonlight Sonata," *All About Ludwig van Beethoven,* accessed February 16, 2015, http://www.all-about-beethoven.com/moonsonata.html.

59. Robert Schumann, "Carnaval: Scènes mignonnes sur quatre notes, Op.9," *Classical Archives,* accessed February 16, 2015, http://www.classicalarchives.com/work/25359.html#tvf=tracks&tv=about.

60. Robert Schumann, "Kreisleriana, Op.16," *Classical Archives,* accessed February 16, 2015, http://www.classicalarchives.com/work/25407.html#tvf=tracks&tv=about.

61. "Modest Mussorgsky, Pictures at an Exhibition," *Classical Archives,* accessed February 16, 2015, http://www.classicalarchives.com/work/91268.html#tvf=tracks&tv=about.

62. "Franz Liszt, Piano Sonata in B Minor, S.178," *Classical Archives,* accessed February 16, 2015, http://www.classicalarchives.com/work/147272.html#tvf=tracks&tv=about.

63. "Josef Hofmann," *Naxos,* accessed February 16, 2015, http://www.naxos.com/person/Josef_Hofmann_3657/3657.htm.

64. Robert Cummings, "Anton Rubinstein," *ALLMUSIC,* accessed February 16, 2015, http://www.allmusic.com/artist/anton-rubinstein-mn0000683409/biography

65. "Nikolai Medtner," *Piano Society,* accessed February 16, 2015, http://pianosociety.com/cms/index.php?section=890.

66. James M. Ketter, "Dmitri Shostakovich, Concerto No. 1 in C Minor for Piano, Trumpet, and Strings, Opus 35," San Francisco Symphony, accessed February 16, 2015, http://www.sfsymphony.org/Watch-Listen-Learn/Read-Program-Notes/Program-Notes/SHOSTAKOVICH-Concerto-No-1-in-C-minor-for-Piano,-T.aspx.

67. "Ludwig van Beethoven, Piano Sonata No.23 in F Minor, Op.57 (Appassionata)," *Classical Archives,* accessed February 16, 2015, http://www.classicalarchives.com/work/3997.html#tvf=tracks&tv=about.

68. "Vladimir Lenin is Dead," *Marxists.org,* accessed February 16, 2015, http://www.marxists.org/archive/gorky-maxim/1924/01/x01.htm.

69. "Paul Lewis," Ingpen & Williams, accessed February 16, 2015, https://iw.overturehq.com/mediapage/20004888/paul-lewis.

70. Tadmor, Tetlock, & Peng, 2009, quoted in Seth J. Schwartz and Jennifer B. Unger, "Biculturalism and Context: "What is Biculturalism, and When is it Adaptive?" *Human Development* 53(1) (2010): 26–32.

71. Alfred Brendel, accessed February 16, 2015, http://www.alfredbrendel.com.

72. "Richard Strauss, Ein Heldenleben," LAPHIL, accessed February 16, 2015, http://www.laphil.com/philpedia/music/ein-heldenleben-richard-strauss.

73. Ludwig van Beethoven, Piano Sonata No. 29 in B flat Major, Op. 106, known as the *Große Sonate für das Hammerklavier.*

74. Tom Service, "A guide to György Kurtág's music," *The Guardian,* March 12, 2013, accessed February 16, 2015, http://www.guardian.co.uk/music/tom-serviceblog/2013/mar/12/contemporary-music-guide-gyorgy-kurtag.

75. Rovi Staff, "Erik Satie," *ALLMUSIC,* accessed February 16, 2015, http://www.allmusic.com/artist/erik-satie-mn0000675185/biography.

76. "Alexander Scriabin," Scriabin Society of America, accessed February 16, 2015, http://www.scriabinsociety.com/biography.html.

77. Ibid.

78. "Franz Schubert, *Die Schöne Müllerin,* D.795," Franz Peter Schubert, accessed February 16, 2015, http://www.franzpeterschubert.com/die_schone_mullerin.html.

79. Robert Cummings, "Franz Schubert, Piano Sonata No. 20 in A Major, D. 959," *ALLMUSIC,* accessed February 16, 2015, http://www.allmusic.com/composition/piano-sonata-no-20-in-a-major-d-959-mc0002370927.

80. Robert Cummings, "Ludwig van Beethoven, Piano Sonata No. 32 in C Minor, Op. 111," *ALLMUSIC*, accessed February 16, 2015, http://www.allmusic.com/composition/piano-sonata-no-32-in-c-minor-op-111-mc0002365634.

81. "Ludwig van Beethoven Symphony No. 4 in B flat Major, Op. 60," *ALLMUSIC*, accessed February 16, 2015, http://www.allmusic.com/composition/symphony-no-4-in-b-flat-major-op-60-mc0002366807.

82. "Aleksandar Madžar," *Festival Resonances in Belgium*, accessed February 16, 2015, http://www.festival-resonances.be/artist/aleksandar-madzar.

83. "Aleksandar Madžar," medici.tv, accessed February 16, 2015, http://www.medici.tv/#!/aleksandar-madzar.

84. "Hugo von Hofmannsthal," *art directory*, accessed February 16, 2015, http://www.hofmannsthal-von-hugo.com.

85. "Synopsis: Der Rosenkavalier," The Metropolitan Opera, accessed February 16, 2015, http://www.metoperafamily.org/metopera/history/stories/synopsis.aspx?customid=21.

86. "Synopsis: Ariadne auf Naxos," The Metropolitan Opera, accessed February 16, 2015, http://www.metoperafamily.org/metopera/history/stories/synopsis.aspx?customid=34.

87. "Alex Henery," zoominfo, accessed February 16, 2015, http://www.zoominfo.com/p/Alex-Henery/690762556.

88. "Kees Boersma," *Musica Viva Festival 2011*, accessed February 16, 2015, http://www.abc.net.au/classic/viva/artists/kees-boersma.htm.

89. Lauren Ronda, "Explaining Beethoven's Music: 7th Symphony, Allegretto," *laurenrondaHub*, accessed February 16, 2015, http://laurenronda.hubpages.com/hub/Explaining-Beethovens-7th-symphony-Allegretto.

90. Wayne Reisig, "Anton Bruckner, Symphony No. 7 in E Major, WAB 107," *ALLLMUSIC*, accessed February 16, 2015, http://www.allmusic.com/composition/symphony-no-7-in-e-major-wab-107-mc0002368842.

91. Roger Dettmer, "Franz Joseph Haydn, Symphony No. 100 in G Major ("Military") H. 1/100," *ALLMUSIC*, accessed February 16, 2015, http://www.allmusic.com/composition/symphony-no-100-in-g-major-military-h-1-100-mc0002379964.

92. "Lake Ice: (Missed Tales No. 1) by Mary Finsterer," Australian Music Centre, accessed February 16, 2015, http://www.australianmusiccentre.com.au/work/finsterer-mary-lake-ice.

93. "Mary Finsterer," Mary Finsterer, accessed February 16, 2015, http://maryfinsterer.com.

94. String Quintet in C Major (D. 956, Op. posth. 163). See "Schubert Most Sublime: The String Quintet in C," *nprmusic*, accessed February 16, 2015, http://www.npr.org/2011/07/18/111631425/schubert-most-sublime-the-string-quintet-in-c.

95. "Ole Böhn," Alice and Eleonore Schoenfeld International String Society, accessed February 16, 2015, http://schoenfeldcompetition.com/en/ole.php.

96. "Music Therapy for Drug and Alcohol Treatment," *SoberRecovery*, accessed February 16, 2015, http://www.soberrecovery.com/drug-rehabilitation-al-

cohol-treatment/addiction-treatment/addiction-treatment-methods/music-therapy-for-drug-and-alcohol-treatment.html.

97. Elliott Carter, accessed February 16, 2015, http://elliottcarter.com.

98. Krzysztof Penderecki, accessed February 16, 2015, http://www.krzysztof-penderecki.eu/en/3/0/2/Brief%20Biography.

99. "*Don Giovanni*," The Metropolitan Opera, accessed February 16, 2015, http://www.metopera.org/metopera/season/synopsis/don-giovanni?customid=14.

100. "*Rigoletto*," The Metropolitan Opera, accessed February 16, 2015, http://www.metoperafamily.org/metopera/history/stories/synopsis.aspx?-customid=134.

101. "Edward Dusinberre," Janklow & Nesbit UK, accessed February 16, 2015, http://www.janklowandnesbit.co.uk/edward-dusinberre.

102. National Youth Orchestra of Great Britain, accessed February 16, 2015, http://www.nyo.org.uk.

103. "Tolstoy's *Kreutzer Sonata*," British Library, accessed February 16, 2015, http://www.bl.uk/reshelp/findhelplang/russian/tolstoycentenary/kreutzer-sonata/kreutzersonata.html.

104. "Takács Quartet, Beethoven, Große Fuge, op. 133," YouTube video, 14:28, posted by "My channel – that sums it up," October 14, 2010, https://www.youtube.com/watch?v=xjUh11EPGcM.

105. "Franz Schubert, String Quartet No. 15 in G Major, D. 887," *earsense—chamber music database*, accessed February 16, 2015, http://earsense.org/chamberbase/works/detail/?pkey=605.

106. "Ludwig van Beethoven, String Quartet No. 15 in A Minor, Op. 132," *earsense—chamber music database*, accessed February 16, 2015, http://www.earsense.org/blog/?p=68.

107. Ted Libbey, "Pastoral Passion: Ravel's 'Daphnis and Chloe,'" *nprmusic*, accessed February 16, 2015, http://www.npr.org/2011/07/18/106615205/pastoral-passion-ravels-daphnis-and-chloe.

108. "Grieg, Piano Concerto in A Minor, Op. 16," *Favorite Classical Composers*, accessed February 16, 2015, http://www.favorite-classical-composers.com/grieg-piano-concerto.html.

109. "Bartók: The 6 String Quartets / Takács Quartet," ArkivMusic, accessed February 16, 2015, http://www.arkivmusic.com/classical/album.jsp?album_id=6012.

110. "Takács to Premiere Vine's Fourth Quartet (Sep 2, 2004)," Faber Music, accessed February 16, 2015, http://www.fabermusic.com/news/tak%C3%A1cs-to-premiere-vines-fourth-quartet-839.

111. Rovi Staff, "Franz Schubert, String Quartet No. 14 in D Minor ('Death and the Maiden'), D. 810," *ALLMUSIC*, accessed February 16, 2015, http://www.allmusic.com/composition/string-quartet-no-14-in-d-minor-death-and-the-maiden-d-810-mc0002370327.

112. "Donald Grant," Elias String Quartet, accessed March 20, 2015, http://eli-asstringquartet.com/about-2/donald/.

113. Beethoven, String Quartet No. 15 in A Minor, Op. 132.

114. Ted Libbey, "Schubert Most Sublime: The String Quintet in C," *nprmu-sic*, accessed March 20, 2015, http://www.npr.org/2011/07/18/111631425/schubert-most-sublime-the-string-quintet-in-c.

115. "Henri Dutilleux," *Bach Cantatas*, accessed February 16, 2015, http://www.bach-cantatas.com/Lib/Dutilleux-Henri.htm.

116. The Elias String Quartet performed their last concert in the Beethoven Project on March 7, 2015.

117. Tully Potter, "Exploring the Beethoven Quartets on disc: Many Paths to Nirvana," Elias String Quartet Beethoven Project, accessed February 17, 2015, http://thebeethovenproject.com/exploring-the-beethoven-quartets-on-disc-many-paths-to-nirvana.

118. Martin Saving, "How Fast Shall We Play?" Elias String Quartet Beethoven Project, accessed February 17, 2015, http://thebeethovenproject.com/how-fast-shall-we-play.

119. Beethoven, String Quartet No. 15 in A Minor, Op. 132.

120. Op. 127: String Quartet No. 12 in E-flat Major, Op. 130: String Quartet No. 13 in B-flat Major, Op. 131: String Quartet No. 14 in C-sharp Minor, Op. 132: String Quartet No. 15 in A Minor, Op. 133: *Große Fuge* in B-flat Major for string quartet, originally the finale to Op. 130, Op. 135: String Quartet No. 16 in F Major.

121. Four movements: I. Allegro II. Molto Adagio. Si tratta questo pezzo con molto di sentimento III. Allegretto – Maggiore (Thème russe) IV. Finale. Presto. John Palmer, "Ludwig van Beethoven, String Quartet No. 8 in E Minor ('Rasumovsky No. 2'), Op. 59, No. 2," *ALLMUSIC*, accessed February 17, 2015, http://www.allmusic.com/composition/string-quartet-no-8-in-e-minor-rasumovsky-no-2-op-59-2-mc0002438318.

122. The three "Rasumovsky" Quartets are comprised of String Quartets No. 7 in F Major, Op. 59, No. 1, No. 8 in E Minor, Op. 59, No. 2, and No. 9 in C Major, Op. 59, No. 3.

123. "Clive Greensmith, Cello," Tokyo String Quartet, accessed February 17, 2015, http://www.tokyoquartet.com/artist.php?view=bio&bid=2025.

124. "Tokyo String Quartet," Harmonia Mundi artists, accessed February 17, 2015, http://www.harmoniamundi.com/mobile/pages/Artiste01.php?lang=UK&id=2037.

125. Eric Siblin, "How Bach's Cello Suites changed Eric Siblin's life," *The Guardian*, January 16, 2010, accessed February 17, http://www.guardian.co.uk/culture/2010/jan/16/bach-cello-suites-eric-siblin.

126. Pru Allington-Smith, "Mental health of children with learning disabilities," BJPsych 12 (2006): 130–38.

127. Jennifer Stephenson, "Music Therapy and the Education of Students with Severe Disabilities," *Education and Training in Developmental Disabilities* 41:3 (2006): 290-99.

128. El Sistema, El Sistema USA.

129. Roger Dettmer, "Ludwig van Beethoven, Symphony No. 3 in E flat Major ('Eroica'), Op. 55," *ALLMUSIC*, accessed February 12, 2015, http://www.allmusic.com/composition/symphony-no-3-in-e-flat-major-eroica-op-55-mc0002396628.

130. "Béla Bartók," Boosey & Hawkes, accessed February 12, 2015, http://www.boosey.com/composer/b%C3%A9la+bart%C3%B3k

131. Beethoven, String Quartet No. 15 in A Minor, Op. 132.

132. Rovi Staff, "Ludwig van Beethoven, Symphony No. 9 in D Minor ('Choral'), Op. 125," *ALLMUSIC*, accessed February 16, 2015, http://www.allmusic.com/artist/ludwig-van-beethoven-mn0000536126.

133. Ted Libbey, "Quiet Anguish in Elgar's Cello Concerto," *nprmusic*, accessed February 17, 2015, http://www.npr.org/2011/07/18/120248259/quiet-anguish-in-elgars-cello-concerto.

134. "Felix Mendelssohn," *earsense—chamber music database*, accessed February 17, 2015, http://www.earsense.org/chamberbase/works/detail/?pkey=650.

135. "Joseph Haydn, The Creation," *Music with Ease*, accessed February 17, 2015, http://www.musicwithease.com/haydn-creation.html.

136. "Joseph Haydn: The Creation," Classic FM, accessed February 17, 2015, http://www.classicfm.com/composers/haydn/music/creation.

137. Joseph Haydn, Quartet No. 36 in B-flat Major, Op. 50, No. 1.

138. Franz Schubert, *Die Schöne Müllerin*, D.795.

139. Gabriel Fauré, *Papillon*, for cello and piano, Op.77.

140. "Amihai Grosz," Victoria Artists Management, accessed February 16, 2015, http://www.victoria-artists.com/soloist/Amihai-Grosz.php.

141. West-Eastern Divan Orchestra, accessed February 16, 2015, http://www.west-eastern-divan.org.

142. Libbey, "Schubert Most Sublime."

143. Guy Dixon, "New Tafelmusik honour is out of this world," The Globe and Mail, April 18 2009, accessed April 1, 2015, http://www.theglobeandmail.com/arts/new-tafelmusik-honour-is-out-of-this-world/article20458322.

144. "Alison Mackay: Double Bass," Tafelmusik, accessed March 7, 2015, http://www.tafelmusik.org/about/orchestra/bios/alison-mackay.

145. "Tafelmusik's Alison Mackay named winner of 2013 Betty Webster Award," Tafelmusik, accessed March 7, 2015, http://www.tafelmusik.org/media-room/media-releases/releases/tafelmusiks-alison-mackay-named-winner-2013-betty-webster-award.

146. "*Baroque Adventure: The Quest for Arundo Donax*," Tafelmusik, http://www.tafelmusik.org/shop/recordings/baroque-adventure-quest-arundo-donax.

147. "Tafelmusik's Alison Mackay named winner of 2013 Betty Webster Award," Tafelmusik, accessed March 7, 2015, http://www.tafelmusik.org/media-room/media-releases/releases/tafelmusiks-alison-mackay-named-winner-2013-betty-webster-award.

148. *"Metamorphoses* by Ovid," *The Internet Classics Archive*, accessed March 7, 2015, http://classics.mit.edu/Ovid/metam.html.

149. Alison Mackay, "The Galileo Project: Music of the Spheres Programme Notes," Tafelmusik, accessed March 7, 2015, http://www.tafelmusik.org/downloads/ Media/Galileo/Galileo_programme_notes.pdf.

150. "Tafelmusik House of Dreams," *Musica Viva Australia*, accessed March 7, 2015, www.musicaviva.com.au/downloads/file/PublicDocuments/ 2015TafelmusikWeb.pdf.

151. "Bach's Leipzig 1725–1750,"baroquemusic.org, accessed March 7, 2015, http://www.baroquemusic.org/bachleipzig.html.

152. "The Book of One Thousand and One Nights," *New World Encyclopedia*, accessed March 12, 2015, http://www.newworldencyclopedia.org/entry/The_Book_ of_One_Thousand_and_One_Nights.

153. Aaron Green, "Antonio Vivaldi's Four Seasons: Notes, Historical Information, and Sonnets,"About.com, accessed March 7, 2015, http://classicalmusic.about.com/od/baroqueperiod/ss/fourseasons.htm.

154. Joshua J Mark, "Silk Road," *Ancient History Encyclopedia*, March 28, 2014, accessed March 12, 2015, http://www.ancient.eu/Silk_Road.

155. "Pipa—a Chinese lute or guitar," Liu Feng, featured artist of Philmultic, accessed March 7, 2015, http://www.philmultic.com/pipa.html.

156. Megan Romer, "Oud," About.com, accessed March 7, 2015, http://worldmusic. about.com/od/instruments/g/Oud.htm.

157. "Raga," *Encyclopedia Britannica*, accessed March 7, 2015, http://www.britannica.com/EBchecked/topic/489518/raga.

158. "Sarangi," *Encyclopedia Britannica*, accessed March 7, 2015, http://www.britannica.com/EBchecked/topic/523956/sarangi.

159. "Throat Singing," *National Geographic* video, 1:25, 2008, accessed March 7, 2015, http://video.nationalgeographic.com/video/exploreorg/inuit-throat-singing-eorg.

160. "Thomas Babington Macaulay, Baron Macaulay," *Encyclopedia Britannica*, accessed March 7, 2015, http://www.britannica.com/EBchecked/topic/ 353722/Thomas-Babington-Macaulay-Baron-Macaulay.

161. Virgil, *The Aeneid*, translated by John Dryden, *The Internet Classics Archive*, accessed March 7, 2015, http://classics.mit.edu/Virgil/aeneid.html.

162. Christian-Pierre La Marca, accessed February 16, 2015, http://www.christianpierrelamarca.com/about.

163. Trio Imàge, "Trio II in One Movement, for Violin, Cello and Piano" by Mauricio Kagel on *Mauricio Kagel: Piano Trios I–III*, recorded September 2011 and April 2012, CAvi-music, compact disc.

164. Blair Johnston, "Franz Schubert Piano Trio No. 2 in E flat Major, D. 929 (Op. 100)," *ALLMUSIC*, accessed February 17, 2015, http://www.allmusic.com/ composition/piano-trio-no-2-in-e-flat-major-d-929-op-100-mc0002368068.

165. Blair Johnston, "Arnold Schoenberg, *Verklärte Nacht* ('Transfigured Night') for string sextet, Op. 4," *ALLMUSIC*, accessed February 17, 2015, http://www.

allmusic.com/composition/verkl%C3%A4rte-nacht-for-string-sextet-op-4-mc0002370233.

166. Brentano Quartet, accessed February 18, 2015, http://brentanoquartet.com.

167. "Nina Lee, cello," Brentano Quartet, accessed February 18, 2015, http://brentanoquartet.com/about/nina-lee.

168. "Oscar Mayer Commercial 1973," YouTube video, 0:31, posted by "ddrower," January 20, 2007, accessed February 18, 2015, http://www.youtube.com/watch?v=rmPRHJd3uHI.

169. The Juilliard School, accessed February 18, 2015, www.juilliard.edu.

170. Robert Cummings, "Ludwig van Beethoven, String Quartet No. 13 in B flat Major, Op. 130," *ALLMUSIC*, accessed February 18, 2015, http://www.allmusic.com/composition/string-quartet-no-13-in-b-flat-major-op-130-mc0002363315.

171. Beethoven, String Quartet No. 15 in A Minor, Op. 132.

172. "Peter Rejto," zoominfo, accessed February 18, 2015, http://www.zoominfo.com/p/Peter-Rejto/13072350.

173. Although often modified and distorted, basic sonata form consists of two themes in the exposition, followed by a development and then a recapitulation and coda, a little tag on the end. There are similarities here with a story that starts with a protagonist and an antagonist, followed by conflict and a resolution. It affects us because we are responding to the story. The recapitulation looks back to the beginning and puts us in touch with the feelings of relief in going home. The last movement is usually fast, in order to leave people in a positive frame of mind (Peter Rejto).

174. Aspen Music Festival, accessed February 18, 2015, http://www.aspenmusicfestival.com.

175. In music theory, the intervals between notes are considered either consonant, which sound pleasant, or dissonant, which sound unpleasant. The tension caused by a dissonant interval causes a longing to resolve it in a consonant interval.

176. "Ludwig van Beethoven, String Quartet No. 16 in F Major, Op. 135," *earsense—chamber music database*, accessed February 18, 2015, http://earsense.org/chamberbase/works/detail/?pkey=570.

177. "Mstislav Rostropovich Quotes," Brainy Quote, accessed February 18, 2015, http://www.brainyquote.com/quotes/authors/m/mstislav_rostropovich.html.

178. Tom Huizenga,"A Visitor's Guide To Bach's 'St. Matthew Passion,'" *nprmusic*, accessed February 16, 2015, http://www.npr.org/blogs/deceptivecadence/2014/04/17/298773771/a-visitors-guide-to-bachs-st-matthew-passion.

179. A musical idea is presented initially. A second idea follows that may have nearly or exactly the same melodic or rhythmic sequence. However, the third is often significantly different (though still recognizable as "similar" to the initial fragment) and moves the composition toward new material. This simple "rule" has profound consequences. It reinforces the idea that the brain seeks out patterns, (hence the second nearly exact repetition), but can become easily bored, there-

fore the necessity that the third "repetition" be different. In baroque music, there is not much evidence of this type of patterning. The one, two, three rule is flagrantly violated! However, as music evolved it does seem that this rule was applied either consciously or unconsciously by composers. The performer needs to take great pains not to become predictable or fully anticipated. The one, two, three rule easily facilitates this requirement (Peter Rejto).

180. "Pieter Wispelwey, Cello," ArtsManagement, accessed February 18, 2015, http://www.artsmanagement.com.au/main/?c=sb-plugin-gocontacts&sb-plugin-gocontacts_task=view_item_details&id=30014.

181. Blair Sanderson, "Pablo Casals, J.S. Bach: Six Suites for Solo Cello," *ALLMUSIC*, accessed February 18, 2015, http://www.allmusic.com/album/js-bach-six-suites-for-solo-cello-mw0001813352.

182. Ibid.

183. Diana Doherty, Oboe, ArtsManagement, accessed February 18, 2015, http://www.artsmanagement.com.au/main/?c=sb-plugin-gocontacts&sb-plugin-gocontacts_task=view_item_details&id=30010.

184. "Franz Haydn Oboe Concerto in C Major, H. 7g/C1 (doubtful)," *ALLMUSIC*, accessed February 18, 2015, http://www.allmusic.com/composition/oboe-concerto-in-c-major-h-7g-c1-doubtful-mc0002357258.

185. "Fantasia on a Theme by Thomas Tallis (1910)," *Classical Net*, accessed February 18,2015, http://www.classical.net/music/comp.lst/works/v-w/tallisfantasia.php.

186. "*Dialogues des Carmélites*," The Metropolitan Opera, accessed February 18, 2015, http://www.metopera.org/metopera/history/stories/synopsis.aspx?customid=38.

187. "Classical from the Beethovenfest—Poulenc: Oboe Sonata," *Deutsche Welle (DW)*, accessed February 18, 2015, http://www.dw.de/classical-from-the-beethovenfest-poulenc-oboe-sonata/a-16242459.

188. Roger Dettmer, "Sergey Rachmaninov, Piano Concerto No. 2 in C Minor, Op. 18," *ALLMUSIC*, accessed February 18, 2015, http://www.allmusic.com/composition/piano-concerto-no-2-in-c-minor-op-18-mc0002386092.

189 A musical key refers to the scale on which a composition is based.

190. "Fibonacci Numbers and The Golden Section in Art, Architecture and Music," Fibonacci Numbers and the Golden Section, accessed March 31, 2015, http://www.maths.surrey.ac.uk/hosted-sites/R.Knott/Fibonacci/fibInArt.html.

191. John Mangum, "Johann Sebastian Bach, Sonata in B Minor for Flute, Harpsichord, and Continuo, Bwv 1030," LAPHIL, accessed February 18, 2015, http://www.laphil.com/philpedia/music/sonata-b-minor-for-flute-harpsichord-and-continuo-bwv-1030-johann-sebastian-bach.

192. Michael Rodman, "Ludwig van Beethoven, Violin Concerto in D Major, Op. 61," *ALLMUSIC*, accessed February 18, 2015, http://www.allmusic.com/composition/violin-concerto-in-d-major-op-61-mc0002357517.

193. Kathryn Meyrick, *The Musical Life of Gustav Mole*, Swindon, UK: Child's Play, 2006.

194. Vikram Seth, *An Equal Music: A Novel*, New York: Vintage,2000.

195. "Béla Bartók, Concerto for Orchestra," *Classical Notes*, accessed March 24, 2015, http://www.classicalnotes.net/classics/bartok.html.

196. Michael Rodman, "Robert Schumann, Piano Concerto in A Minor, Op. 54," *ALLMUSIC*, accessed February 18, 2015, http://www.allmusic.com/composition/piano-concerto-in-a-minor-op-54-mc0002357317

197. James Zychowicz, "Richard Strauss, Oboe Concerto in D Major, Op. 144 (TrV 292, AV 144)," *ALLMUSIC*, accessed February 18, 2015, http://www.allmusic.com/composition/oboe-concerto-in-d-major-oop-144-trv-292-av-144-mc0002371246.

198. "Der Rosenkavalier," The Metropolitan Opera, accessed March 24, 2015, http://www.metopera.org/metopera/season/synopsis/rosenkavalier?customid=789.

199 Allen Schrott, "Joaquín Rodrigo, Concierto de Aranjuez, for guitar & orchestra," *ALLMUSIC*, accessed February 18, 2015, http://www.allmusic.com/composition/concierto-de-aranjuez-for-guitar-amp-orchestra-mc0002391137.

200. "Romeo e Giulietta (1968) di Franco Zeffirelli. Musica di Nino Rota," YouTube video, 6;20, posted by "Caribuk," January 25,2012, accessed February 18, 2015, http://www.youtube.com/watch?v=bSFEkWOFZKs.

201. Yvonne Kenny, accessed February 18, 2015, http://www.yvonnekenny.com/main.html.

202. "Autistic, Blind Man a Musical Savant," ABC News video, 2:47, September 28, 2011, accessed February 18, 2015, http://abcnews.go.com/WNT/video/autistic-blind-man-a-musical-savant-14626121.

203. Merry Makers Australia, accessed February 18, 2015, http://www.merrymakers.com.au.

204. Allen Schrott, "Benjamin Britten, *Peter Grimes*, opera, Op. 33," *ALLMUSIC*, accessed February 18, 2015, http://www.allmusic.com/composition/peter-grimes-opera-op-33-mc0002362842.

205. "Les Six," *ALLMUSIC*, accessed February 18, 2015, http://www.allmusic.com/blog/post/les-six-2.

206. "Gustav Mahler, Symphony No. 4 in G Major," *Classical Notes*, accessed February 18, 2015, http://www.classicalnotes.net/classics/mahler4.html.

207. Karajan.org, accessed February 18, 2015, http://www.karajan.org/jart/prj3/karajan/main.jart?reserve-mode=active&rel=en.

208. Roy Brewer, "Roger Norrington Biography," *ALLMUSIC*, accessed February 18, 2015, http://www.allmusic.com/artist/roger-norrington-mn0000041799/biography.

209. Chris Morrison, "Ralph Vaughan Williams, Serenade to Music ('How sweet the moonlight sleeps upon this bank!') for 16 soloists (or soloists & chorus) & orchestra," *ALLMUSIC*, accessed February 18, 2015, http://www.allmusic.com/composition/serenade-to-music-how-sweet-the-moonlight-sleeps-upon-this-bank!-for-16-soloists-or-soloists-chorus-orchestra-mc0002369083.

210. "Maria Callas," *Biography*, accessed February 19, 2015, http://www.biography.com/people/maria-callas-9235435.

211. Biography, amarcord, accessed February 19, 2015, http://www.amarcord.de/en/about.php#.VDI9L-ecZ0E.

212. Ibid.

213. Biography supplied by Daniel Knauft. amarcord, vocal ensemble, Colbert Artists Management, accessed March 31, 2015, http://www.colbertartists.com/ArtistBio.asp?ID=amarcord.

214. "St. Thomas Boys Choir," Thomas Kirche, accessed February 20, 2015, http://www.thomaskirche.org/r-st-thomas-boys-choir.html.

215. Tom Service, "Carlo Gesualdo: composer or crazed psychopath?" *The Guardian*, March 19, 2010, accessed February 20, 2015, http://www.guardian.co.uk/music/tomserviceblog/2010/mar/18/carlo-gesualdo-composer-psychopath.

216. "Stasi," *Conservapedia*, accessed February 20, 2015, http://www.conservapedia.com/Stasi.

217. Motet by Bach BWV 225, *Singet dem Herrn ein neues Lied* ('Sing a new song to the Lord').

218. *Sehet, wir gehn hinauf gen Jerusalem* (Behold, let us go up to Jerusalem), BWV 159, is a church cantata by Johann Sebastian Bach. Bach composed the cantata in Leipzig for the Sunday Estomihi, the Sunday before Ash Wednesday, and probably first performed it on 27 February 1729.

Final Chorale

5. Choral

Oboe e Violino I col Soprano, Violino II coll' Alto, Viola col Tenore, Continuo

| | |
|---|---|
| *Jesu, deine Passion* | Jesus, Your passion |
| *Ist mir lauter Freude,* | is pure joy to me, |
| *Deine Wunden, Kron und Hohn* | Your wounds, thorns and shame |
| *Meines Herzens Weide;* | my heart's pasture; |
| *Meine Seel auf Rosen geht,* | my soul walks on roses |
| *Wenn ich d'ran gedenke,* | when I think upon it; |
| *In dem Himmel eine Stätt* | grant a place in heaven |
| *Mir deswegen schenke.* | for me for its sake. |

(English translation by Pamela Dellal, http://www.emmanuelmusic.org/notes_translations/translations_cantata/t_bwv159.htm#pab1_7).

219. Stephen Cleobury, accessed February 20, 2015, http://www.stephencleobury.com.

220. "War Requiem," *Benjamin Britten*, accessed February 20, 2015, https://www.its.caltech.edu/~tan/Britten/britwar.html.

221. Beethoven's Symphony No. 5, The Destiny Symphony.

222. "Dimity Hall, violinist," UNSW Australia Music Performance Unit, accessed February 20, 2015, http://www.music.unsw.edu.au/australia-ensemble/about-australia-ensemble/dimity-hall.

223. "Julian Smiles," Goldner String Quartet, accessed February 20, 2015, http://goldnerquartet.com/portfolio/julian-smiles.

224. "Maurice Ravel, Piano Concerto in G," Classic FM, accessed February 20, 2015, http://www.classicfm.com/composers/ravel/music/piano-concerto-g.

225. Max Derrickson, "Rachmaninov—Symphony No. 2 in E-minor, op. 27," *Music Program Notes*, accessed March 25, 2015, http://www.musicprogramnotes.com/rachmaninoff-symphony-no-2-in-e-minor-op-27/.

226. "Shostakovich's Symphony No. 5," *Keeping Score*, accessed February 20, 2015, www.pbs.org/keepingscore/shostakovich-symphony-5.html.

227. Kronos Quartet, accessed February 20, 2015, http://www.kronosquartet.org.

228. Graham Olson, "Dmitry Shostakovich, Piano Concerto No. 2 in F Major, Op. 102," *ALLMUSIC*, accessed February 20, 2015, http://www.allmusic.com/composition/piano-concerto-no-2-in-f-major-op-102-mc0002357470.

229. The group of composers that comprised Arnold Schoenberg, his pupils and close associates in early twentieth-century Vienna.

230. Steven Coburn, "Alfred Schnittke," *ALLMUSIC*, accessed February 20, 2015, http://www.allmusic.com/artist/alfred-schnittke-mn0001169129/biography.

231. "Peter Sculthorpe," Australian Music Centre, accessed February 20, 2015, http://www.australianmusiccentre.com.au/artist/sculthorpe-peter.

232. Mike D. Brownell, "Messiaen: *Quartet for the End of Time*," *ALLMUSIC*, accessed February 20, 2015, http://www.allmusic.com/album/messiaen-quartet-for-the-end-of-time-mw0001864073.

233. Stefan Heinemeyer, *atostrio*, accessed February 20, 2015, http://www.atos-trio.de/atos/page.php?go=sp&pid=1.

234. Atos Trio, accessed February 16, 2015, http://www.atos-trio.de/atos/page.php?go=sp&pid=14.

235. Thomas Hoppe, accessed February 20, 2015, http://www.thomashoppe.com/piano/page.php?go=sp&pid=17.

236. Blair Johnston, "Johannes Brahms, Piano Concerto No. 1 in D Minor, Op. 15," *ALLMUSIC*, accessed February 20, 2015, http://www.allmusic.com/composition/piano-concerto-no-1-in-d-minor-op-15-mc0002357319.

237. "Dene Olding," UNSW Australia Music Performance Unit, accessed March 26, 2015, http://www.music.unsw.edu.au/australia-ensemble/about-australia-ensemble/dene-olding .

238. Irina Morozova, *Australia Ensemble*, accessed February 20, 2015, http://www.music.unsw.edu.au/australia-ensemble/about-australia-ensemble/irina-morozova.

239. "Goldner String Quartet," Australian Strings Association, accessed February 20, 2015, http://austa.asn.au/imgs/page%2016-18.pdf.

240. Goldner String Quartet, accessed February 20, 2015, http://goldnerquartet.com.

241. Pietro Amedeo Modesti, et al,"Psychological predictors of the antihypertensive effects of music-guided slow breathing," *Journal of Hypertension* 28(5) (2010):1097-1103, accessed February 20, 2015, doi: 10.1097/HJH.0b013e3283362762.

242. Jorge G. Camara, Joseph M. Ruszleowski, Sandra R. Worak, *"The effect of live classical piano music on the vital signs of patients undergoing ophthalmic surgery,"* Medscape J Med 10(6) (2008):149, accessed February 20, 2015, http://www.ncbi.nlm.nih.gov/pmc/articles/PMC2491669/.

243. Jane Collingwood, "Music Benefits Preterm Babies," *PsychCentral*, accessed February 20, 2015, http://psychcentral.com/lib/2010/music-benefits-preterm-babies.

244. Peter Gutmann, "Ludwig van Beethoven Symphony No.6 in F Major, Op. 68, 'Pastoral,'" *Classical Notes*, accessed February 20, 2015, http://www.classicalnotes.net/classics4/pastoral.html.

245. "Music helps children learn maths," *The Telegraph*, March 22, 2012, accessed February 20, 2015, http://www.telegraph.co.uk/education/9159802/Music-helps-children-learn-maths.html.

246. "Michael Powell," Conn-Selmer, accessed February 20, 2015, http://www.conn-selmer.com/en-us/artist-information/centerstage/artist-roster/michael-powell.

247. American Brass Quintet, accessed February 20, 2015, http://www.americanbrassquintet.org.

248. "Kevin Cobb, trumpet," American Brass Quintet, accessed February 20, 2015, http://www.americanbrassquintet.org/about.

249. "Sergei Rachmaninov," *goodreads*, accessed February 20, 2015, http://www.goodreads.com/author/show/144683.Sergei_Rachmaninov.

250. Peter Gutmann, "Alban Berg Wozzeck," *Classical Notes*, accessed March 27, 2015, http://www.classicalnotes.net/classics/wozzeck.html.

251. Claudio Monteverdi, *Four Monteverdi Madrigals*, Raymond Mase, ed., American Brass Quintet Series (Montrose, CA: Balquhidder Music, 1997).

252. John Palmer, "Guiseppe Verdi, Requiem Mass, for soloists, chorus and orchestra (Manzoni Requiem)," *ALLMUSIC,* accessed February 21, http://www.allmusic.com/composition/requiem-mass-for-soloists-chorus-orchestra-manzoni-requiem-mc0002363805.

253. The involuntary association of pitch with color is known as chromesthesia, or sound-color synesthesia.

254. "Alina Ibragimova," Askonas Holt, accessed February 21, 2015, http://www.askonasholt.co.uk/artists/instrumentalists/violin/alina-ibragimova.

255. "Cédric Tiberghien," Askonas Holt, accessed February 21, 2015, http://www.askonasholt.co.uk/artists/instrumentalists/piano/cdric-tiberghien.

256. Their repertoire includes the Beethoven, Debussy, and Ravel sonatas for piano and violin.

257. Wass, Miller, & Redditt, 1991, cited in "Sexuality and Violence in Metal Music," *Pointersviewpoint*, May 29, 2010, accessed February 21, 2015, http://pointersviewpoint.wordpress.com/2010/05/29/sexuality-and-violence-in-metal-music.

258. Wade Bradford, "'Amadeus' by Peter Shaffer," *About.Education*, accessed February 20, 2015, http://plays.about.com/od/plays/a/amadeus.htm.

259. Biographies supplied by Andreas Loewe and Katherine Firth.

260. Rick Marschall, Johann Sebastian Bach, Tennessee: Thomas Nelson, 2011. p.72.

261. Johann Mattheson and Hans Lenneberg, "Johann Mattheson on Affect and Rhetoric in Music (1)," Journal of Music Theory, Vol. 2, No. 1 (1958): 47–84.

262. "Gerardus Willems," The University of Sydney, accessed February 20, 2015, http://sydney.edu.au/music/staff-profiles/gerard.willems.php.

263. "Beethoven's Piano Sonata No. 29, Op. 106—'Hammerklavier': Creation History and Discussion of Musical Content," *Raptus Association*, accessed February 20, 2015, http://raptusassociation.org/son29e.html.

264. Blair Johnston, "Ludwig van Beethoven, Piano Sonata No. 26 in E flat Major (*'Les Adieux'*), Op. 81a," *ALLMUSIC,* accessed February 20, 2015, http://www.allmusic.com/composition/piano-sonata-no-26-in-e-flat-major--quot-les-adieux-quot--op-81a-mc0002365329.

265. Beethoven's Moonlight Sonata.

266. Rovi Staff, "Ludwig van Beethoven, Symphony No. 9 in D Minor ("Choral").

267. Beethoven's Symphony No. 5. The Destiny Symphony.

268. "Ludwig van Beethoven, Triple Concerto," The Kennedy Center, accessed February 16, 2015, http://www.kennedy-center.org/calendar/?fuseaction=-composition&composition_id=4609.

269. Ludwig van Beethoven, Große Fuge, Op. 133 (or string quartet),

270. "Esterházy family," *Encyclopaedia Brittanica*, accessed February 16, 2015, http://www.britannica.com/EBchecked/topic/193439/Esterhazy-Family.

271. Roger Dettmer, "Johannes Brahms, Symphony No. 1 in C Minor, Op. 68," *ALLMUSIC*, accessed February 20, 2015, http://www.allmusic.com/composition/symphony-no-1-in-c-minor-op-68-mc0002366601.

272. Robert Cummings, "Ludwig van Beethoven, An die ferne Geliebte, song cycle for voice & piano, Op. 98," *ALLMUSIC,* accessed February 20, 2015, http://www.allmusic.com/composition/an-die-ferne-geliebte-song-cycle-for-voice-piano-op-98-mc0002369069.

273. Alfred Brendel, accessed February 21, 2015, http://www.alfredbrendel.com.

274. See "Must Classical Music Be Entirely Serious?" in Alfred Brendel, *Alfred Brendel on Music: His Collected Essays* (Chicago: A Capella, 2001).

275. "Ludwig van Beethoven, Piano Sonata No. 16 in G Major, Op. 31 No. 1," *ALLMUSIC*, accessed February 20, 2015, http://www.allmusic.com/composition/piano-sonata-no-16-in-g-major-op-31-1-mc0002404708.

276. Blair Sanderson, "Beethoven, *Diabelli Variations*," *ALLMUSIC*, accessed February 21, 2015, http://www.allmusic.com/album/beethoven-diabelli-variations-mw0002650770.

277. Beethoven's *Moonlight Sonata*.

278. "Ludwig van Beethoven, Piano Sonata No. 29 in B flat Major, Op. 106, *Hammerklavier*," *Raptus Association,* accessed February 21, http://raptusassociation.org/son29e.html.

279. Berenikaonline, accessed February 20, 2015, http://berenikaonline.com/about/culture.

280. "Dana Point Symphony Sets First Season," *Orange County Register*, accessed February 20, 2015, http://www.ocregister.com/articles/point-318757-artist-dana.html.

281. Peter Gutmann, "Johannes Brahms, 'Double' Concerto for Violin and Cello, Op. 102," *Classical Notes,* accessed February 20, 2015, http://www.classical-notes.net/classics4/brahmsdouble.html.

282. Berenika's Facebook page, accessed April 16, 2015, https://www.facebook.com/pages/Berenika/156857957686991.

283. "Mary Jo Capps," zoominfo, accessed February 21, 2015, http://www.zoominfo.com/p/Mary-Capps/253057920.

284. Gerard Manley Hopkins, "Spring and Fall: to a Young Child," *Poem of the Week,* accessed February 20, 2015, http://www.potw.org/archive/potw29.html.

285. "Live Performance Plus," Musica Viva, accessed February 20, 2015, http://www.musicaviva.com.au/education/liveperformanceplus/about.

286. Christina Davies, "The Impact and Effectiveness of the Musica Viva Live Performance Plus Program on Regional Western Australian Children 2013 Report," School of Population Health, University of Western Australia, accessed February 20, 2015, http://www.musicaviva.com.au/downloads/file/PublicDocuments/ImpactandEffectivenessofLPP.pdf

287. El Sistema, *El Sistema USA.*

288. "William Lyne CBE," zoominfo, accessed February 20, 2015, http://www.zoominfo.com/p/William-Lyne/76555382.

289. AFCM Australian Festival of Chamber Music, accessed April 16, 2015, http://issuu.com/oraclestudio/docs/afcm_2013_programme_web.

290. Kuhmo Chamber Music Festival, accessed April 16, 2015, http://www.kuhmofestival.fi/inenglish.htm.

291. Aaron Green, "Beethoven's *Eroica Symphony*, Ludwig van Beethoven's Symphony No. 3, Op. 55," *Classical Music*, accessed February 21, 2015, http://classicalmusic.about.com/od/symphonies/a/aaeroica.htm.

292. Greg Johnson, "Sir Reginald Goodall: An Appreciation," *The Occidental Quarterly*, May 30, 2009, accessed February 21, 2015, http://www.toqonline.com/blog/reginald-goodall.

293. Tim Franks, "Andras Schiff: Why I won't perform in Hungary," *BBC News Magazine*, December 23, 2013, accessed February 21, 2015, http://www.bbc.com/news/magazine-25450716.

294. Jessica Elgot, "Interview: Dame Fanny Waterman," *The Jewish Chronicle*, accessed February 20, 2015, http://www.thejc.com/arts/arts-interviews/34489/interview-dame-fanny-waterman.

295. "Dr. Fanny Waterman," zoominfo, accessed February 20, 2015, http://www.zoominfo.com/p/Fanny-Waterman/39824632.

296. "Dame Fanny's Message to Competitors," The Leeds International Piano Competition, accessed February 21, 2015, http://leedspiano.com/News.

297. "Dr. Fanny Waterman CBE," zoominfo.

298. "Dame Fanny Waterman, Desert Island Discs," *BBC Radio 4*, accessed February 20, 2015, http://www.bbc.co.uk/programmes/b00sw7fd.

299. Murray Perahia, accessed February 21, 2015, http://www.murrayperahia.com.

300. Rovi Staff, "Sviatoslav Richter," *ALLMUSIC*, accessed February 20, 2015, http://www.allmusic.com/artist/sviatoslav-richter-mn0000818152/biography.

# GLOSSARY OF MUSICAL TERMS

**Allemande:** A dance of German origin, and in baroque music, one of the movements of a suite.

**A cappella:** A solo or group of singers without instrumental accompaniment.

**Antiphony:** A style of call and response in which separate musicians or groups such as choirs perform alternately.

**Atonal:** Refers to music that lacks a key and traditional harmony.

**Baroque:** A musical style from mid-seventeenth to mid-eighteenth centuries, characterized by ornamentation, grandeur, a strict form and repeated bass line.

**Cavatina:** A short, simple melody, as opposed to an aria.

**Chamber music:** A genre of classical music written for a small group of instruments, each with one part, and originally played in private homes by amateur musicians.

**Chorale:** A hymn sung by the choir and congregation in a German Protestant Church.

**Chord:** A set of three or more notes played together in harmony.

**Classical:** The period of Western music history dated from about mid-eighteenth to mid-nineteenth centuries. The music was lighter and more emotionally reserved than that of the romantic or baroque eras.

**Concerto:** A composition, usually in three movements, written for a solo instrument accompanied by an orchestra.

**Conductor:** Someone who directs a group of performing musicians by gestures, indicating the tempo, dynamics and phrasing.

**Contralto:** The lowest range for a female singer. Equivalent to the alto voice and the male countertenor.

**Counterpoint:** Two or more melodic lines played simultaneously.

**Dissonance:** Conflicting or discordant sounds. Also, a chord or combination of tones that suggests tension and requires a harmonious resolution.

**Ensemble:** A group of musicians who perform together.

**Fugue:** A polyphonic composition based on a theme, which is stated and developed in a fixed number of voices.

**Harmony:** A pleasing combination of tones or chord progressions.

**Hymn:** A song of praise and thanksgiving to a divinity.

**Interpretation:** A performer's personal version of a piece of music.

**Interval:** The difference in pitch between two notes.

**Intonation:** The production of tones with regard to accuracy of pitch.

**Key:** Refers to the major or minor scale, or system of seven notes on which the harmony of a composition is based.

**Major:** One of the two modes of the tonal system, identifiable by its positive, bright mood. It can refer to chords, keys or scales.

**Mezzo:** The voice between *soprano* and *contralto*. Also refers to dynamics, e.g., *mezzo forte* ('medium-loud') and *mezzo piano* ('medium-soft').

**Minor:** One of the two modes of the tonal system, identifiable by its mood of melancholy. It can refer to chords, keys or scales.

**Modulation:** Changing from one key to another.

**Motif:** A distinctive theme that is repeated or developed.

**Movement:** A self-contained section of a longer composition.

**Musicology:** The academic study and research of the history, theory and performance of music.

**Notation:** A system of symbols that represent music. Commonly refers to the method developed in Europe in the Middle Ages.

**Octave:** A progression of the eight notes in a musical scale.

**Opera:** A dramatic work with words sung to instrumental accompaniment.

**Opus:** A numbered composition usually in order of publication. The number follows the word "opus," e.g., Beethoven's Sonata Opus 111.

**Orchestra:** A large group of performers who play together on various musical instruments.

**Orchestration:** The composition or arrangement of a piece of music for an orchestra.

**Passacaglia:** An early Spanish or Italian dance based on a series of variations.

**Piano:** An instruction to play softly.

**Pitch:** Variations in notes, depending on the rate of vibration.

**Polyphony:** Combining two or more independent harmonizing melodies played simultaneously. Also known as counterpoint.

**Recapitulation:** A modified restatement of themes that were introduced earlier, particularly in sonata form.

**Recital:** A concert performed by one or more musicians.

**Resonance:** Reverberation through vibrations of strings.

**Rhythm:** A regular pattern of strong and weak beats.

**Romantic:** An era of Western classical music during the eighteenth and early nineteenth centuries, characterized by a more expressive and emotional style.

**Score:** Sheet music containing the notation of musical symbols; also film and theater music.

**Sarabande:** A stately Spanish dance; also, movement of a musical suite.

**Sonata:** A composition in three or four movements typically for keyboard or other solo instrument with keyboard accompaniment. The movements are in various forms and related keys; the first movement is usually in sonata form.

**Sonata form:** Usually the first of many movements of a piece of music. It consists of three segments, an exposition, development and recapitulation, often ending with a coda.

**Soprano:** The highest tonal range of a singing voice.

**Stave:** The staff or stave in Western music consists of five horizontal lines for notation of different musical pitch on the lines and spaces in between.

**String Quartet:** An instrumental ensemble consisting of two violins, viola and cello.

**Symphony:** Three to four movements of an orchestral piece, generally in the form of a sonata.

**Syncopation:** A shift of accent to stress a weak beat.

**Temperament or Equal Temperament:** The common tuning system in Western music that divides the octave into twelve equal parts. Fixed pitch instruments, such as keyboard, can then be played in all keys without extra tuning.

**Tempo:** An indication of the speed at which a composition is to be played.

**Theme:** A melodic subject in a musical composition.

**Tonal:** Relating to notes, conventional harmony and keys.

**Tonality:** A system of seven tones based on the first note of a scale. The musical key of a piece.

**Tone:** The character of a note, e.g., intonation, pitch, intensity, timber.

**Tonic:** The first note or keynote of a scale.

**Tuning:** Adjusting the pitch of an instrument to produce the correct intervals between tones.

**Vibrato:** A pulsating, rapid change of pitch.

**Virtuoso:** A performer with outstanding technical ability.

**Voice:** A musical line for a singer or instrument. One of the parts, lines, or melodies in counterpoint.

# ABOUT THE AUTHOR

IDA LICHTER is a psychiatrist based in Sydney, Australia. She has been involved with music for most of her life and studied piano performance and theory before taking up a career in medicine, specializing in psychiatry. An interest in performance anxiety led her to work in the field of therapy for musicians who were trying to master symptoms inhibiting their ability to play in public.

For many years she lived in London, and together with her family, was intimately involved with Wigmore Hall, one of the world's leading venues for the performance of chamber music.

She is a founder and director of Music in the Hunter, a chamber music festival inaugurated in 1991 to commemorate the bicentenary of Mozart's death. It takes place in the Hunter Valley wine-growing district of New South Wales, Australia, and celebrated its twenty-fifth successful year in 2015. Members of the Goldner String Quartet, who are the core performers, have played at every festival, together with guest artists. Audience numbers are limited in order to maintain an intimate, collegial atmosphere.

Dr. Lichter is committed to enhancing audience enjoyment of music and exploring the links between music and other specialties, such as art, architecture, wine, and archeology.